Uruguay

Uruguay

The History of a South American Success Story

Peter V. N. Henderson

ROWMAN & LITTLEFIELD
Lanham • Boulder • New York • London

Rowman & Littlefield
Bloomsbury Publishing Inc, 1385 Broadway, New York, NY 10018, USA
Bloomsbury Publishing Plc, 50 Bedford Square, London, WC1B 3DP, UK
Bloomsbury Publishing Ireland, 29 Earlsfort Terrace, Dublin 2, D02 AY28, Ireland
www.rowman.com

Copyright © 2025 by The Rowman & Littlefield Publishing Group, Inc.

All rights reserved. No part of this publication may be: i) reproduced or transmitted in any form, electronic or mechanical, including photocopying, recording or by means of any information storage or retrieval system without prior permission in writing from the publishers; or ii) used or reproduced in any way for the training, development or operation of artificial intelligence (AI) technologies, including generative AI technologies. The rights holders expressly reserve this publication from the text and data mining exception as per Article 4(3) of the Digital Single Market Directive (EU) 2019/790.

British Library Cataloguing in Publication Information available

Library of Congress Cataloging-in-Publication Data Available

ISBN 9798881807733 (cloth : alk. paper) | ISBN 9798881807740 (pbk. : alk. paper) | ISBN 9798881807757 (ebook)

For product safety related questions contact productsafety@bloomsbury.com.

♾™ The paper used in this publication meets the minimum requirements of American National Standard for Information Sciences—Permanence of Paper for Printed Library Materials, ANSI/NISO Z39.48-1992.

Contents

List of Figures		vii
List of Textboxes		xi
Preface		xiii
1	Uruguay: Land and People in Colonial Times	1
2	Uruguay's Struggle for Independence, 1808–1828	25
3	The Near-Death of the Republic, 1828–1875	51
4	Forming the Nation: Progress and Order, 1876–1903	79
5	Uruguay in the Age of Batlle, 1903–1930	109
6	There Is Nowhere Like Uruguay, 1930–1955	137
7	Batllismo Challenged: Things Fall Apart, 1955–1985	163
8	The Renaissance: Uruguay, 1985–2024	189
Select Bibliography		213
Index		217
About the Author		229

List of Figures

CHAPTER ONE

Map 1.1	Contemporary Uruguay	2
Figure 1.1	Early Hunters Pursuing a Glyptodon	4
Figure 1.2	Charrúa Warrior Attacking a Spaniard with a *Rompecabeza*	7
Figure 1.3	Portuguese Home in Colonia	15
Figure 1.4	"Gaucho and His China at the Well," by Melchor Méndez Margariños	18
Figure 1.5	"Montevideo at the End of Eighteenth Century"	20

CHAPTER TWO

Figure 2.1	"Gaucho in the Countryside," by Juan Manuel Blanes	29
Figure 2.2	"The Rapto," (Kidnapping) by Juan Manuel Blanes	30
Figure 2.3	"Surrender of José Posadas at the Battle of Las Piedras," by Juan Manuel Blanes	33
Figure 2.4	"Artigas on the Meseta," by Carlos Maria Herrera	36
Figure 2.5	"The Instructions of 1813," by Pedro Blanes Viale	37
Figure 2.6	"Oath of the 33 Orientals," by Juan Manuel Blanes	43

CHAPTER THREE

Figure 3.1	"Sketch for the People's Oath to the Constitution of 1830," by Pedro Blanes Viale	53
Figure 3.2	*Divisas* from the Battle of Carpintería	56
Figure 3.3	"President Fructuoso Rivera," by Juan Manuel Blanes	58
Map 3.1	Map of the Revision of the Brazilian Border in 1851	62
Figure 3.4	Portrait of Bernadina Fragosa de Rivera, by Amadeo Gras	63
Figure 3.5	"The Assassination of Venancio Flores," by Juan Manuel Blanes	70
Figure 3.6	"The Yellow Fever Epidemic," by Juan Manuel Blanes	72

CHAPTER FOUR

Figure 4.1	"Machero of General Santos," by J. M. Correa	83
Figure 4.2	"Artigas's Remains Being Repatriated," by Domingo Rois	86
Figure 4.3	Aguas Corrientes Water Works. Museo del Agua. Aguas Corrientes	88
Figure 4.4	Tool for Installing Barbed-Wire Fence	90
Figure 4.5	Advertisement for LEMCO Meat Extract	93
Figure 4.6	Female Students at the Normal School	100

CHAPTER FIVE

Figure 5.1	Poster of Aparicio Saravia	111
Figure 5.2	Portrait of José Batlle y Ordoñez	113
Figure 5.3	Photograph of Francisco Piria	118
Figure 5.4	"Processing Beef at the Swift *Frigorífico*"	119
Figure 5.5	Baltasar Brum with Robert Lansing	125
Figure 5.6	The Palacio Salvo: Latin America's Tallest Skyscraper in 1928	131

CHAPTER SIX

Figure 6.1	The ANCAP Petroleum Refinery at La Teja	140
Figure 6.2	Torres-García's School with the Maestro	143
Figure 6.3	The Scuttling of the *Graf Spee*	146
Figure 6.4	Punta del Este, Uruguay's Premier Beach Resort	149
Figure 6.5	The 1950 World Cup Presentation	155

CHAPTER SEVEN

Figure 7.1	Evacuees from the Floods of 1959	166
Figure 7.2	Raúl Sendic Leading March of Sugar Cane Workers	170
Figure 7.3	Carnival Parade in Montevideo	177
Figure 7.4	Poster: José Batlle Would Vote No	181
Figure 7.5	The Statue of the Door, La Libertad	182

CHAPTER EIGHT

Figure 8.1	A Group of Gauchos Drinking Yerba Mate	208

List of Textboxes

Box 2.1	Artigas in His Lair: A British Merchant at Purificación	35
Box 2.2	Juan Manuel Blanes	39
Box 3.1	Massacre of the Charrúa	55
Box 3.2	A Caudillo's Wife: Bernadina Fragosa de Rivera	62
Box 3.3	Gauchesca Literature and National Identity	67
Box 4.1	An Immigrant Success Story	89
Box 4.2	The Teatro Solís: Opera and Orchestral Performances in the Golden Age	96
Box 5.1	Francisco Piria and Entrepreneurship in the Batlle Years	117
Box 5.2	The Workings of El Anglo's *Frigorífico*	120
Box 5.3	The Legalization of Dueling in 1920	126
Box 6.1	The Modernist Movement	143
Box 6.2	The *Graf Spee* Incident	145
Box 6.3	Highlight of the Postwar Era: The World Cup Victory of 1950	156
Box 7.1	The Miracle in the Andes, Flight 571	173
Box 7.2	Candombé in Montevideo	176
Box 8.1	Energy	198
Box 8.2	Philanthropy and the MEVIR Program	204
Box 8.3	COVID-19 and Yerba Mate	206

Preface

Hopefully, this book's provocative title, *Uruguay: The History of a South American Success Story*, will encourage readers to consider the reasons why the history of the continent's smallest Spanish-speaking nation has evolved so differently from that of its neighbors. By the 1920s, international observers and Uruguayans themselves commonly referred to the nation as the "Switzerland of the Americas," not because of its towering mountains (Uruguay's tallest peak registers only 1,644 feet above sea level), its well-crafted precision watches, or its tasty cheeses. Rather, Uruguay achieved this notoriety because of its broad-based democracy, its prosperity, its sizable middle class, its high literacy rate, its secular values, and its progressive legislation on women's rights, social welfare programs, and pension systems. Unlike other Latin American nations with enormous disparities between the few rich and the many poor, Uruguay's relatively egalitarian society minimized social conflict and made the country the envy of its neighbors. During the twenty-first century, the nation has built upon these successes and invested in a green economy and legislated additional progressive reforms that provided rights to an even broader spectrum of its citizens.

Despite this popular image, Uruguayans have also faced the stark reality of its Latin American heritage because for lengthy periods, its history differed little from that of its neighbors. Its wars for independence lasted longer than any other nation in Latin America, and involved the intervention of five other countries: Spain, Portugal, Argentina, Brazil, and Great Britain. Its weak post-independence government failed to form an effective state for fifty years, during which time endless caudillo wars between the leaders of the Red (Colorado) and White (Blanco) factions engendered a culture of violence and invited Argentine and Brazilian intervention. The early state massacred its indigenous people and "disappeared" its Black population, unnoticed in the massive wave of European immigrants who by 1910 constituted a significant proportion of South America's "white nation." Like its neighbors, nineteenth-century Uruguay remained a supplier of primary products and relied upon the British for investment funds, technology, and infrastructure. Following the dramatic successes from 1910 to 1955, the alternative reality mentioned earlier, Uruguay again fell victim to its Latin American heritage. The excesses of state intervention in the economy and the inability to reform the overextended social welfare and pension systems led to a declining standard of living in the late 1950s, unrest and urban guerrilla warfare during the late 1960s, and then a brutal dictatorship that lasted from 1973 to 1985, during which time the words "the Switzerland of South America" became a mockery.

Through the good times and bad, Uruguay has participated in a transnational community. Its geography and its proximity to South America's two largest nations predetermined this experience. Beginning in the late colonial period, Uruguay was swept into a political, economic, and cultural relationship with the Atlantic world, particularly Great Britain, and later, the United States. During the twentieth century, Uruguay led the South American response to numerous transnational movements such as the struggle for universal suffrage and democracy, the quest for greater social and economic equality. In the twenty-first century, transnationalism has become increasingly global, as Uruguay joined its neighbors in the Southern Cone's common market known as Mercosur, and China has become its largest trading partner. It has outpaced its neighbors by promoting green energy and implementing new progressive social policies. In short, Uruguay's complex history must not be read in isolation.

For nearly sixty years, I have either studied, taught, researched, or published on topics about Latin American history. In so doing, I have incurred numerous intellectual and personal debts for which I must express my gratitude. First, I would like to thank the community of scholars at the University of Texas–Austin who provided such a stimulating intellectual and social climate. Scholars like Virginia Garrard, Seth Garfield, Alan Knight, Jonathan Brown, Ann Twinam, Andrew Villalon, and Lina del Castilla contributed to several of my books, as did the directors and staff of the Nettie Lee Benson Library. More recently, the librarians at Florida Gulf Coast University have provided me with the resources I needed to complete this text. Rocio Suárez and her staff at the Columbus Memorial Library provided several outstanding photographs. Several of the individuals mentioned above overlap with the colleagues I shared great conversations with at the Rocky Mountain Council of Latin American Studies, which include my decades long-friends John Sherman, Kris Lane, Susan Ramírez, Kim Morse, Monica Rankin, William Beezley, Jonathan Truit, Iñigo García Bryce, Steve Bunker, Jeffrey Shumway, and some of more recent vintage such as Lisa Edwards and Alisha Loftin. Colleagues who have assisted with other book projects deserving thanks include Charles Walker, Brian McCann, and Nicola Foote. For this book I owe special thanks to Matias Quincke, who guided me throughout Uruguay and who shared his extensive knowledge of his nation with me. My editor at Rowman & Littlefield, Michael Tan, and his assistant, Hollis Peterson, have transformed my text into a polished book. Thank you all!

Finally, I must thank family, former colleagues, and nonacademic friends. My Winona State University compatriots, Marianna Byman, Seymour Byman, Gregory Schmidt, and my replacement, Juandrea Bates, have always provided friendship and encouraged my efforts. Our former president, Darrell Krueger, a strong supporter of the liberal arts and scholarship, enthusiastically funded academic work. My good friend Aurea Osgood has willingly shared her knowledge of technology and bailed me out on numerous occasions. My sister, Anne Finucane, photo-manipulated the images that I took and made them look professional. My brother-in law, Brendan, improved my faulty understanding of economics. I also must thank my lifelong friends and their spouses: Bryan and Naomi Weare, Dan and Felicia Miller, and Doug and Nancy Brown, who provided safe haven from two hurricanes. My daughter, Courtney Starnes, and her husband, Christian, bring joy to my life as do my wonderful grandchildren: Jackson, Liliana, Olive, and Liev.

One

Uruguay

Land and People in Colonial Times

Uruguay, originally known as the *Banda Oriental* (Eastern Bank), offered few temptations for prospective settlers for nearly two hundred fifty years following Christopher Columbus's encounter with the Americas in 1492. Unlike Peru and Mexico with their vast riches and sophisticated sedentary populations suitable for forced labor, early visitors to the Río de la Plata River basin found the Eastern Bank an inhospitable land, lacking gold or silver, and populated largely by a hostile, nomadic indigenous foe, the Charrúa. By the eighteenth century, however, the smattering of cattle that a Spanish governor had once loosed onto the prairielands had multiplied into vast herds that encouraged scattered Spanish outposts where ranchers and their gauchos (cowboys) rounded-up and slaughtered cattle for their hides. Meanwhile, Spain and Portugal challenged one another militarily for possession of the Eastern Bank, the frontier of empire. By the end of the eighteenth century, the once entirely ignored Banda Oriental had attracted a sparse civilian population engaged in either one or both of these enterprises. This chapter will introduce the reader to the land, its society, and the Banda Oriental's evolving history through the year 1806.

THE LAND

Bordered by the Atlantic Ocean on the east, the estuary of the Río de la Plata on the south, and the Río Uruguay on the west, South America's smallest Spanish-speaking nation lies trapped between the continent's two largest nations, Brazil and Argentina. As a result, Uruguay experienced a transnational existence from its colonial beginnings. Over time, the fortunes of war shrank Uruguay's northern frontier with Brazil, where no natural border existed, to a negotiated line terminating in the Laguna Merín. Containing a little over 66,200 square miles (about the size

Map 1.1 Contemporary Uruguay. *Source*: cc Graphics, Cape Coral, Florida.

of Oklahoma or North Dakota), Uruguay's landscape is an extension of the Argentine pampas, an undulating plain that early visitors described as a "green ocean" of grasslands and shrubs, broken only by occasional chains of hills capped with granite ridges called *cuchillas*.[1]

The highest peak in the country, the Cerro Catedral, rises to an elevation of a mere 1,685 feet and is barely distinguishable from surrounding hills. The sandy Atlantic coastal region gives way to occasional marshes and shallow lagoons, while the broader, fertile coastal plains along the La Plata estuary and the Uruguay River eventually merge into the hillier interior. The latter body of water, whose name comes from an indigenous language meaning either "river of shell-fish" or "the water of colorful birds," is navigable as far north as the city of Salto. Cuchillas divide the land into four regions: the West, the South, the East, and the much less populated interior.[2]

Because of its rolling terrain, the landscape resembles that of Iowa or western Nebraska; nevertheless, subtle topographical and climatic differences do occur. Today, in the coastal regions from Montevideo to the west, fertile soils make truck farming possible, producing most of the fruits and vegetables consumed in the capital. Rich soils along the shore of the Uruguay River allow farmers to engage in grain production, largely wheat, but also yield decent amounts of corn and oats for animal feed. Although thin soils in the interior make agriculture difficult, some four hundred varieties of native grasses flourish there, and provide excellent pasture for both cattle and sheep. In the north, the hotter climate near the Brazilian border allows sugarcane and semi-tropical fruit orchards to flourish. The flat, wet, and swampy lands in the far east around Laguna Merín sustains extensive rice production. In short, Uruguay's wealth lies on its surface and not underground in mines as was the case in colonial Mexico and Peru.[3]

Blessed with generous rainfall, Uruguay's numerous lakes, streams, and rivers promote dense, almost impenetrable groves along their banks on the otherwise unbroken plains. A high water-table drawing from the enormous Guaraní Aquifer provides additional moisture for the ranches that dominate the interior. The country lies entirely in the temperate zone, the only South American nation to fully do so. As a result, the spring is cool and damp, summers are hot, autumns mild, and winters cold and dry, especially if the cold wind called the *pampero* blows from Argentina. (Being in the Southern Hemisphere, the months for these seasons are the reverse of those in the Northern Hemisphere.) Rains, however, can be fickle, leading to floods during one growing season and drought in the next. In addition to the Río de la Plata and the Uruguay River, two other significant bodies of water help nourish the nation's soils. In the central region, the River Yí feeds the Río Negro, the country's largest source of water. The Río Negro bifurcates the country from the northeast to the southwest.[4]

THE INDIGENOUS INHABITANTS

Had you spoken with a Uruguayan a century ago, they would have boasted about their European heritage and denied any indigenous forbears. Today, many Uruguayans revere their indigenous heritage, as roughly 5 percent of the population claims some such ancestry. At the time of the encounter with Europeans, four groups, the Charrúa, the Minuane, the Chaná, and the Guaraní, occupied portions of today's Uruguay. The European encounter significantly disrupted these societies. As archaeologists have recently discovered, however, the indigenous presence dates back for perhaps eleven thousand years.

During antediluvian times, large animals known as megafauna populated the land along with birds and small mammals. Uruguayan museums showcase dinosaur eggs as well as individual fossilized bones from giant ground sloths and mastodons, as well as full skeletons of glyptodons (giant armadillos) and a recently discovered enormous rodent weighing over a ton. The eminent biologist Charles Darwin unearthed a partial fossil of a giant toxodon (hippopotamus or rhinoceros) in 1832. By the early twenty-first century, archaeologists proved with certainty that some of these animals, especially the glyptodon and perhaps the giant sloth, shared the countryside with early humans. For decades experts debated whether humans or dramatic climate change caused the extinction of the megafauna. Recent research suggests that both contributed. By the time of recorded history, only small deer, *carpincho* (capybara) and *ñandu* (rheas) that Spanish explorers called ostriches remained as game. Fish filled the many streams, providing another source of nutrition for indigenous people.[5]

The hunter-gatherers arrived in three successive waves. After Asians first crossed the Bering Strait roughly twenty thousand years ago, the first wave slowly migrated southward, entering northwestern Uruguay between 8000 BCE and 6000 BCE, an inexact timeframe because neither group (the *catalanense* and the *cuareimense*) made ceramics whose botanical contents would have allowed for carbon dating. The *catalanense* and *cuareimense* settled along the Cuareim River in Artigas department on the Brazilian border. Both groups used shaped, stone-tipped wooden spears to hunt. Archaeologists can distinguish the two groups because the catalanense fashioned rougher, rounded stone tips, while those of the cuareimense were thinner and more pointed. When successful, the group devoured the results of the day's hunt immediately, having no capacity for food storage. Each day began with hunters stalking fresh game after breakfasting on the remnants of the previous day's kill.[6]

Roughly around 3000 BCE, the second wave of hunter-gatherers, larger numerically and more technologically sophisticated, spread into Uruguay, some in the east in Rocha department and others scattered in the west. Although Stone Age people,

Figure 1.1 Early Hunters Pursuing a Glyptodon. Anthropologists continue to debate whether humans or climate change caused the extinction of megafauna in South America. This drawing depicts a scene where humans and megafauna coexisted simultaneously. Jared Diamond in his bestseller, *Guns, Germs, and Steel*, theorizes that because of their size, megafauna like the glyptodon had no fear of humans with weapons, ultimately to their detriment. *Source*: Museo Histórico, Paysandú, Uruguay.

these groups had developed improved weaponry, specifically bows and arrows and a multi-purpose tool unique to the pampas-grasslands called a *boleadora* (popularly called a *bola*) to hunt game or make war. Hunters swung the boleadora (grass rope lariats with two or sometimes three stones attached to the end of the lariat) over their head and threw it like a lasso. Once released, the hurled bola wrapped itself around the pursued animal's legs, bringing it to the ground where it could be killed and skinned with a stone knife. After the hunter stripped off its hide, stone scrapers allowed him to remove the hair and fat, making the hide usable for clothing or for covering a framed shelter (a *toldo*).

The most carefully studied group of the second wave, a semisedentary group, occupied Rocha department around the Laguna Merín in the east where they moved seasonally from fishing camps along the Atlantic to higher ground in the west. By 2000 BCE, they began constructing the *cerritos de indios* (indigenous earthen mounds) from sixty to a hundred and seventy feet in diameter and as high as seven feet. Although the earliest mounds solely served as boundary markers between groups; in time the semicircular mounds became living spaces, burial grounds, and ceremonial sites. When archaeologists discovered ceramics and stone mortars in the most recent mounds, they concluded that these people cultivated corn, squash, and peas, the first evidence of agriculture in Uruguay. With a more reliable food supply, the population increased and developed hierarchical social groups with chieftains. The pre-Hispanic people of Rocha carved stones and shaped them into human figures. Their earthen mounds and their inhabitants' lifeways resemble those of the mound cultures of the Mississippi Valley and the Calusa in southwestern Florida. These people disappeared in the sixteenth or seventeenth century, perhaps because of deaths from European diseases, raids by enslavers from Brazil, or resistance to missionaries' evangelical work.[7]

By the time Spaniards first contacted Uruguay's indigenous people in 1516, a third wave had entered the country: the Charrúa (who lived mostly in western Uruguay); the Guaraní (mostly along the La Plata in the area of today's Colonia and San José departments as well in much larger numbers in Brazil and Paraguay); the Chaná (who lived along the Uruguay River) and the Minuane (situated in the same area in the 1500s). None of these groups had developed writing; hence the stories about their origins and lifeways come from the impressions of Spanish explorers, missionaries, and government officials. Because the Guaraní and Chaná practiced agriculture, they more readily coexisted with the Europeans. Unlike the Guaraní and Chaná, the Charrúa showed no interest in abandoning their culture or their nomadic lifestyles and resisted attempts to force them into missions.[8]

The largest group, the Charrúa, probably numbered between five thousand and ten thousand people at the time of the encounter and have had the greatest cultural impact on Uruguay. Anthropologists base this population estimate on the sparse resources available in the sixteenth century as well as the reported size of the typical Charrúa band, a kinship group consisting of between a few dozen to one hundred people. Over the course of a given year, the Charrúa typically migrated seasonally from south to north, depending on the weather to maximize the exploitation of available game. A soldier who accompanied the 1535 Spanish expedition, one of the earliest to explore the region, left the following short description: "These Indian people go quite naked, the women leaving only their privities covered, from the navel to the knee, with a small piece of . . . cloth. The Zechurias (Charrúa) have nothing to eat but fish and meat."[9]

Charrúa men attained an average height of about five-and-a-half feet, while women were slightly shorter, making them essentially the same height as the Europeans and taller than indigenous people Spaniards encountered elsewhere. In addition, they were athletically built, with strong cheekbones and dark eyes. Even after European contact, the Charrúa retained their pre-Hispanic lifeways, moving from one encampment site (*toldería*) to the next, never practicing agriculture, and sleeping in open *toldos* (initially deerskin, later cowhide). Engineered for local conditions, the Charrúa designed their *toldos* with openings at the bottom because the fierce *pampero* winds that blew from May to September would have carried away enclosed tents. The Charrúa developed a reputation for ferocity because of the gruesome story about their first encounter with Spaniards in 1516 and because of the determination with which they defended their lands, making Uruguay nearly impossible to settle for nearly two hundred years. Because of their heroic resistance to outsiders, the Charrúa eventually became a patriotic symbol for twentieth-century Uruguayans (and the name of the national soccer team).[10]

The Charrúa had limited tools and weapons at their disposal. Some early explorers claimed that the Charrúa were so fleet afoot that they chased down their game, deer, or the *ñandu* bird. They consumed their meat raw, sun-dried, or roasted. To make fire, the Charrúa rubbed two sticks together and used hollowed-out stones as cooking vessels. Bolas proved fearsome tools for hunting and weapons in times of war, as did *rompecabezas* (literally head smashers). These deadly weapons made by attaching a multipointed stone to twine were swung like *bolas* or tied to wooden handles like mace heads to kill or maim enemies. Charrúa warriors also used bows and arrows, spears, and slings in battles with enemies. Quivers filled with arrows lay flat on warriors' backs, enabling them to fire rapidly. Men took charge of the hunt, led battles, and located new campsites. Women apparently gathered edible *ceiba* shoots and *butia* nuts, carried the portable *toldos* when the band moved, and cared for the children in the camp. The Charrúa never developed agriculture because the pampas offered no varieties of wild plants suitable for domestication. Because of the nature of their nomadic culture, the Charrúa placed little value on the acquisition of material goods.[11]

SPANISH EXPLORERS AND SETTLERS, 1516–1680

Juan Díaz de Solís, Spain's Pilot Major (most eminent navigator), arrived in southern South America with three ships in the spring of 1516 seeking a passage through or around the continent that would enable Spanish ships to reach Asia. Portugal had already secured access to Asia's coveted spices by sailing east around Africa, and the

Figure 1.2   Charrúa Warrior Attacking a Spaniard with a *Rompecabeza*. Archeologists and museum curators still debate the manner in which the Charrúa employed the *rompecabeza*. The striations on the stones suggest that they were either tied to a club or, alternatively, to a cord similar to the ones used on a *bola* and swung over the head, enabling the warrior to attack an enemy while maintaining a safe distance as this image suggests. *Source*: Museo Indígena, Parque Nacional San Miguel.

Spanish monarchy intended to compete for the trade. South of Brazil, Solís's expedition discovered the widest estuary in the world, a one-hundred-forty-mile-wide river of fresh water that met the Atlantic at today's Punta del Este. Hoping that this estuary might provide the route to Asia, Solís sailed his ship west to the conjunction of the Río de la Plata with the Río Uruguay. As the river narrowed and seemed unlikely to be the passage to the Pacific, Solís reversed course and rejoined his fleet.

Meanwhile, the Indigenous people on the eastern bank had waved to the Spaniards in what the impetuous Solís interpreted as a friendly gesture. He and several crewmembers rowed a longboat ashore to investigate. The landing place, allegedly at the Arroyo de Solís (although some writers claim the incident occurred on Martín García Island), marked the spot of the first European encounter with Indigenous people in Uruguay. Apparently Solís attempted to seize captives to take to Spain and train as interpreters. (Hernán Cortés three years later employed the same strategy to great benefit during the conquest of Mexico.) But the Indigenous people took umbrage at Solís's effrontery, killed him and several of his companions, cut off their heads, arms, and legs before roasting their bodies in front of the horrified crew, and then "devouring them." "Thus was the unhappy end of Juan Díaz de Solís, an abler pilot than commander." Only the cabin boy Francisco del Puerto survived before being rescued by the next expedition that reached the Uruguayan shore. This widely circulated tale painted the Charrúa as vicious cannibals and savages and became common lore in Uruguay's national history. The Charrúa, however, rarely ate human flesh except under extraordinary circumstances. Other writers have suggested that Solís and his crew had actually encountered Guaraní, known cannibals who also inhabited this territory along the La Plata River.[12]

A decade later, Pilot Major Sebastián Gaboto (Sebastian Cabot) entered the estuary, at that time named after its ill-fated discoverer. He sailed upstream, rescued Solís's cabin boy, and established San Salvador fortress on one of the islands where the San Salvador River meets the Uruguay River in Soriano department, the first European settlement in Uruguay. He left a few soldiers and two ships there while he reconnoitered the Paraná River, which looked like a more probable passageway to Asia until it to narrowed when he arrived at the present-day location of Asunción, Paraguay. There, the Guaraní greeted him adorned with thin sheets of silver on their chests, obtained through their interactions with the Inka of Peru. This sign of material wealth led Cabot to rename the estuary the Río de la Plata (Silver River). In 1531, he enthusiastically returned to Spain with news about the wealth he had witnessed. Meanwhile the sailors on San Gabriel, beset by Charrúa attacks, had abandoned Fort San Salvador and returned to Spain.[13]

Cabot's stories of silver inspired King Charles V to authorize a large-scale expedition under the leadership of court-favorite Pedro de Mendoza in 1535. With five thousand men and women, Mendoza attempted to found a settlement at Buenos Aires, which he named for the fresh breezes that blew from the pampas. After a disastrous defeat at the hands of the Argentine Indigenous people, the sickly Mendoza and most of the expedition returned to Spain while some survivors escaped to Asunción. Only in 1580 would Paraguayans resettle Buenos Aires. In the sixteenth century, the Eastern Bank offered nothing but hardship, poverty, hunger, danger and death at the hands of hostile Charrúa who, left alone, continued to live as they had for generations.[14]

Hernando Arias de Saavedra (commonly referred to as Hernandarias), the son of a soldier who had settled in Paraguay, became the first *criollo* (Spaniard born in the New World) governor of the La Plata region. In 1608 he proposed several visionary ideas to transform the "land of hunger" into a land of plenty. His report to King Philip brimmed with *enthusiasm* for the region's prospects. According to legend, Hernandarias, the first *estanciero* (large-scale rancher) in Argentina, released one hundred cows and an unspecified number of bulls at the Arroyo de Vacas near present-day Carmelo in Colonia department. Their progeny took advantage of the rich grasslands, rapidly reproducing and creating enormous herds of perhaps a million head by the end of the century. He refused to release horses in Uruguay because mounted Charrúa would make even more ferocious enemies.

Despite his well-equipped forces of five hundred men, more than once Hernandarias met defeat at the hands of the Charrúa. Therefore, he proposed pacifying the region by providing missions for indigenous peoples to minimize hostilities on the frontier. As a result, in 1624 the Franciscans (later Jesuits) established the mission of Santo Domingo de Soriano on Isla Vizcaino, the first permanent settlement in Uruguay (the mission soon moved to Villa Soriano on the mainland). Hernandarias also urged ambitious colonists to move to the Eastern Bank. These early transients founded outposts, often named for the intrepid Spanish trader who collected hides there, thus beginning the "age of leather," increasingly important in European markets. Settlers lived a precarious existence because well into the eighteenth century, the Charrúa and Minuane *tolderías* dominated the interior, feasting on the "creole cattle" (in the U.S. West, cowboys named the cousins of these shaggy-coated cattle "longhorns") beyond the pale of Spanish trading posts, missions, or towns.[15]

The arrival of Spaniards and their ungulates moderately changed Charrúa lifeways. In the beginning, the remarkable fecundity of Hernandarias's cattle produced a bounty of food unimaginable to earlier generations of Charrúa. Because of their lifeways and the prolific number of cattle, the Charrúa never attempted to corral or domesticate them. Their weaponry, bolas, and bows and shaped-stone arrows proved more than adequate to slay their new game. Steel knives, obtained from Spanish traders, made stripping hides from animals and carving meat simpler. The Charrúa thought of cattle like deer or *ñandu*, mere sources of food, which later led to conflict with Spanish ranchers.

Cattle also enabled the Charrúa to fashion warmer, more protective clothing called *quillapís* (essentially hides decorated with red and blue geometric designs that covered men and women from shoulder to ankle; women also continued to wear loincloths). Cowhides also permitted the construction of larger *toldos*. The Charrúa traded hides and enslaved captives to the Spanish for knives, alcohol, tobacco, yerba mate (a tea-like herb), sugar, playing cards and beads. As the Charrúa gained more material wealth, the social status of each band's leader increased, allowing him to have multiple wives. Charrúa women intermarried with Spanish traders and gauchos (the cowboys of the pampas).[16]

Over time, as the number of Spanish ranches increased, the Charrúa ran afoul of the European idea of private property. Some *estancieros* (ranchers) acquired royal land grants; others relied upon usufruct rights (mere usage) of the open range to acquire color of title. In either instance, ranchers asserted possessory rights to the cattle on their range. Both legal concepts conflicted with the Charrúa concept of *tolderías* (seasonal hunting grounds). Thus, under Spanish law, the Charrúa rustled privately owned stock and had to be punished for doing so. The Charrúa also retained their traditional spiritual beliefs and resisted conversion to Christianity, one of the fundamental justifications for Spanish claims to the New World. Franciscan attempts to found missions in western Uruguay for the Charrúa, who rejected the sedentary lifestyle, failed utterly. The combination of Charrúa misappropriation of cattle and their refusal to convert to Christianity allowed the Spaniards to dismiss Charrúa as heathens and savages.

Elsewhere in the Americas, diseases for which native people had no immunities caused a rapid demographic decline of indigenous populations. Because of their nomadic ways and the sparse Spanish contact, the Charrúa postponed this fate for almost two centuries. Eventually, increased interactions between European traders, ranchers, and the Charrúa brought the latter smallpox, flu, tuberculosis, and whooping cough epidemics that decimated their numbers. Ranchers retaliated and killed Charrúa who raided their livestock. Charrúa surprise attacks at dawn punctuated with fierce cries proved no match for European weapons and the rural police of the late colonial period. Because the European ethos of the eighteenth and early nineteenth century accepted as normal the extermination of "barbarians and heathens" in the name of "civilization," many colonial Uruguayans had little compunction about massacring the Charrúa.[17]

RELIGIOUS MISSIONS ON THE URUGUAYAN FRONTIER

Beginning in the seventeenth century, the Jesuits advanced the rim of Christendom southward from Paraguay into Uruguay. In pre-Hispanic times, extensive Tupi-Guaraní populations occupied wide swaths of territory in Brazil, Argentina, Paraguay, and Uruguay, living by slash-and-burn agriculture, growing corn and manioc, and supplementing their diet by hunting and fishing. Fierce warriors, they expanded against their weaker neighbors and by 1300 had established themselves around the La Plata estuary. Because of their sedentary lifeways, the Jesuits organized their Banda Oriental *reducciones* (mission communities) principally for the Guaraní and the Chaná, although they hoped to entice the Charrúa to submit to the mission regimen as well.

As in other places in the Americas, the Jesuits took advantage of similarities between Guaraní practices and Christian doctrine to convert neophytes. In addition, the Jesuits protected them from both Portuguese *bandeirantes* (slave raiders seeking workers for Brazilian sugar plantations). The missionaries organized Guaraní militias to defend the reducciones, and by 1640 had beaten back the bandeirante threat. Afterward, they expanded into Uruguay. Some of the Guaraní from the Misiones district (now part of northeastern Argentina and southwestern Brazil, see map 1.1) along with enslaved Africans and members of the Chaná settled in the missions established along the Uruguay River.[18]

Within reducciones, the Jesuits enforced communal living and instructed the Guaraní in handicrafts and elements of European culture (especially music).

Although some writers have portrayed the *reducciones* as socialist utopias, others found that more coercive conditions prevailed. Indigenous workers in Paraguay raised yerba mate (a local tea plant, high in caffeine, still very popular in Uruguay and Paraguay) on plantations, or in the case of the Uruguayan missions, herded cattle and horses and engaged in agriculture. Each family raised corn, sweet potatoes, beans, and manioc, and received a ration of approximately four pounds of beef per week, which they consumed raw, parasites and all. As might be expected, the Guaraní retained many of their traditions including polygamy for community leaders and shamanic religious practices undertaken in the guise of Christianity.[19]

The Franciscan mission of Santo Domingo de Soriano, first established for the Chaná on Vizcaino Island, moved to the mainland at Villa Soriano in 1624 and became the first permanent Spanish settlement on the Eastern Bank. As the Franciscan conversion effort waned, the Jesuits replaced them and founded seven missions in "greater Uruguay," four in the western Missiones District and three in present-day Uruguay (the Calera de las Huérfanes, the Orphans' lime kiln mission outside Carmelo); the convent in Colônia (San Francisco Xavier) both in ruins, and the estancia Nuestra Señora de los Desamparados, now the tourist hotel San Pedro de Timote, which features a restored chapel.[20]

The Calera de las Huérfanes differed from other *reducciones* because it produced lime for construction projects. Workers ground up rocks high in calcium carbonate and heated them in wood-burning kilns to over fifteen hundred degrees Fahrenheit to remove the carbon dioxide. When mixed with sand and water, lime served as mortar to bind together stones or bricks. Because of small local demand, the Jesuits shipped most of the mortar to Buenos Aires and used the profits generated for charitable purposes. After the expulsion of the Jesuits in 1767, the Sisters of Charity took possession of the kiln and used its proceeds to maintain a girls' orphanage in Buenos Aires. The father of José de San Martín, the hero of Argentine independence, managed this kiln site for several years, leading to disquieting rumors that his son had been born in Uruguay.

Jesuit *reducciones* in Uruguay managed extensive ranches and farms that sustained the workers on the complexes, provided food for poorhouses, and sold hides for revenue. For example, Jesuits at the Calera de las Huérfanes managed the Estancia del Río de las Vacas that grazed cattle and horses on almost 350,000 acres. In Florida department in contemporary Uruguay, the Jesuit aforementioned *estancia* named Nuestra Senora de las Desamparados, founded in 1740, owned nearly a quarter of a million acres of excellent grazing land supporting large herds of cattle whose hides, the principal item of commerce in the colonial Banda Oriental, was part of the expanding Atlantic trade network.[21]

SPANISH-PORTUGUESE RIVALRY OVER THE EASTERN BANK, 1680–1777

In 1680, Portugal made the claim that the boundary line separating Spanish and Portuguese possessions in the Americas established by the Treaty of Tordesillas of

1593 lay further west than previously understood. Having finally escaped from what the Portuguese referred to as the "Babylonian Captivity" (the period between 1580 and 1640 when Spanish kings ruled Portugal), it wanted to reassert its sovereignty in South America. While the Pope adjudicated the merits of the rival Spanish and Portuguese claims, Prince Pedro acted, ordering Governor Manoel Lobo in Río de Janeiro to secure a foothold on the La Plata estuary, which Pedro argued was Brazil's natural southern boundary.[22]

Lobo's expedition of four hundred soldiers, three priests, thirty enslaved Africans (probably artisans), and a few women founded Colônia do Sacramento. They constructed stone walls, city gates, a military garrison, a church, and a governor's palace on a peninsula thirty miles across the estuary from Buenos Aires. Although Spanish governor José de Garro's troops ousted the Portuguese in 1681, a treaty returned Colônia to Portugal the following year, a scenario repeated five times throughout the eighteenth century. The Portuguese colonists began smuggling hides, enslaved Africans, and British manufactured goods into Buenos Aires in exchange for silver from the mines of Potosí. Portugal's colonization of Colônia initiated trans-imperial squabbles over the Banda Oriental that led one early twentieth-century traveler to refer to Uruguay as "the Flanders of South America."[23]

The inclusion of the La Plata region into Atlantic-World commerce heightened the transnational rivalry between Spain and its ally France against Portugal and its protector, Great Britain. Portugal seized an opportunity to expand in 1724 and placed some fortifications on Montevideo Bay, an excellent horseshoe-shaped, deep-water port about 110 miles to the east of Colônia. Uruguayan schoolchildren learn that Ferdinand Magellan, passing by the area in 1519 during his circumnavigation of the globe, had named the future town of Montevideo ("the mountain I saw") referring to the *cerro* (hill) that stood in stark contrast to the otherwise uniform flatness of the bay's shore. Because that grammatical construction does not work in Portuguese, more recent writers have suggested that the "video" refers to a famed Portuguese bishop, or more probably, a geographical reference to the city being the sixth (roman numerals) hill in a westerly direction from Punta de Este (*vi-deo*, direction east to west).[24]

In response to the Portuguese, Governor Bruno Mauricio de Zabala of Buenos Aires attacked their outpost in January, 1724, removed the intruders, and planted a rudimentary settlement of six families there. By December 1726, Governor Zabala had distributed land in Montevideo to a second group of colonists from Galicia and the Canary Islands, who settled in the "Old City" along with roughly one hundred Guaraní and a number of enslaved Africans. These early pioneers constructed their homes mostly from leather: the doors, beds, even the fasteners holding the structure together were bound by moistened leather. Montevideo became the center of the Spanish presence in colonial Banda Oriental and has remained Uruguay's largest urban area to the present.[25]

During the next decades, Colônia remained an entrepôt for trade and a transit point for smuggled goods and enslaved people destined for Buenos Aires. Colônia had a very high percentage of Black people in its population, perhaps as much as

58 percent of its total in 1760. Portuguese settlers fanned out into the interior and established farms. Despite being Spain's international rivals, the merchants of Colônia forged practical networks with their counterparts in Buenos Aires and Montevideo based on marriage, religious organizations, and friendships.[26]

The marriage of Portuguese princess María Bárbara to Spain's King Ferdinand VI offered a rare opportunity for the two Iberian powers to resolve the disputed border between their colonies. The Treaty of Madrid of 1750 transferred Colônia as well as lands farther north on the Río Uruguay to Spain while ceding to Portugal expanded borders west and north, including the Seven Missions territory in what today is the Brazilian state of Río Grande do Sul. The treaty required a joint commission to survey and delineate fixed boundaries that would enable better prosecution of smugglers.[27]

The commission's process demonstrated a bias in favor of sedentary populations and ignored the rights of the Charrúa and Minuane to their tolderías, leading to numerous skirmishes between the indigenous and the surveyors. Further, the Treaty of Madrid required the Jesuits to abandon their missions now located in Portuguese territory. Some Jesuits prevaricated, as did the Guaraní. The treaty left the Guaraní a difficult choice: whether to live as individual families under the flag of their longtime tormentors, the Portuguese; or to abandon their ancestral lands for an uncertain future in the Spanish colony where hostile Charrúa contested the land assigned to Guaraní settlers. This impossible choice led to the Guaraní War (1753–1756), in which Spain and Portugal jointly fought the indigenous and the Jesuits. At the battle of Batoví in 1756, the Spaniards killed the Guaraní captain, ending the war. The ensuing treaty theoretically returned the Seven Missions territory to Spain although the border commission's work remained incomplete in exchange for Colonia. Because some Jesuits had fought alongside the Guaraní, Portuguese prime minister Sebastião José Carvalho e Melo, the Marquis of Pombal, expelled the Jesuits from Portuguese territory in the Americas. Spanish King Charles III followed suit in 1767, ending the Jesuit presence in Uruguay.[28]

In 1776 France and Spain sided with the thirteen British colonies in the U.S. War for Independence, and for once, enjoyed success. King Charles III strengthened his empire by reforming the colonial administrative and economic systems. To shore up vulnerable areas, he appointed viceroys in northern South America and the La Plata region. The following year, Pedro de Cevallos, the first viceroy of La Plata, captured Colônia after a month-long siege. In the aftermath, Cevallos destroyed the city walls and the governor's palace. He forced its Portuguese soldiers to sail to Brazil, while allowing civilians to remain in Spanish territories if they swore a loyalty oath. Because Buenos Aires needed artisans and laborers, many of the workers in Colônia (now spelled Colonia) ended up in Argentina, while others, especially the merchants, relocated to Montevideo where they constituted over 50 percent of the foreign-born population through the colonial period. These Portuguese assimilated quickly into Uruguayan society because of their long-standing familial, commercial, and friendship ties with Montevideo's merchant class. Other Portuguese ex-patriots settled near Maldonado and Soriano.[29]

The Treaty of San Ildefonso in 1777 projected Spain's undisputed imperial sovereignty over the entire Eastern Bank. Once again, Spain and Portugal created a joint mapmaking commission to delineate the border. When the cartographers arrived in northern Uruguay, the Charrúa clans blocked their passage, extracting payments for the right to cross indigenous lands. The Charrúa *tolderías* continued to control portions of the interior, impeding prospective *estancieros*' plans to create large ranches. By the end of the eighteenth century, Spanish attitudes about nomadic people had hardened. Spaniards rationalized the imprisonment, resettlement, and even murder of indigenous people because the Charrúa continued to rustle cattle and restrict Spanish settlement. As the violence escalated, some Charrúa fled to towns or ranches. Others moved north. Commander Félix de Araza encouraged them to settle in the town of Batoví, now in Brazil, opening the ranchland to the south to *estancieros*. The mapmakers' failure to agree on the Banda Oriental's northern border, would lead to further disputes during the first half of the nineteenth century.[30]

THE BLACK POPULATION IN THE COLONIAL PERIOD

The first enslaved Africans arrived in Montevideo from Buenos Aires in the mid-1720s and built the fortifications and the few stone structures in what is today known as the Old City. Thereafter, enslavers from Portugal, Great Britain, Spain, France, and the Netherlands exchanged their human cargo for hides and tallow at the port of Montevideo. The numbers of enslaved people increased over time with most captives destined for Buenos Aires and thereafter to the mines of Peru and Bolivia. When slave ships first arrived in Montevideo, traders housed their charges in the *Caserío de los Negros* in the *Barrio Sur* (south neighborhood) until sold. According to census records, enslaved people and free *pardos* (mixed-race mulattoes) comprised slightly more than one-third of Montevideo's population in the 1770s, a percentage that remained consistent throughout the remainder of the colonial period. After the destruction of Colônia, many enslaved men joined the free Black militia or fled into the interior, where in at least one instance, they formed a *quilombo* (a community of runaway slaves).[31]

Enslaved people performed many roles in colonial Uruguay. Because no sugar, cotton, or coffee plantations existed on the Eastern Bank, enslaved Afro-Uruguayan males worked as skilled artisans (tailors, cobblers, blacksmiths, masons, jewelers, bullfighters, musicians, and barbers). Women labored as domestic servants and wetnurses for the children of the wealthy. A few enslaved men became ranch hands, stripping hides from cattle and performing other such functions, while others labored in the *saladeros* (meat-salting plants) that produced *tasajo* (beef jerky), a new industry that supplied the protein that plantation owners in Brazil and Cuba provided to their enslaved workers. Although some writers have argued that because of the nature of the work performed, slavery was less harsh in the Río de la Plata region than on plantations in Cuba, Brazil, or the southern United States, others have refuted this justification. Owners chained their slaves, whipped them, and forced

Figure 1.3 Portuguese Home in Colonia. This home, now the Hotel Charco, is one of a handful of eighteenth-century Portuguese dwellings remaining in Colonia, a UNESCO World Heritage site. The stonework used in Portuguese homes differed from the Spanish style houses built after 1776. Colonia retains its colonial-era cobblestone streets, such as the Calle de los Suspiros, the Street of Sighs, named either by the Portuguese garrison soldiers who longed to return home, or by the sex workers in houses along the street who hoped to enthrall a handsome soldier. *Source*: Author photo.

female laundry workers to sleep outside the city gates amid rats and refuse. Because most of the enslaved population arrived in the late eighteenth century, few could purchase their manumission before the independence era. Others resisted slavery by escaping or by seeking redress from the law in cases of mistreatment.[32]

By becoming *vecinos* (citizens), freed Afro-Uruguayans could improve their social position. To do so, *morenos* (free blacks) and *pardos* (free people of mixed race) needed to demonstrate their *calidad* (quality), which depended upon their skin color, occupation, legitimacy, family background, and, most importantly, honor. As military threats to the Spanish Empire increased after 1777, King Charles organized militias comprised entirely of free people of color. The Guaraní militias, for example, defended Montevideo and the eastern frontier at the fortress of Santa Teresa. Afro-Uruguayans who achieved the rank of a militia officer gained privileges and enhanced social prestige, especially within the Black community. These distinguished men also played leadership roles in the Afro-Uruguayan *cofradia*, the lay brotherhood of St. Benedict. Both the militia and the lay brotherhood provided Afro-Uruguayans with a social network that often began as shipmates among unwilling passengers from Africa.[33]

Even during the colonial period, the enslaved population took steps to preserve its African heritage. They created mutual aid social networks called *salas de nación*, based on African ethnic identities. On holidays such as the Day of Kings (Epiphany–January 6), the African community created a parade of the nations. Members would dress to the nines and process in a drum-and-dance ritual called *tambo*, later known as *candombé*, a rich tradition still observed (see chapter 7). The nations marched to the cabildo and proclaimed their loyalty to the governor. Their music and dancing, however, invoked the image of a world turned upside down, disconcerting some Europeans.[34]

URUGUAY AT THE END OF THE COLONIAL ERA

The tempo of change sped up at the end of the eighteenth century. Until then, the geographical territory today known as Uruguay did not even possess a consistent name. During the eighteenth century, travelers and officials referred to it as the *Otra Banda* (Other Bank), the *Banda Norte* (Northern Bank), the *Banda Charrúa*, the Province of Montevideo, or the Fields of Montevideo. By the end of the colonial period, official maps designated it as the Banda Oriental. The region's economy flourished. Its military significance as the principal barrier against Portuguese expansion plans helped it secure its own identity. These two developments led to the widespread recognition that the Banda Oriental was a distinctive region within the Viceroyalty of La Plata, which also included Paraguay and Bolivia.

Montevideo gained new status as the seat of a governorship beginning in 1751. After Charles III's reforms, the city also became the mandatory port of call for all Spanish shipping in the South Atlantic as well as Spain's official naval base because of its deep harbor, far superior to that of Buenos Aires. To bolster Montevideo's defenses, the Crown built a new hundred-gun fortress on the cerro. Despite recognition of its growing significance, Montevideo remained the jealous junior partner of Buenos Aires in the La Plata region. Because the latter enjoyed the greater volume of commerce, it housed the viceroyalty's *Consulado de Comercio* (Chamber of Commerce), which decided disputes between any two merchants, often between individuals in the rival cities. It could use tariff proceeds to promote commerce, agriculture, and industry, which also favored *Porteños* (citizens of Buenos Aires). Montevideo wanted a consulado of its own as well as an intendency, a subdivision of the viceroyalty that would have granted it more autonomy. The king denied both requests.[35]

Despite Pedro de Cevallos's success in expelling the Portuguese from Colônia and razing its fortifications in 1776, he feared that Portugal's ambition to secure its "natural" southern border at the Río de la Plata would again threaten the Banda Oriental. Thus, he devised a new defensive strategy: to block potential by occupying the recently captured fortresses of Santa Teresa and San Miguel in the north and settling new towns in the interior. Settlers moved north from Maldonado to San Carlos, Minas, Melo, and as far east as Rocha. As officially sanctioned towns, its *vecinos* (citizens, whose obligations included militia service) chose a *cabildo*, which distributed land to community members, a powerful inducement for settlement. The redistribution of property caused legal conflicts between the settlers and absentee landlords, many of them wealthy merchants from Montevideo, who dreamed about creating huge estancias in the same territory. When Portugal went on the offensive in 1801 (the brief War of the Oranges) and seized Batoví (now in Brazil), Spain allowed the absentee landlords to regain their property north of the new jurisdictions. By then, Spain also relied on a rural police force, the Blandengues, to patrol the border.[36]

Commerce expanded significantly during the latter part of the eighteenth century as Uruguay became deeply entwined in the Atlantic trade network, benefiting from the empire's new *comercio libre* (literally free trade or better said, direct trade) policy under which ships departing from any Spanish port could trade with any Spanish colonial port. But Montevideo merchants and their counterparts in Río de Janeiro and Great Britain flouted even that liberal policy by invoking two tenets of international law to facilitate contraband trade. The first subterfuge allowed ships of neutral nations in time of war to engage in commerce with both combatants. (The United States would fight the War of 1812 in defense of this principle.) The second law allowed ships in distress to seek refuge in the nearest port to make "repairs" (the doctrine of *arribadas*) to save its crew and cargo (although legally it could not unload said cargo). Taking advantage of these loopholes, both the Portuguese and the British smuggled enormous quantities of sugar, textiles, and enslaved Africans into Montevideo in the years after 1778. More illicit commerce flowed overland from Brazil in exchange for hides and tallow that Uruguayans smuggled northward.[37]

The Río de la Plata's rapidly growing economy resulted from a demand for these two products derived from the plentiful cattle roaming the open range. Although historically the Charrúa *tolderías* had proven an effective obstacle to the expansion of Spanish ranches, the Cédula of 1754 authorized governors to grant huge tracts of land in the interior to bolster Spain's claim to disputed territory by rights of

Figure 1.4 "Gaucho and His China at the Well," by Melchor Méndez Margariños. This painting depicts a gaucho and his partner in a typical rural scene. Women performed domestic chores and cared for children, but when their gaucho took a job on a distant estancia, women also had to care for any livestock the family owned. On days when the weather prevented outdoor work, the couple might invite neighbors to share the custom of "rain, mate, and tortas." The woman would fry tortas made from flour and fresh rainwater and the group would brew and communally sip yerba mate tea. *Source*: Museo Histórico Nacional, Casa de Rivera, Montevideo.

occupation. As the demand and prices for hides grew in the post-1777 era, absentee landowners secured grants for new *estancias* (ranches). Because the wood of the hollow native *ombú* tree proved too flimsy to serve as a building material, *estancieros* (estate owners) built stone homes that doubled as fortresses where employees could take refuge and fend off indigenous attacks. Over time, *estancieros* claimed ever-larger parcels as notables came forward requesting grants in the interior and the north.[38]

Estancias needed labor. To minimize expenses, the *estanciero* hired a handful of well-paid permanent employees (the administrator, foremen, and skilled artisans) who oversaw a few enslaved people and *gauchos* (cowboys) who broke horses, built corrals, branded cattle, fed livestock during droughts, and raised crops. Gauchos had various backgrounds and heritages: *criollo* (Spanish), Afro-Uruguayan, Guaraní, or *mestizos* (mixed race). Each year, the administrator hired additional gauchos to supplement the full-time employees and assist with the round-up and transport of cattle to market. As the value of cattle increased, estancieros began branding their cattle to minimize rustling. The Crown's policy favoring large estates had two negative consequences. First, the policy of granting huge tracts of the open range limited the number of towns in the interior. Second, it negatively affected smallholding ranchers who found that in desperate times they had to sell their holding to the *estanciero*.[39]

As the gentry of rural Uruguay, *estancieros* expected to be treated as such. In such a sparsely settled land, travelers hoped that their day's journey would find them in sight of an estancia at nightfall. To obtain a meal and lodging, travelers followed a strict protocol, according to British biologist Charles Darwin: "At night we came to the house of Don Juan Fuentes, a rich landed proprietor, but not known personally to either of my companions. On approaching the house of a stranger, it is usual to follow several little pieces of etiquette: riding slowly up to the door, the salutation of "Ave María" is given, and until somebody comes out and asks you to alight, it is not customary to even alight from your horse. Having entered the house, some general conversation is kept up for a few minutes, till permission is asked to pass the night there. This is granted as a matter of course."[40]

During the 1790s and into the early nineteenth century, hides and tallow commanded high prices in the transatlantic marketplace. The Banda Oriental's export of hides fluctuated between slightly more than four hundred thousand hides annually to well over a million. Europeans found new uses for leather in addition to the traditional footwear, gloves, saddles, bridles, and harnesses. For example, factories during the early years of the Industrial Revolution used leather belts to move rollers on machinery. As demand for leather increased, smaller ports like Paysandú emerged on the Río Uruguay that shipped hides and tallow to Montevideo, where warehouses piled high with hides drew swarms of rats searching for food. Tallow could be manufactured into candles (whale oil was the only competing source of light) or could be used to lubricate Industrial Revolution–era machinery. Hides remained Uruguay's most important export for the next seventy-five years.[41]

In the midst of Montevideo's growing prosperity, the city's small elite of absentee estancieros and merchants held tightly onto their privileges based on birthright, race, and honor, dominating membership in the *cabildo*, religious brotherhoods, and merchant guilds. They viewed the Afro-Uruguayan population with much suspicion, especially as disorder mounted in the 1790s. They demanded that social order and the proprieties be respected. As a result, they proved the most loyal of the king's subjects, which they would demonstrate during the early stages of the independence movement (chapter 2). While one would expect the elite to live well, during this

Figure 1.5 "Montevideo at the End of Eighteenth Century." This anonymous painting depicts Montevideo and its city walls at the end of the colonial period. Across the bay, the Cerro's newly constructed fortress looms ready to defend the city. The tallest building in colonial Montevideo is the Church on the Plaza Matriz, across from which sits the Cabildo, the seat of government. *Source*: Museo Histórico Nacional, Casa de Rivera, Montevideo.

era artisans and even the poor in Montevideo enjoyed a relatively high standard of living. The abundance of grain, grown in the region around Montevideo, and inexpensive beef, meant that Uruguay no longer was the "land of hunger."[42]

CONCLUSION

Spaniards' initial impression of the Banda Oriental, devoid of mineral wealth and inhabited by the hostile Charrúa, convinced the intruders that this was a land left well enough alone. But Hernandarias's providential introduction of cattle reversed this opinion, as enormous herds of bovines laid the groundwork for what would become South America's twenty-first-century success story. The rich, undulating grassy plains that challenged the survival of Indigenous clans was by 1800 transformed into a virtual paradise for cattle and sheep. Although the Charrúa initially benefited from the introduction of a new source of meat, by the end of the colonial period the encroachment of European ranchers threatened their tolderías, and European diseases, their very survival. Enslaved Africans literally built Montevideo and soon constituted a third of its population. Most importantly, the Banda Oriental became the scene of trans-imperial rivalries in the eighteenth century as Spain and Portugal jousted for control of the strategic region. After 1776, Portuguese merchants and workers, displaced from Colônia, became the first contingent of foreigners to integrate themselves into Montevideo's population. New prosperity based on transatlantic commerce, a relatively homogeneous population, immigrants, and transnational rivalries provided the

Banda Oriental with an atypical colonial heritage. By the late colonial period, many Uruguayans felt a sense of autonomy that would intensify after 1808, as chapter 2 will relate.

NOTES

1. R. B. Cunninghame Graham, *The Conquest of the River Plate,* London: The Hakluyt Society, 1891, 9–12. See also Charles Darwin, *The Voyage of the Beagle,* abridged ed. London: Penguin Books, 1989, 71, 139–40.

2. Rex A. Hudson and Sandra W. Meditz, eds., *Uruguay: A Country Study,* Washington, DC: Government Printing Office, 1992, 52–62.

3. Ernst Clark Griffin, "Causal Factors Influencing Agricultural Land Use Patterns in Uruguay," *Revista Geográfica,* No. 80 (June 1974), 13–33. Anon., *Uruguay,* Washington: Bureau of the American Republics, 1892 (reprint 2019), 1–6.

4. George Pendle, *Uruguay,* third ed., London: Oxford University Press, 1965, 1–5. Thomas Dawson, *The South American Republics: Part I,* New York: G. P. Putnam's Sons, 1906, 227–29; Hudson and Meditz, *Country Study,* 55–56.

5. R. A. Fariña et al., *Megafauna: Giant Beasts of Pleistocene South America,* Bloomington: Indiana University Press, 2013. More recently, geologists uncovered the remains of a dinosaur in Tacuarembó department. José L. Prado, Cayetana Martínez-Maza, and María T. Alberdi, "Megafauna Extinction in South America: A New Chronology for the Argentine Pampas," *Paleography, Palaeoclimatology, and Paleoecology,* Vol. 421, May 1, 2015, 41–49. A replica of the skull Darwin found can be seen at the Museo Roselli in Nueva Palmira. The Museo Paleontológico Alejandro Berro in Mercedes contains numerous megafauna bones and skulls, including a glyptodon.

6. Renzo Pi Hugarte, *El Uruguay Indígena,* Montevideo: Editorial "Nuestra Tierra," 1969, 13–17. Gustavo Verdesio, *Forgotten Conquest; Rereading the New World History from the Margins,* Philadelphia: Temple University Press, 2001, 147.

7. José M. López Mazz, "*Las estructuras tumulares (Cerritos) del Litoral Atlantico,*" *Latin American Antiquity,* Vol. 12, No. 3 (September 2001) 231–55; Renzo Pi Hugarte, *Los Indios del Uruguay,* Quito: Abya-Yala, 1995, 24–25, 42–53. Another second-wave site, Chamangá in Flores department, features still indecipherable abstract pictographs (paintings on stone).

8. The Chaná settled on the islands in the Río Uruguay in the west of the country as well as in Argentina. A numerically small group, they raised corn and fished in the rivers and by the end of the colonial period had been assimilated either into other indigenous groups or the Spanish population. Their use of pottery suggests that they had become primarily agricultural people. The Guaraní will be treated later in this chapter as most of the Uruguayan Guaraní became converts on Jesuit or Franciscan missions. Pi Hugarte, *Indios,* 59–67.

9. The quoted language is from Ulrich Schmidt (Hulderico Schmidel in sixteenth century German) who participated in the Mendoza expedition of 1535. See Ulrich Schmidt (Luis L. Domínguez, trans.), *The Conquest of the River Plate, 1535–1553,* London: The Hakluyt Society, 1891, 6–7. For the information about the Charrúa bands, see Jeffrey Alan Erbig, Jr., *Where Caciques and Mapmakers Met: Border-Making in Eighteenth Century South America,* Chapel Hill: University of North Carolina Press, 2020, 9 and 184, note 41.

10. The recent data from anthropologists is in Pi Hugarte, *Indios,* 104, 145–46. Verdesio, *Forgotten Conquests,* 151. Spanish chronicler Pedro Lozano blamed the Charrúa for the 1516 encounter.

11. Pi Hugarte, *Indios,* 90–104, 68–73; Erbig, *Mapmakers,* 24; J. H. Parry and Robert G. Keith edited a five-volume series of colonial documents titled *New Iberian World: A Documentary History of the Discovery and Settlement of Latin America to the Early Seventeenth Century,* 5 Vols., New York: Times Books, 1984. Volume 5 contains the documents from the La Plata area. The tale of Charrúa running down deer is the testimony of Luis Ramírez, Sebastian Cabot's cabin boy, 249–52, taken from J. Toribio Medina, "El Veneciano Sebastiáno Caboto al servicio de España." Museum directors disagree on the use of the *rompecabeza;* some claiming they were thrown by sling; others make the case for the club or the *bola.* Given the time it must have taken to fashion a *rompecabeza,* I am skeptical about throwing it away in a sling. On the lack of agriculture, see Jared Diamond, *Guns, Germs, and Steel: The Fates of Human Society,* New York: W.W. Norton & Company, 1999, 153, although agriculture may have migrated from southern Brazil.

12. Verdesio, *Forgotten Conquests,* 15–26, debates the evidence about Charrúa cannibalism from conflicting accounts. The story originated from Martín Fernández de Enciso's *Suma de Geografía,* Seville: J. Cromberger, 1519. Anthropologist Pi Hugarte uses considerable evidence to demonstrate that Solís encountered the Guaraní, not the Charrúa, and that the Guaraní had long engaged in ritual cannibalism. Pi Hugarte, *Indios,* 23; Parry and Keith, *Documentary History,* Vol. V, 248–49, from Antonio de Herrera's *The General History of the Vast Continent and Islands of America,* and Sebastian Cabot's testimony, Parry and Keith, VI, 252–57.

13. Cunninghame Graham, *Conquest of the River Plate,* 27–28.

14. Cunninghame Graham, *Conquest of the River Plate,* 3, 28–38, 194, 241–59.

15. Because of his significant role in both Argentine and Uruguayan history, Hernandarias has been the subject of several biographies. See Raúl Molina, *Hernandarias: Primer gran estanciero criollo del Río de la Plata,* Buenos Aires: Lancestremere, 1948, and Raúl Iturria, *Hernandarias: De tropero a estadista,* Montevideo, Tierradentro Ediciones, 2007, 126–27, 143–55. The cities of Rocha and Pando were named for these pioneers. See also Verdesio, *Forgotten Conquests,* 63–71; Erbig, *Mapmakers,* 14–22; Eduardo Acevedo Vásquez, *Anales Históricos del Uruguay,* 6 Vols., I, Montevideo: Casa A. Barreiro y Ramos, S.A., 1933–1934, 13. Acevedo Vásquez was not related to famous Uruguayan novelist Eduardo Acevedo Díaz.

16. Pi Hugarte, *Indios,* 98–113. Verdesio, *Forgotten Conquests,* 123; Erbig, *Mapmakers,* 30–38. Hernandarias, the first Spaniard to encounter yerba mate, burned huge piles of it, arguing that it would lead the Guaraní to ruination. Ultimately it became the national drink of Uruguay, Argentina, and Paraguay. See Rebekah E. Pite, *Sharing Yerba Maté: How South America's Most Popular Drink Defined a Nation,* Chapel Hill: University of North Carolina Press, 2023, 19.

17. Pi Hugarte, *Indios,* 143–59, 177–80; Pi Hugarte, *Uruguay Indígena,* 43–44, 56–57; Verdesio, *Forgotten Conquests,* 124–33.

18. Barbara Ganson, *The Guaraní under Spanish Rule in the Río de la Plata,* Palo Alto: Stanford University Press, 2003, 45–47; Julia S. J. Sarreal, *The Guaraní and Their Missions: A Socioeconomic History,* Stanford: Stanford University Press, 2014, 29–34.

19. For an excellent overview of the Guaraní and the mission system, see Ganson, *Guaraní under Spanish Rule,* 19–47. Sarreal, *Socioeconomic History,* 27–48, 67–70, 75–76. See also Pi Hugarte, *Indios,* 132–41.

20. Pi Hugarte, *Indios,* 189–93.

21. Tim Burford, *Uruguay: The Bradt Travel Guide*, third ed. New York: The Globe Pequot Press, 2017, 174. The *Calera Real del Arroyo Dacá* (Soriano department) famous as Uruguay's first industrial enterprise, dates back to 1722, and engaged in lime production under governmental auspices.

22. Mario Rodríguez, "Dom Pedro of Braganza and Colônia de Sacramento," in *Hispanic American Historical Review*, Vol. 38 (1958), 179–208.

23. Verdesio, *Forgotten Conquests*, 73–83. The quote is from Thomas Dawson, *The South American Republics, Part I*, New York: G. P. Putnam Sons, 1906, 227–28.

24. Rodríguez, "Dom Pedro of Braganza," 197–208; Erbig, *Mapmakers*, 48.

25. Raúl Montero Bustamante and Julio M. Llamas, *Fundación de Montevideo*, Montevideo: Instituto histórico y geográfico del Uruguay, 1976, 9–37, esp. 13. Historians had long debated whether the founding occurred in 1724 when Zavala expelled the Portuguese, or in 1726 when settlers arrived and Zavala granted them lots in the Old City to build their homes. Bustamante and Llamas indicted that the documents favored 1726. Pendle, *Uruguay*, 67.

26. Fabrício Prado, *Edge of Empire: Atlantic Networks and Revolution in Bourbon Río de la Plata*, Oakland: University of California Press, 2015, 14–33.

27. Erbig, *Mapmakers*, 65–68.

28. Erbig, *Mapmakers*, 68–70. Ganson, *Guaraní under Spanish Rule*, 89–117; Sarreal, *Socioeconomic History*, 104–6. Pi Hugarte, *Indios*, 193–196; Erbig, *Mapmakers*, 40–76.

29. Jonathan C. Brown, *A Brief History of Argentina*, second ed., New York: Checkmark Books, 2011, 51–53, 62–63; David Rock, *Argentina: 1516–1982: From Spanish Colonization to the Falklands War*, Berkeley: University of California Press, 1985, 40–42. Fabrício Prado, "Trans-Imperial Dynamics and the Making of Independent Uruguay: The Portuguese Presence in the Formation of the Banda Oriental (1716–1810), in Pedro Cameselle-Pesce and Debbie Sharnak, *Uruguay in Transnational Perspective*, New York: Routledge 2024, 17–34, especially 22–33. Colonia, largely fell into disuse, and as a result, many portions of the old city have been perfectly preserved. Today, the city enjoys its status as a UNESCO World Heritage site and is a popular destination for international visitors and day-trippers from Argentina.

30. Erbig, *Mapmakers*, 107–36.

31. Irene Diggs, "The Negro in the Viceroyalty of the Río de la Plata," *The Journal of Negro History*, Vol. 36, No. 3 (July 1951), 281–301. Juan Carlos Pedemonte, *Hombres con dueño: crónica de la esclavitud en el Uruguay*, Montevideo: Editorial Independéncia,1943, 23–30; Alex Borucki, *From Shipmates to Soldiers: Emerging Black Identities in the Río de la Plata*, Albuquerque: University of New Mexico Press, 2015, 25–39. See also his chapter, "Rethinking Trans-Local Black Communities in Uruguay across the Southern Cone," in Cameselle-Pesce and Sharnak, *Transnational*, 55–61.

32. George Reid Andrews, *Blackness in the White Nation: A History of Afro-Uruguay*, Chapel Hill, University of North Carolina Press, 2010, 5–23; Prado, *Edge of Empire*, 20–23; Diggs, "The Negro," 290–92; Tulio Halperín-Donghi, *Politics, Economic and Society in Argentina during the Revolutionary Period*, Cambridge: Cambridge University Press, 1975, 23–32; Peter Blanchard, *Fearful Vassals: Urban Elite Loyalty in the Viceroyalty of Río de la Plata, 1776–1810*, Pittsburgh: University of Pittsburgh Press, 2020, 116–17; Borucki, *Shipmates*, 8.

33. Borucki, *Shipmates*, 85–99; Sarreal, *Socioeconomic History*, 157–57.

34. Andrews, *Blackness*, 23–28; Diggs, "The Negro," 291–92; Blanchard, *Fearful Vassals*, 109–15, 126–32; Borucki, *Shipmates*, 99–104. Pedemonte, *Hombres con dueño*, 33–37.

35. Prado, *Atlantic Networks*, 118–29, 182–83. Blanchard, *Fearful Vassals*, 66–87.

36. Prado, *Atlantic Networks*, 83–120; Blanchard, *Fearful Vassals*, 23–24; Julio Dejendererdijan, "Roots of Revolution: Frontier Settlement Policy and the Emergence of New Spaces of Power in the Río de la Plata Borderlands, 1776–1810," *Hispanic American Historical Review*, 88, No. 4, Nov. 2008) 639–68. Forty families settled the town on Minas in 1784. Each family received a plot of land and a two-room home consisting of one bedroom and one living room. Independence hero Juan Lavalleja's birthplace in Minas, now a museum, is a good example. The strategic forts squeezed invaders onto the Atlantic coast where theoretically they could be trapped.

37. Prado, *Atlantic Networks*, 30–34, 61–85; Blanchard, *Fearful Vassals*, 32–35.

38. William H. Katra, *José Artigas and the Federal League in Uruguay's War of Independence (1810–1820)*, Teaneck, PA: Farleigh Dickenson University Press, 2–6.

39. Ricardo Salvatore and Jonathan C. Brown, "Trade and Proletarianization in Late Colonial Banda Oriental: Evidence from the Estancia de las Vacas, 1791–1805, *Hispanic American Historical Review*, Vol. 67, No. 3 (August 1987), 431–59.

40. Griffin, "Causal Factors," 24; Charles Darwin, *The Works of Charles Darwin*, 74. The same custom is described in W. H. Hudson, *The Purple Land: Being the Narrative of One Richard Lamb's Adventures in the Banda Oriental as Told by Himself*, second ed., New York: Grossett & Dunlop, 1904, p. 21.

41. Sarreal, *Socioeconomic History*, 192–215, 295, note 62. Drying hides and getting them to market promptly was imperative for maximum profits. A good hide could last for eight or ten months, but moths loved to eat the fat on hides which could make them lose value.

42. Juan Carlos Garavaglia, "Economic Growth and Regional Differentiations: The Río de la Plata Region at the End of the Eighteenth Century," *Hispanic American Historical Review*, Vol. 65, No. 1 (February, 1985), 51–89. Blanchard, *Fearful Vassals*, 43–65, also notes that many merchants living in Montevideo had Basque or Catalan origins.

Two

Uruguay's Struggle for Independence, 1808–1828

For most Latin American nations, the brave deeds undertaken during the lengthy, bloody conflict that took an inordinate toll in lives and treasure and resulted in the winning of independence represented the first step in the formation of their national identity. Uruguay experienced the longest, most transnational and circuitous path to independence of all the republics, requiring its liberators to overcome British, Spanish, Portuguese, Brazilian, and Argentine opposition, and succeeding only when Great Britain intervened diplomatically to serve as midwife to the birth of the nation. For most of two decades, Uruguayans themselves disagreed about the optimal result with a small minority favoring an independent nation, but most advocating becoming part of a larger territorial project. Because of foreign interventions and internal disagreements, Uruguay's independence movement experienced multiple phases as charismatic leaders with different visions competed to achieve their objectives. These disagreements posed challenges for the formation of the country's national identity until the 1870s. This chapter will unravel the many twists and turns of the story that ultimately resulted in Uruguayan independence.

GROWING TENSIONS AND BRITISH INTERVENTION IN THE RÍO DE LA PLATA, 1806–1808

As noted in chapter 1, the Bourbon reforms had increased the rivalry between Buenos Aires and Montevideo. The following issues motivated Spanish Americans elsewhere to seek independence: Enlightenment notions of republican government and individual liberties; the successful U.S. independence movement against the world's greatest power; the example of the French Revolution embodying Enlightenment political theory, and the tensions between local elites (*criollos*) and Spaniards (*peninsulares*) for offices, played almost no role in fomenting unrest in the Banda Oriental. Even increased sin taxes on playing cards and alcohol impacted few people because gauchos lived off the land and limited their purchases at the *pulperia* (store that doubled as a bar) to locally made booze, cigars, and yerba mate imported from nearby Paraguay. Even the short-lived Guaraní War in the 1750s hardly qualified as an anti-Colonial rebellion. Simply stated, the Napoleonic Wars primarily initiated the independence movements in southern South America.

Bonaparte's decision to resume fighting in 1805 dragged Spain and Portugal into the continental conflict as partners with their respective allies: Spain with France and Portugal with Great Britain. Napoleon recognized that British strength resulted from its dominance of the seas and the profits resulting from selling manufactured goods in Europe. To weaken the British, he organized the Continental Blockade; closing European harbors to British ships. This decision led the British to seek trade opportunities elsewhere, such as with the rich colonies of France's ally, Spain.

After the definitive naval battle of Trafalgar in 1805 that destroyed the French and Spanish fleets, Britannia ruled the waves. Aware that his government sought new markets beyond Europe, Sir Home Riggs Popham, the Naval Commander of the British fleet at the Cape of Good Hope, South Africa, on his own initiative decided to turn vague policy into action. Possessed with a reputation for brilliance, Popham, who pioneered the use of chronometers to measure longitude (the distance west or east from the Greenwich meridian), set out to liberate the La Plata region with his fleet and about 1,300 soldiers under the command of Colonel William Beresford.

On June 8, 1806, the British arrived off the coast of the Banda Oriental, bypassed the fortified city of Montevideo, and landed near Buenos Aires. As Popham's fleet approached, the Spanish Viceroy, the Marquis Rafael de Sobremonte, shored up Montevideo's garrison, sent the treasury into the interior, and then took charge of the defense of Buenos Aires. After Popham and Beresford took Buenos Aires, the former offered the *porteños* an "enlightened regime" under the auspices of the British Crown (but not independence), protection of the Catholic Church, and free trade. Much to his surprise, the proclamation received a chilly response. Montevideo's cabildo provided funds for the resistance. Santiago de Liniers, a French-born militia officer, took charge of the counteroffensive with 550 soldiers from the Montevideo garrison and four hundred volunteers, including future Uruguayan independence hero José Gervasio Artigas. Liniers landed his troops just north of Buenos Aires, took Beresford and his men prisoners and held them captive.[1]

Montevideo's *cabildo* lauded its contributions to Liniers's triumph in a letter to King Carlos IV. The city officials contrasted their loyalty to Sobremonte's lackluster leadership, itemized the resources it expended in the recapture of Buenos Aires, and again requested its own consulado and its own intendancy, including the entirety of the Banda Oriental. Spain rejected these requests. Meanwhile, the optimistic British cabinet sent a second expedition to reinforce Popham. After taking aboard the two thousand Redcoats who had captured Maldonado, the British laid siege to Montevideo and its five thousand defenders. After an intense battle during which more than six hundred Spanish regulars were killed, the city fell on February 3, 1807, as Artigas escaped across the estuary. Montevideo remained in British hands until September.[2]

Lieutenant General John Whitelocke took command and resumed the attack on Buenos Aires. Unfortunately, his strategy proved disastrous. He ordered his troops to occupy the city without first bombarding it, and in so doing exposed his soldiers to withering fire from the parapets of the roofs of the city's homes. Bloody street fighting broke out. Liniers's appeal to local patriotism coupled with Whitelocke's incompetence resulted in victory for the Spanish loyalists. In September 1807, the British withdrew their troops from Buenos Aires and Montevideo and returned to the European theater. Angry at the incompetence of the colonial administration, the *porteños* grew increasingly disenchanted with their colonial status.

What had caused the British intervention to fail? First, the British cabinet's belief that "all right-minded people wanted to be British" proved erroneous. The people of the La Plata area had no desire to exchange Spanish overlordship for British suzerainty (or as historian Peter Winn more humorously put it, had "no enthusiasm for exchanging the rule of a senile Bourbon for that of a mad Hanoverian"). More importantly, Liniers's successes against the British weakened Spain's prestige, now vested in Buenos Aires and Montevideo's cabildos. As a sign of their displeasure, the revenues that ordinarily would have flowed to Seville to fight Napoleon now remained in Buenos Aires and Montevideo to pay the local militia.[3]

When the British army departed, several British merchants remained in Montevideo, wholesaling goods valued at more than a million pounds sterling to Montevideo's merchants who profitably retailed the goods. Neutral nations like the United States also began trading with the Banda Oriental, much to the resentment of the porteño business community. Promoted to Viceroy permanently as a reward for his military successes, Liniers vehemently opposed Montevideo's renewed petition for an intendancy and *consulado* and even sought to strip Montevideo of its status as the South Atlantic's sole naval base and official port. Liniers's appointee as the governor of the Banda Oriental, Colonel Francisco Javier de Elío, however, stood firm against his superior, arguing to King Charles that the Banda Oriental deserved greater autonomy, which won him considerable popularity in Montevideo. In short, the British intervention in the La Plata region and its aftermath deepened tensions between Buenos Aires and Montevideo.[4]

JOSÉ ARTIGAS: GAUCHO EXTRAORDINAIRE AND SPANISH OFFICER, 1780s–1810

Today, Uruguayans universally recognize José Gervasio Artigas, the grandson of one of the six founders of Montevideo, as their national hero. Born in 1764, young Artigas acquired a rudimentary education at a Franciscan school in Montevideo, but rejected the soft life managing his family's estancia, instead spending the majority of his formative years as a working gaucho where he displayed the attributes that made him popular with his fellows. An outstanding equestrian (like Simón Bolívar and George Washington), his colleagues admired his ability to mingle freely with other gauchos, enjoying their comradery (like England's King Henry V with his troops before the battle of Agincourt), that inspired their loyalty. As one historian has noted, Artigas had "an almost uncanny knowledge of the psychology of the gauchos." Like his fellows, he roamed throughout the country and lived for a while with the Charrúa, learning their language and fathering a child (rumors claimed multiple women and multiple children). His activities took him to the Brazilian frontier, where he smuggled hides into Río Grande do Sul. His forceful personality won him many friends although he could be stubborn, temperamental and irascible at times.[5]

Certain individuals like Artigas utilized their charismatic personalities to play decisive roles in history. Defined as "heroes on horseback" in the nineteenth century, such leaders, later called *caudillos* (strongmen or warlords), utilized their genius, vision, courage, strength, boundless energy, and personal magnetism to unite disparate communities, particularly during wartime. These military heroes transformed the usual relationship between a leader and his people through an emotional bond, a commanding personality and an image sometimes cultivated in print media. During the Age of Atlantic Revolutions, individuals like George Washington, Napoleon Bonaparte, Toussaint Louverture, and Simón Bolívar personified the traits of a charismatic leader.[6] Artigas, as well as three other figures associated with Uruguay's independence movement, would exhibit charisma to motivate their followers.

Earning the respect of independent gauchos required significant leadership skills. Gauchos proudly lived in a male dominated world in which they avoided long-term estancia work, rustling, smuggling and living off the land independently as long as possible. They randomly killed wild or branded cattle and ate only the choicest cuts, leaving the remainder to rot in the sun. They fashioned much of what they wore from hides, including their famous *botas de potro* (boots made from the skin of a horse's shank). When temporarily hired on an *estancia*, gauchos rounded up cattle and slaughtered them, stripping the carcass for its hide and scraping off the fat to be rendered into "grease" (tallow).

These semi-nomadic gauchos dwelled in homes with walls of mud, sticks and straw rooves. With few available women in the countryside, they sometimes resorted to the practice of *rapto* (kidnapping), furthering their outlaw image. Gauchos valued their freedom and independence above wealth. As seasonal ranch hands during their time on the estancia, they earned just enough money to meet their annual necessities: yerba mate tea, black tobacco from Brazil, clothes, and pocket change to spend carousing in *pulperías*. Described as the nerve center of rural areas, the *pulperías* sold groceries, provided a place for locals to swap stories and news, and doubled as bars where brawling and knife fights commonly took place. The term gaucho became a pejorative one in the eyes of Montevidean city-dwellers, who lumped gauchos together as cattle thieves and smugglers and referred to them as the "pariah class." But, as the gauchos' relationship with Artigas demonstrates, theirs was a much more egalitarian society than the one that existed in Montevideo.

Charles Darwin provided an excellent description of the gaucho: "During the evening a great number of gauchos came in (to the *pulpería*) to drink spirits and

Figure 2.1 "Gaucho in the Countryside," by Juan Manuel Blanes. Juan Manuel Blanes, Uruguay's best-known nineteenth-century artist, painted many of his country's most famous historical episodes. He also depicted ordinary figures, such as gauchos or *estancieros*, in the genre known as costumbrista painting. This painting depicts a typical gaucho, probably from the region around Salto, Blanes's birthplace. *Source*: Museo de Bellas Artes, María Irena Olarreaga Galino, Salto, Uruguay.

smoke cigars. Their appearance is very striking, they are tall and handsome but with a proud and dissolute expression. They frequently wear their mustaches long, their long black hair curling down their backs. With their brightly colored garments, great spurs clanking about their heels, and knives (*facóns*) stuck as daggers at their waist . . . they seem ready, if occasion demanded it, to cut your throat."[7]

In part because of the gauchos' reputations, the propertied class prevailed upon the Spanish Crown in 1797 to establish a rural police force, the *Blandengues de la Frontera* (Royal Lancers), to maintain law and order in the countryside. The Crown hired former bandits and other shady characters as police because the latter knew both the outlaws and the territory in which they operated. Artigas received an amnesty for his past misdeeds and joined the *Blandengues* as an officer initially stationed in Maldonado's Cuartel de Dragones. His commanding personality and his equestrian skills won him the loyalty of his subordinates, two of whom, Fructuoso Rivera, an estanciero from Durazno, and Fernando Otorgués, a fellow Blandengue, would serve as his primary officers during the war for independence. Artigas's Blandengues reduced rural crime, winning him the praise of *estancieros*.

In 1801, the government assigned Artigas as the assistant to Captain Félix de Azara, tasked with promoting settlement in the northern Banda Oriental to fend off Portuguese incursions across the frontier. Azara described the gauchos as follows:

> Their nakedness, their long beards, their ever uncombed hair and the uncleanliness and brutishness of their appearance, make them horrible to see. For no motive or interest will they work for anyone, and besides being thieves, they also make off with women. These they take to the woods, and they live with them in huts, catching wild cattle for their food. When the gaucho has some necessity or caprice to satisfy, he steals a few horses or cows, takes them to Brazil where he sells them and where he gets what he needs.

Figure 2.2 "The Rapto," (Kidnapping) by Juan Manuel Blanes. Elites typically regarded gauchos as lawless individuals. Here, a gaucho is carrying off a white woman after a *rapto* (kidnapping). Given the shortage of women in the interior, *rapto* was sufficiently common that Blanes thought it worth memorializing. In some instances, however, the woman colluded with the kidnapper when her father refused to sanction a suitor's request to marry his daughter because he was from a lower social class and therefore unsuitable. *Source*: Museo de Artes Decorativas (Palacio Taranco), Montevideo.

Azara proposed a plan to establish towns (like Batoví, today in Brazil) in the far north of the Banda Oriental within Spanish territory described in the Treaty of San Ildefonso, as well as to distribute medium-sized parcels of unoccupied land to people willing to ranch and provide a zone of Spanish occupation in this empty space. As noted in chapter 1, the Spanish government traditionally granted huge spreads to favored individuals, many of whom lived in Buenos Aires, but that policy had failed to accomplish the government's goal of effectively occupying the land. Unfortunately, Azara's inability to attract settlers to the north forced him to revert to larger grants; however, Artigas remembered Azara's proposal and made it a centerpiece of his agrarian reform vision in 1815. Artigas did convince some Guaraní to settle in the north. Both Charrúa and Guaraní would fight for him during the wars of independence.[8]

THE OPENING SALVOS OF THE INDEPENDENCE MOVEMENT, 1810–1813

The resumption of the Napoleonic Wars provided an opening for Spanish American regions to secure greater autonomy from Spain. By 1808, Napoleon recognized that his Continental Blockade against British trade had developed a leak in the Iberian Peninsula, which he was determined to plug. Therefore, he invaded Portugal and Spain, forced King Charles IV to abdicate and imprisoned his heir, Prince Ferdinand. As a final blow to Spanish sensibilities, Napoleon imposed his brother Joseph as king. Napoleon's coup had great consequences for Latin America as a whole and especially for the growing dissention between Montevideo and Liniers's government in Buenos Aires. Governor Elío questioned Liniers's loyalty because of his French ancestry, and successfully lobbied for his replacement. Meanwhile, the Portuguese royal court fled Napoleon's invasion and sailed to Brazil under the protection of the British Navy.[9]

Following the lead of many other Spanish American cities, Buenos Aires refused to accept Napoleon's brother as Spain's legitimate king, and on May 10, 1810 (today celebrated as Argentina's May Revolution), called a *cabildo abierto* (open town meeting) of its notable citizens. They deposed Liniers's unpopular replacement and created a junta (governing committee) to rule in the name of the absent King Ferdinand VII (really a convenient guise to prevent accusations of treason, but in reality, a declaration of autonomy). The junta demanded that Montevideo, where the Spanish garrison resided, recognize the transfer of authority. Elío, newly cloaked with the title of viceroy by the Cortes of Cádiz, reaffirmed his loyalty to Spain and rejected the authority of the Buenos Aires junta. As a result, Elío and the leading citizens of Montevideo remained Spanish loyalists for the time being.[10]

Elío's forces blockaded Buenos Aires in the hope of strangling commerce and forcing the city to surrender. But Elío's popularity waned, especially in rural areas, when the Cortes raised taxes on *estancia* owners by requiring them to prove clear title (which few had) to their ranches or else to purchase said titles from the Spanish government. In addition, the Cortes insisted that ranchers purchase the open range lands they had traditionally used freely. *Estancieros* resisted. Elío's forces also raided farms in nearby Canelones district to secure foodstuffs for the garrison and the people of the city, further antagonizing the rural population. Dissent mounted.[11]

ARTIGAS AND THE MILITARY CONFLICT IN THE BANDA ORIENTAL, 1811–1815

Even before the May 10 declaration, a few Uruguayans had conspired against the viceroy. One, a wealthy *estanciero*, Joaquín Suárez, turned down Elío's commission as lieutenant in the royal army and authored anti-Spanish tracts. When discovered, he and his associates escaped to Buenos Aires where they continued their work. In February 1811, Suárez joined other pro-autonomy *criollos*, leading gaucho bands in rural Uruguay. Although disaffected *estancieros* provided the leadership for the popular uprising, gauchos constituted its core. They brought their own equipment with them: their *tropilla* (string of mounts), their *bolas*, and their spears. The very nature of pastoral work transformed its cowboys into a well-armed cavalry.[12]

With Artigas still in Argentina, the Uruguayan anti-Spanish movement erupted spontaneously in the western Banda Oriental. Two men from Soriano department, one a ranch foreman and the other a retired militia corporal, rallied about one hundred gauchos on February 26, 1811, in a field and issued the *Grito de Asencio* (the "Admirable Alarm") repudiating the Elío government. Two days later, the patriots successfully captured the nearby towns of Mercedes and Villa Soriano and then marched toward Colonia, which proved too strongly guarded to capture. Artigas resigned his commission in the Blandengues and crossed the Río de la Plata to serve the cause of Buenos Aires' junta. Other contingents of independently acting gauchos joined the rebellion and soon coalesced under Artigas's leadership.[13]

Within two months, the patriots had taken most of rural Banda Oriental. Artigas and his gauchos, supplemented by soldiers from Buenos Aires, approached Montevideo, where a royalist army of about 1,500 protected the supply route from Canelones' farms to the capital. On the morning of May 18, Artigas delivered an inspiring speech to his troops at Las Piedras, telling them that their deeds that day would immortalize them. He then outfoxed the Spanish commander, drawing him into a trap that allowed the patriots' superior cavalry forces to triumph. While the Spaniards lost over one hundred men killed and another five hundred captured, the patriots suffered only eleven fatalities. Following Artigas's decisive triumph (the only major battle in which he personally led troops), the patriots controlled the entire countryside, leaving the Spanish garrison in Montevideo surrounded. The triumph at Las Piedras boosted Artigas's reputation and confirmed his status as Banda Oriental's patriot leader.[14]

Desperate, Viceroy Elío appealed to Portuguese prince João for assistance against the rebels. Prince João ordered his army to cross the border, closing in on Maldonado in the east and Villa Soriano in the west, leaving Artigas's army sandwiched

Figure 2.3 "Surrender of José Posadas at the Battle of Las Piedras," by Juan Manuel Blanes. In this work, Blanes portrays José Artigas's brilliant victory at Las Piedras in 1811. He drew Colonel Posadas into a trap, ordered the two wings of his army to close on the Spanish, and secured the first major victory of the wars for independence. Located near Montevideo, the battle of Las Piedras enabled Artigas to besiege the capital with the assistance of troops from Buenos Aires. *Source*: Museo Militar, Montevideo.

between the invaders and Elío's garrison. In October, the British envoy to Brazil, Lord Strangford, who sought peace in the La Plata region (not on humanitarian grounds, but to protect British commercial interests), negotiated an agreement with the Buenos Aires government that guaranteed Viceroy Elío's control over the Banda Oriental and required patriot troops to withdraw across the river. The Portuguese agreed to withdraw to Brazil, which they belatedly did in August 1812. Artigas reluctantly accepted this arrangement in the name of patriot unity, although he felt betrayed by the *porteños*.[15]

Artigas gathered his army of four thousand soldiers and as many as sixteen thousand civilians who spontaneously followed him in the "great Exodus" of October 1811 that crossed the Uruguay River into Argentina. In addition to thousands of gauchos and their families, Artigas's compatriots included a company of Blandengues, numerous enslaved persons and free Blacks, hundreds of Charrúa garbed in feather headdresses, and many Guaraní. The Indigenous men hunted game and helped to feed the starving civilians who had abandoned their homes and possessions, taking what they could on their backs or in ox-drawn carts. By undertaking the great Exodus, the population of rural Uruguay demonstrated its affection for Artigas, now the personification of the Uruguayan nation, as suggested by his unofficial title, *Jefe de los Orientales*. The participants crossed the Uruguay River just north of Salto at Ayuí and up the adjacent river to Entre Ríos, where they remained for almost one year.[16]

Despite British hopes that the truce would hold, the junta in Buenos Aires resumed its attack on Spanish forces in the Banda Oriental a year later. José Rondeau's army took Colonia, swept eastward along the coastal plain and defeated the Spaniards at the Cerrito (Little Hill), just east of Montevideo, isolating them in the capital's fortress. Artigas, miffed because Rondeau had not consulted him, nonetheless led his soldiers and civilian followers back to Montevideo. In concert with his principal officers, Fructuoso Rivera, Juan Antonio Lavalleja, both veterans of Las Piedras, and Fernando Otorgués, the Uruguayans assisted in the siege. Both Rondeau's and Artigas's armies recruited numerous enslaved Argentines and Uruguayans who gained their emancipation by enlisting. Many enslaved men found the patriot slogan of "Freedom and Equality" a persuasive enticement. Enslaved camp followers who worked as nurses, cooks, spies and servants found that their services did not always warrant emancipation.[17]

Artigas and Rondeau's fragile friendship fractured over competing views about the future of the Banda Oriental. Rondeau and the *porteño* leadership sought to create a Buenos Aires dominated, centralized state, which would have returned the Banda Oriental to its subservient status. Artigas envisioned a federal union with virtually autonomous provinces, including the Banda Oriental. Artigas took affront at what he perceived as Rondeau's personal snubs. For both reasons, Artigas withdrew his soldiers from the siege at the beginning of 1814. Rondeau's military successes gained him a promotion to commander in chief of the patriot forces in Peru, replacing the Argentine general José de San Martín, who retired to England. Meanwhile, British-born admiral William Brown, in the employ of the United Provinces of Argentina, improvised a navy and against all odds defeated the Spanish fleet at Buceo (the port at the Cerrito). Unable to procure more supplies, on June 20, 1814, the Spanish garrison in Montevideo surrendered to Argentine general Carlos Antonio de Alvear. In Artigas's opinion, however, Montevideo remained under alien rule.[18]

The war between Buenos Aires centralists and Artigas's federalists proved more destructive than had the battle for Montevideo. Under Alvear's command, the centralists swept through the Banda Oriental. Atrocities, on and off the battlefield, marred the conflict. When Argentine general Manuel Dorrego entered Colonia, he sponsored a ball for the elite of the town. Allegedly, his officers put "Spanish fly" in the ladies' beverages, including that of General Otorgués daughter, and took advantage of them. After January 1815, when Alvear was assigned to Peru, the Orientals' resistance to Argentine occupation strengthened. General Fructuoso Rivera defeated the porteño army at Arroyo Guayabos (near Paysandú) and forced the survivors to retreat to Montevideo. As General Otorgués approached the capital, Artigas demanded that the Argentines depart, which they did in February, but not before looting the city. Artigas and his popular movement took charge of Uruguay.[19]

After the Argentines left, Artigas demonstrated his disdain for the city by refusing to enter it. Nevertheless, its elite initially accepted his administration because he promised to restore order, which would allow the devastated pastoral economy to recover. Because of Artigas's predilection for life in the countryside (some contemporaries referred to him as the "man of the open space"), he founded his government's capital in a new community that he named Purificación, located about seven miles north of the *Meseta de Artigas*, a bluff on the eastern side of the Uruguay

River between Paysandú and Salto. This location placed him closer to the Argentine provinces that he hoped to bind with the Banda Oriental into a great federation.[20]

BOX 2.1: ARTIGAS IN HIS LAIR: A BRITISH MERCHANT AT PURIFICACIÓN

J. P. Robertson, the British merchant who, along with his brother William, provided one of the best accounts of the La Plata region during the wars for independence, stopped at Artigas's rural capital in Purificación in 1816 to complain about the treatment he had received at the hands of some of Artigas's federalist allies. Not only had his cargo been seized, but he had been imprisoned and threatened with execution. Robertson found the Protector "seated on a bullock's skull, eating beef off a spit, and drinking gin (aguardiente) from a cow horn. He was surrounded by a dozen officers in weather-beaten attire, similarly occupied." Two secretaries took dictation, and couriers rushed in and out of headquarters delivering or carrying off new messages. According to Robertson, "He seemed . . . like the greatest commander of the age" (Wellington). Artigas displayed the common touch as he interacted with his men. They called him "*Mi general*" as a gesture of respect.[21]

Artigas appointed General Otorgués as military governor of Montevideo. A rough countryman with no administrative experience, this assignment soon caused friction with the urban elite. First, Artigas ordered Otorgués to round up recalcitrant Spanish merchants and dispatch them to Purificación for political reeducation. (Allegedly, the settlement received its name because of this program). Although rumors spread about the use of tortures like the "waistcoat" (sewing prisoners into the hide of a recently slain bull and exposing it to the sun, which shrank and suffocated the victim), Artigas's defenders deny such tales and claim that he merely required the prisoners to farm and earn their keep. Otorgués found it impossible to rein in the gauchos who roamed the streets at night, drinking, brawling in *pulperías*, and taking full advantage of the "fleshpots" of the city. After many complaints, Artigas reassigned Otorgués elsewhere and allowed Montevideo's citizens to elect a *cabildo*.[22] Artigas continued to ignore Montevideo and turned his attention to the remainder of the Banda Oriental and the Argentine interior provinces with whose gaucho leaders he hoped to ally.

THE INSTRUCTIONS OF 1813, THE PATRIA VIEJA, AND THE FEDERAL LEAGUE, 1813–1816

Meanwhile, in 1813, the government of the United Provinces of the Río de la Plata had called for a constitutional assembly. The assembly asked the regions of the former viceroyalty to recognize Buenos Aires' sovereignty and to send delegates (neither Bolivia nor Paraguay expressed interest). Artigas organized an election and

Figure 2.4 "Artigas on the Meseta," by Carlos María Herrera. As the Exodus of 1811 proceeded, Artigas stood on this meseta, over one hundred feet above the Uruguay River, to search for a safe crossing into Argentina. Such a place existed just north of the city of Salto. Upon the return from Entre Ríos in 1813, Artigas set up his civilian encampment and capital at Purificación, just north of the Meseta. Today, an enormous monument dedicated to Artigas stands on this spot. *Source:* Museo Histórico Nacional, Casa de Rivera, Montevideo.

asked the delegates to debate the specific proposals he presented to them. When they met at Tres Cruces (today a neighborhood of Montevideo), he addressed the members, mostly ranchers and merchants, saying, "My authority springs from you and it ceases by virtue of your sovereign appearance." Nevertheless, Artigas's beliefs significantly influenced their proposals. He made it clear that he wanted a constitution that guaranteed the autonomy of the Banda Oriental and embraced popular sovereignty.[23]

Within a week, Artigas's congress completed the document known as the "Instructions of the Year 1813," agreeing that it would accept the sovereignty of the Buenos Aires' Constituent Assembly, but *only* if its final product met certain conditions. The Instructions included a declaration of independence from Spain (a step Buenos Aires had not yet taken), the creation of the *Provincia Oriental* conforming to the 1777 boundaries of colonial Banda Oriental, the right for provinces to legislate their own taxes and maintain their own armies, and provincial autonomy within a loose confederation. The document further demanded a limit on the national government's diplomatic powers, and the placement of the national capital elsewhere than in Buenos Aires. The Tres Cruces meeting appointed five delegates (four of them priests) to the Constituent Assembly, but in June, the assembly refused to seat the Banda Oriental delegates. Because the Uruguayan group had articulated provincial demands so well, several Argentine interior provinces followed its lead. The Constituent Assembly, however, rejected these ideas and wrote its own constitution mandating centralism.[24]

As relations between Buenos Aires and the interior provinces deteriorated in 1815, Artigas organized the Banda Oriental's first autonomous government, later called the Patria Vieja (Old Fatherland), which lasted only twenty-two months but allowed Artigas to outline his vision for the Banda Oriental. His ideas have provided historians with considerable fodder for generations. First, Artigas expressed a desire to instill democratic institutions. He called for the election of a new Congress in

Figure 2.5 "The Instructions of 1813," by Pedro Blanes Viale. In 1813 Artigas's Assembly reviewed the Instructions that he had drafted. Artigas wanted these Instructions to become the basis of the union of the provinces of the former viceroyalty. The political leadership in Buenos Aires completely disagreed and insisted upon a centralized system of governance in which they dominated the provinces. Artigas and the *caudillo* governors of Argentina's interior provinces disagreed and eventually formed the Federal League in opposition. *Source*: Palacio Legislativo, Montevideo.

which all "citizens" could vote. Artigas also hoped to broaden democracy by authorizing elected cabildos in smaller municipalities. In 1815, one representative from each eligible town traveled to Montevideo to elect a new administrative council to govern the entire Banda Oriental and to assure that Montevideo's *cabildo* (largely merchants with royalist sympathies) did not dominate provincial government. The final arrangement decentralized the government and gave rural communities more influence.[25]

In Artigas's era, democracy and popular republicanism had a more limited meaning than it does today. Only *vecinos* (citizens) could cast ballots, and, by definition, only qualified males could be *vecinos*. Nevertheless, the entire community could gather in the town square where all persons, including women, verbally expressed their opinions about the candidates or a document. Although the balloting occurred in secret, the presence of the entire population influenced elections and created nascent democratic moments, a more representative system than Spanish colonial procedures. The elections of 1815 followed the model Artigas laid out in 1813 and represented the first wide-scale exercise of the franchise in Uruguay even though the process resulted in the election of landowners and merchants.[26]

Artigas's popular principles featured a more egalitarian landholding system as Félix de Azara had proposed years before. The details laid out in the "Provisional Ordinance for Progress in the Rural Districts and the Security of Ranchers" would have restructured the pastoral system and reoriented Uruguay's future economy. The ordinance confiscated *estancias* belonging to all royalists and those who had abandoned their ranches for redistribution to "the most unfortunate who shall be the most privileged" in medium-sized *estancias* of 7,500 hectares (roughly 18,500 acres). These *"Americanos"* included free Blacks, free *zambos* (mixed-race Black and indigenous people), Indigenous individuals, especially the Guaraní, and poor *criollos*. Although 18,500 acres sounds substantial, colonial Spanish inheritance laws (forced heirship) required that a deceased's property be divided among all his children, which after several generations could significantly reduce the size of the ranch. To induce settlement, Artigas's decree required grant recipients to construct a house and two corrals within three months after taking possession. The grantees had to measure and stake out the property's boundaries, secure a source of water, and could not sell the land under any circumstance.[27]

By rewarding his loyal followers from the popular classes who had idolized him since the time of the Exodus, Artigas believed that he could curb rural lawlessness and reinforce property rights. During the years of conflict, impoverished people and billeted armies simply slaughtered cattle, eating the choicest cuts and selling their hides. Artigas hoped that land redistribution would both reward his popular followers, appease pro-Artigas landowners' demands for the restoration of order that would allow herds to multiply and punish those who opposed him.[28]

The ordinance appointed Artigas's *Alcalde Provincial* and four subordinates to redistribute property once they determined it belonged to "bad Europeans or worse Americanos" (royalists), a litigious process at best. Notice of this reform turned many *estancieros*, who had once favored Artigas, against him. The redistribution experiment did create some smaller-scale ranches whose ownership rights would be challenged after independence, but the short duration of the Patria Vieja limited its effect. To restore order, he revived the Blandengues to prevent rustling and outlawed vagrancy. As a result of the reforms, large landowners and mercantile interests in Montevideo invited the Portuguese to invade the Banda Oriental in January of 1816, marking the effective end of the Patria Vieja.[29]

The long-term viability of Artigas's plan for rural development poses interesting questions. Had small ranches existed in significant numbers, would they have contributed as much to national prosperity as did the great *estancias* that produced beef and wool for the global marketplace and fueled the development of Uruguay's economy in the late nineteenth and early twentieth centuries? Schemes like Artigas's land redistribution plan would be revived by reformers in the 1870s, and periodically thereafter, but they were never enacted.

Simultaneously, Artigas presided over the *Liga Federal,* or Federal League, a confederation of provinces comprised of the Banda Oriental and four interior Argentine provinces: Corrientes, Misiones, Santa Fe, and Entre Ríos. Between 1816 and 1820, the Federal League fended off the centralizing aspirations of Buenos Aires. In common with Artigas, the governors leading these provinces shared the vision of popular sovereignty, self-determination, and provincial autonomy, which included a tariff protected, self-sufficient economy favoring artisanal craftsmen rather than British manufacturers.[30]

As the proclaimed "Protector" of the Federal League, Artigas faced numerous challenges, not the least was ongoing warfare against the porteños. In addition, controlling the willful, ambitious and egocentric provincial caudillos who had their own ideas about their respective provinces constituted another major headache. They respected Artigas when they needed his troops to defend them, but in the end turned out to be unreliable allies when the situation reversed itself.[31]

BOX 2.2: JUAN MANUEL BLANES

Uruguayans today revere the artistic works of Juan Manuel Blanes (1833–1901) because of his naturalistic portrayal of the nation's landscape, its people, and, perhaps most importantly, its notable historic events. Born of parents of modest means, Blanes displayed an early aptitude for portraiture. Unable to earn a living in Montevideo, he moved to Salto and then to Entre Ríos where he completed a number of battle scenes for General Justo José Urquiza. Returning to Montevideo, he received a grant to study in Florence, where he sharpened his technique. In 1871, he scored a major triumph with his portrayal of a yellow fever victim in Buenos Aires, followed by dramatic historical scenes such as the assassination of Venancio Flores, independence-era battle scenes, landscapes with gauchos, and a portrait of José Artigas. Blanes won his nickname "painter of the homeland" because of his magnificent "Oath of the

Thirty-Three," a depiction of the arrival of liberators on the Uruguayan shore in 1825. Known for his meticulous attention to detail, Blanes stayed at an *estancia* near Agraciada so that he could study the terrain where the liberators landed. He returned to Italy in the 1890s to try and locate his missing son, and died there after finishing his final masterpiece, a rendition of the battle of Sarandí.[32]

THE PORTUGUESE, THE BRAZILIANS, AND THE CISPLATINE PROVINCE, 1816–1828

The end of the Napoleonic Wars in 1815 profoundly affected the Latin American independence movements and in southern South America, allowed the Portuguese to reassert their historic claim to the Río de la Plata as Brazil's natural southern border. After the Portuguese Queen died in 1816, Prince João became king of the kingdom of Portugal, Brazil, and the Algarve. With the conclusion of the European war, British influence over João waned; he then used his freer hand to plan an invasion of the Banda Oriental. A full division of the Portuguese army, ten thousand veterans of the continental wars under the command of Major General Carlos Federico Lecor, arrived in Río de Janeiro, ready to transform João's hopes into reality.

Lecor divided his forces into two. One army entered Eastern Misiones province, traditionally part of Brazil, but since 1813 occupied by Artigas's army. The Portuguese battled with Artigas's Guaraní troops led by his Guaraní son, Andrés "Andrecito" Guacaraví Artigas. The Guaraní fought hard despite having many fewer men and more antiquated equipment. The invaders burned the Guaraní villagers' fields, tore down their dwellings, and killed most of the Guaraní troops. Captured by the Portuguese, Andrecito died in prison the following year.[33]

As the Brazilian invasion unfolded, Artigas pleaded with the Buenos Aires government for assistance, but the Buenos Aires government prevaricated, entering into a secret arrangement with Prince João, offering to allow him to annex the Eastern Bank in exchange for guaranteeing Argentine independence. The Buenos Aires regime feared Artigas and the Federal League far more than it did the Portuguese, and so acted duplicitously, promising aid to Artigas but in reality, sending only minimal amounts.[34]

The second army under General Lecor marched south, skirting the fortress of Santa Teresa along Uruguay's eastern border. After overwhelming Fructuoso Rivera's smaller army at the arroyo of India Muerte in November, Lecor's army hastened down the Atlantic coast, joined reinforcement in Maldonado, and marched to Montevideo, which Artigas ordered evacuated in January, 1817. Lecor offered the political elite of Montevideo the opportunity to join with the Portuguese against Artigas and promised emancipation to Uruguayan Blacks who would enlist. Montevideo's support for Artigas dwindled after 1815 because of his social and agrarian reform agenda and his failure to restore order in the countryside. Not surprisingly, the city's elite *cabildo* members opened its gates to Lecor without resistance.[35]

As the patriots retreated, they rejoined Artigas in Purificación. As Lecor consolidated his control over the Eastern Bank, Artigas's lieutenants resorted to guerrilla warfare without much success. The Portuguese soon captured Artigas's lieutenants Juan Lavalleja and Fernando Otorgués and imprisoned them in Brazil. In October, 1819. Manuel Oribe, another important Artigas follower, defected from the Protector's army and joined the Portuguese army in Montevideo.[36]

Artigas urged his fellow *caudillos* in the Federal League to assist him, but they preferred to further their own interests. Over the next year, Artigas's influence rapidly waned. Younger federalist *caudillos* displaced the once all-important "Protector." The Federal League's chances diminished because Buenos Aires and Portugal controlled all ports of entry along the Atlantic coast, depriving the patriot armies of military provisions. As a result, the effective leader of the Federal League, Francisco Ramírez, without even consulting Artigas, signed the Treaty of Pilar in February 1820, ending the conflict between Buenos Aires and the interior for the moment.[37]

The Artigas movement received its final blow after the Portuguese drubbed his remaining supporters at Tacuarembó on January 22, 1820. Two months later, Fructuoso Rivera, Artigas's most competent commander, surrendered and accepted Lecor's offer to become a colonel in the Portuguese army. Lecor's generous offer provided Rivera with a high rank and salary (Rivera was an inveterate gambler who frequently lost). He accepted command of a regiment of Uruguayan defectors, including recently paroled Lavalleja, all tasked with pacifying the interior of the Banda Oriental.[38]

In September 1820, Artigas and his faithful Black adjutant Manuel Antonio Ledesma (Ansina) crossed the border into Paraguay and accepted dictator José Gaspar Rodríguez de Francia's terms for refuge. Francia kept Artigas and Ansina as virtual prisoners, offering the general a small stipend, a plot of land, and some tools as he, numerous Guaraní, and roughly two hundred Black followers settled in Curaguati. Why did Artigas remain in Paraguay? When President Fructuoso Rivera encouraged him to return in the 1830s, Artigas replied "that he wanted to die in his sweet-smelling wood, the only haven where he had known peace."[39]

As the Portuguese consolidated control, Lecor ingratiated himself with Montevideo's well-to-do. As governor, he granted generous amnesties and incorporated Artigas's officers into the Portuguese army. He pleased ranchers by taking strict measures against rustlers. Merchants applauded when he opened Montevideo to international trade. This paid off. When the Portuguese Cortes forced King João to return home with the Portuguese army in 1821, he ordered Lecor to organize a congress in the Banda Oriental to determine its future. Lecor convinced the delegates to petition Río de Janeiro to have the Banda Oriental incorporated into Brazil as the *Estado Cisplatina* (Cisplatine Province).

After King João's departure, his son Pedro remained behind. When the Portuguese Cortes attempted to recall him, he followed the plan that he and his father had hatched, refusing to return, and declaring Brazil independent on September

7, 1822. Soon he was crowned Emperor Pedro I. Meanwhile, Uruguayans, other than the merchants of Montevideo, grew less enthusiastic about remaining part of Brazil. Brazilians brazenly invaded the northern portion of the Cisplatine Province and occupied land that Uruguayan *estancieros* believed belonged to them. Other Uruguayans felt a greater affinity to Argentina and rejected the idea of becoming Brazilians.[40]

THE IMMORTAL THIRTY-THREE, BRITISH DIPLOMACY, AND INDEPENDENCE, 1825–1828

With the remainder of Spanish South America liberated after the battle of Ayacucho (Bolivia) in December 1824, the Banda Oriental achieved the unenviable status of being the only former Spanish South American region still under foreign rule. In 1823, Juan Antonio Lavalleja (a landowner from Minas) and Manuel Oribe, the son of a Spanish officer, fled to Buenos Aires. There, they joined an anti-Brazilian organization called *Los Caballeros Orientales*. Argentine president Bernadino Rivadavia promised the Uruguayans monetary and military assistance for their ensuing campaign. In Montevideo, Josefa Oribe de Contucci, the granddaughter of the first governor of the city and the wife of a high-ranking Brazilian official, acted as a go-between for Montevideo's patriot sympathizers and the exiles in Buenos Aires.[41]

On April 19, 1825, Lavalleja and the Immortal Thirty-Three (as Uruguayans call them: the landing party actually had several Argentines, two Blacks of unknown nationality, and one Frenchman) eluded Brazilian naval patrols, crossed the river, and landed on the sandy beach of La Agraciada near Nueva Palmira where Lavalleja proclaimed, "Liberty or Death." Soon a collaborator arrived and provided them with several *tropillas* of horses, enabling riders to change mounts and move rapidly. Led by Lavalleja and Oribe, the Immortal Thirty-Three took the historic town of Villa Soriano. As they continued north and east, they rapidly gained recruits. Lavalleja and Oribe sought not an independent Uruguayan state, but rather to join the United Provinces of the Río de la Plata as an autonomous province, independent of Brazilian rule.[42]

The interactions between Lavalleja and the third participant in the liberation of the Banda Oriental, Fructuoso Rivera, remain shrouded in controversy. Rivera and Lavalleja had been colleagues since the beginning of the Artigas revolution. The two both fought in the battle of Las Piedras and Lavalleja later served under Rivera before being captured and imprisoned in Río de Janeiro. From Buenos Aires, Lavalleja had exchanged letters with Rivera, tempting him to join the rebellion against Brazil. Rivera had remained noncommittal in writing. Lavalleja knew, however, that Rivera's military skills would make him an invaluable ally.

Marching north and east along the Río Negro and the Río Yí, Lavalleja's forces encountered Rivera with his escort of twenty-five soldiers and "captured" him, leading to the "abrazo [hug of friendship] de Monzón" where, following two hours of negotiations, the two agreed to collaborate. Because Lavalleja and Rivera became

Figure 2.6 "Oath of the 33 Orientals," by Juan Manuel Blanes. Blanes demonstrated his mastery of the genre of historical painting in this great work. It recreates the moment when the Thirty-Three Orientals landed at the beach of Agraciada on April 19, 1825, and swore an oath to free the Banda Oriental from Brazil. While Blanes worked on this masterpiece in 1875, he stayed at a nearby *estancia*, traveled to the beach regularly to get a sense of the scene, and even took sand to his studio so that his representation would be accurate. The two central figures, Juan Antonio Lavalleja (the shorter man) and Manuel Oribe, became the leaders of the Blanco party. *Source*: Museo Municipal de Bellas Artes Juan Manuel Blanes, Montevideo.

bitter rivals in the 1830s, their adherents have authored wildly different versions of the circumstances surrounding the "*abrazo*." Rivera's supporters claim that he would not have been traveling with such a small escort had not the "capture" been prearranged. They further note that he had been recruiting independence-minded Uruguayan soldiers to his regiment. Lavalleja's supporters claim Rivera was so frightened when captured that he went down on his knees and begged for his life. Whichever the case, during the discussion, Lavalleja probably reiterated that he wanted to see Uruguay join the United Provinces, while Rivera likely proposed the ambitious creation of an independent Uruguayan state including the territory marked out in the Treaty of San Ildefonso. Although these disagreements in the long run proved profound, Lavalleja and Rivera shared an immediate common short-term goal: to liberate Uruguay from Brazilian rule.⁴³

The "*abrazo de* Monzón" made practical sense. Lavalleja and Oribe needed Rivera's military expertise as well as his numerous soldiers, which became the nucleus of the patriot army. By May 1825, the Uruguayan forces completely controlled the interior and had set up camp at the Cerrito just outside Montevideo, where Rivera and Oribe soon defeated the Brazilians, isolating them in their garrison. Then in October, the three leaders took on the second Brazilian army at Rincón and Sarandí in today's Florida department. At the latter, Lavalleja's inspiring shout, "Put your guns aside and charge with your sword in hand," inspired his troops, who split the Brazilian army in half, allowing Rivera and Oribe to gain the field for the Uruguayans.⁴⁴

After these victories, on August 25 (then one of two Independence Days that Uruguayans celebrate), the insurgents' House of Representatives met in the town of Florida, declared the Oriental District's independence *from Brazil* and expressed its eagerness to join the United Provinces of the Río de la Plata if guaranteed autonomy. In October, the Congress of the United Provinces reincorporated the Banda Oriental into Argentina. This event provoked the five-hundred-day long Cisplatine War (1825–1828) between the United Provinces and Brazil. The Uruguayan forces, swollen with additional gaucho and Afro-Uruguayan volunteers, isolated the Brazilians in their fortifications in Colonia and Montevideo.⁴⁵

Both the United Provinces and Brazil claimed to be willing to negotiate, but neither would repudiate its ultimate objective. Brazilian Emperor Pedro I insisted on keeping the Cisplatine Province, while the haughty, vain Argentine President Bernardino Rivadavia demanded the incorporation of the Banda Oriental into the United Provinces. Rivadavia's bluster convinced more Uruguayans to consider outright independence. Pedro attempted to blockade Buenos Aires harbor, but Admiral Guillermo Brown, despite his smaller fleet, inflicted two embarrassing defeats on the Brazilian navy.⁴⁶

For the next year and a half, the military situation stalemated. The battle of Ituzaingó (February 1827) in Río Grande do Sul typified this quagmire. While Argentine Carlos María de Alvear won a tactical victory and eliminated the possibility of a Brazilian invasion of the Banda Oriental, he could not force the Brazilians to forgo their claim. Further, his attempt to absorb the Uruguayan forces into his army angered Lavalleja, whose positive attitude toward the Argentines began to change. Domestic problems limited both belligerents' ability to mount a definitive campaign. Brazil faced a series of uprisings in its northeast, while Rivadavia battled the caudillos of Argentina's interior provinces. Rivera, sent to Buenos Aires to solicit more aid, was briefly imprisoned there, but he escaped to Santa Fe province where the provincial governor helped him raise an army to attack Brazilian territory.⁴⁷

Later in 1827, the United Provinces government forced the unpopular Rivadavia to resign and replaced him with Manuel Dorrego, a moderate federalist, who proved more amenable to diplomatic overtures. Fructuoso Rivera's small army reinforced with Argentine federalists found the Misiones district essentially undefended in April 1828. By August, he had captured the few Brazilian troops stationed there. His victories in Misiones softened Emperor Pedro's negotiating stance. Most importantly, Rivera occupied the town of Bella Unión where he was joined by eight thousand Guaraní from the missions. He refused to hand the town back to the Brazilians, solidifying Uruguay's claim to territories further north. The defeat forced Pedro to face reality and accept British mediation since he did not wish to lose the entire Misiones area.[48]

The British sought to reopen commercial traffic in the La Plata. To achieve this end, Prime Minister George Canning selected Viscount John Ponsonby to negotiate a treaty that would create a buffer state separating Brazil from Argentina. Ponsonby perfectly fit the bill for this delicate mission. His rank in the British nobility ensured his favorable reception by Emperor Pedro I. In addition, Ponsonby's appointment solved a domestic problem for Canning. Reputedly the most handsome man in four kingdoms, Ponsonby had allegedly caught the eye of King George IV's girlfriend, Lady Conyngham. To please the king, Canning sent Ponsonby to the most remote and unpleasant diplomatic post available: Buenos Aires. Ponsonby spent two miserable years shuttling back and forth between Río de Janeiro (which he loved) and Buenos Aires (which he hated). Initially, Ponsonby made no progress negotiating until Rivera's campaign, but by early 1828 both sides wanted a settlement.[49]

Thus, "was Britain midwife at the birth of this, the smallest of the nations of South America." Despite their political disagreements, Lavalleja and Rivera accepted the British solution. On October 4, 1828, the United Provinces and the Empire of Brazil ratified the Treaty of Montevideo, which granted Uruguay independence, returned the Eastern Misiones area to Brazil but left the border at the 1777 line of San Ildefonso, and opened the La Plata to free navigation. After the Uruguayans formed an interim government, ironically led by Artigas's Argentine enemy José Rondeau, it agreed to hold a Constituent Assembly to draft a constitution for the newborn republic.[50]

CONCLUSION

After twenty-two years of conflict involving five nations, the most protracted effort in all of Latin America, the Banda Oriental finally gained independence. Although relatively few Uruguayans perished in battle compared to the bloody slaughters elsewhere in South America or Mexico, the two-decade-long conflict cost Uruguay much of its treasure—the cattle that roamed its prairie. Because of the complex transnational nature of independence, Uruguayans could not point to a decisive battle that secured freedom nor to a clear independence era hero. Three (José Artigas, Juan Lavalleja, and Manuel Oribe) never envisioned Uruguay as a stand-alone state, while the fourth (Fructuoso Rivera) sought an enlarged country that included disputed territory in the Misiones area. The new nation had limited institutional foundations, with neither a significant colonial administrative structure nor a powerful institutional Catholic Church. Not surprisingly, initial attempts to construct a nation from these modest beginnings proved challenging, as chapter 3 will relate.

NOTES

1. Henry Stanley Ferns, *Great Britain and Argentina in the Nineteenth Century*, Oxford: The Clarendon Press, 1960, 18–35; John Street, *Artigas and the Emancipation of Uruguay*, Cambridge: Cambridge University Press, 1959, 75–87; John D. Grainger, *British Campaigns in the South Atlantic, 1805–1807*, Barnsley, Great Britain: Pen & Sword Military Press, 2015, 71–108.

2. Street, *Artigas,* 88–111; Ferns, *Great Britain and Argentina,* 38–51; Peter Blanchard, *Fearful Vassals Urban Elite Loyalty in the Viceroyalty of La Plata, 1776–1810,* Pittsburgh: University of Pittsburgh Press, 2020, 171–80; Grainger, *British Campaigns,* 139–58.

3. Ferns, *Great Britain and Argentina,* 39–51; Tulio Halperín-Donghi, *Politics, Economics and Society in Argentina in the Revolutionary Period,* Cambridge: Cambridge University Press, 1975, 184–91. Peter Winn, "British Informal Empire in Uruguay in the Nineteenth Century," *Past and Present,* No. 73 (November 1976) 100–26, at 102.

4. Street, *Artigas,* 78–90; Fabrício Prado, *Edge of Empire: Atlantic Network and Revolution in Bourbon Río de la Plata,* Oakland: University of California Press, 2015, 155–56; Blanchard, *Fearful Vassals,* 191.

5. William H. Katra, *José Artigas and the Federal League in Uruguay's War of Independence, 1810-1820,* Madison: Farleigh Dickenson University Press, 2017, 9–10; Percy Alvin Martin, "Artigas: The Founder of Uruguayan Nationality," *Hispanic American Historical Review,* Vol. 19, No. 1 (February 1938) 2–15. Artigas quarreled with a number of his followers over the years. A psycho-biography of Artigas would be very interesting. He clearly rejected the lifestyles of his father and grandfather, both pillars of the community of Montevideo, whereas Artigas came to despise the city and everything for which it stood.

6. David A. Bell, *Men on Horseback: The Power of Charisma in the Age of Revolution,* New York: Farrar, Straus, and Giroux, 2020, especially 3–35.

7. Halperín-Donghi, *Politics, Economics, and Society,* 23–24, 50–60; Madeline Wallis Nichols, *The Gaucho: Hunter, Cavalryman, Ideal of Romance,* second ed., New York: Gordian Press, 1968, 4, 12–13, 18–19; Darwin, *Voyage of the Beagle,* 73–74.

8. Street, *Artigas,* 44–74; Katra, *José Artigas,* 11–16; Félix de Azara, *Descripción de la historia del Paraguay y del Río de la Plata,* 2 Vols. (1847), 310; quoted in Nichols, *Gaucho,* 9.

9. Jonathan C. Brown, *A Brief History of Argentina,* second ed., New York: Checkmark Books, 2011, 81–92.

10. John Lynch, *The Spanish American Revolutions,1808–1826,* second ed., New York: Oxford University Press, 1986, 52–71, 91–98. Street, *Artigas,* 104–10.

11. Street, *Artigas,* 124–34; Halperín-Donghi, *Politics, Economics, and Society,* 271–74; Lynch, *Spanish American Revolutions,* 93–94. Lynch's attributes Artigas's success in these early years to his connections with his fellow estancieros rather than his popularity with the gauchos and mixed-race folk of his entourage. Blanchard, *Fearful Vassals,* 202–10. Fernando

López-Alves, *State Formation and Democracy in Latin America*, Durham: Duke University Press, 2000, 74.

12. The two individuals were named Brazilian born Pedro Viera and Venancio Benavides, the ranch foreman respectively. Artigas assigned Benavides to lead the attack on Colônia after these initial successes but refused to promote him. Benavides then joined forces with Belgrano's army bound for Peru, but when they turned back, he deserted and joined the royalists, providing them with important information about the Buenos Aires army. He was killed in battle in 1813; Justo Maeso, *Las Primeros Patriotas Orientales de 1811: Espontaneidad de la Insurrección Oriental contra la España en la Guerra de la Independencia Americana*, second ed., Montevideo: Talleres Gráficos de la Razón, El Siglo y El Telégrafico, 1914, 29–30. The information about Suárez, Maeso gathered from his unpublished autobiography. Suárez's father had a grant of more than two million acres of land. He also contributed financially to the triumph of the Immortal Thirty-Three. Carlos Real de Azúa, *El Patriciado Uruguayo*, Montevideo: Ediciones Asir, 1961, 36–38, 51–52.

13. Maeso, *Primeros Patriotas*, 82–87; Nichols, *Gaucho*, 54.

14. Maeso, *Primeros Patriotas*, 115–23 reproduces the letter from José Artigas to José Rondeau, May 20, 1811, in which the Uruguayan commander describes the battle in detail. See also Acevedo Vásquez, *Anales Históricos*, I, 92–94. Independence leaders Fructuoso Rivera and Juan Antonio Lavalleja served under Artigas at Las Piedras.

15. Prado, *Atlantic Networks*, 159–63; Rock, *Argentina*, 83–84. John Street, "Lord Strangford and the Río de la Plata, 1808–1815, *Hispanic American Historical Review*, Vol. 33, No. 4 (Nov., 1953, 477–510, especially 499–505; Lynch, *Spanish American Revolutions*, 94–96. Maeso, *Primeros Patriotas*, 155, calls the October agreement "one of the most shameful desertions of the American cause."

16. Street, *Artigas*, 147–53.

17. Street, *Artigas*, 164–70; Halperín-Donghi, *Politics, Economics, and Society*, 272–75. Peter Blanchard, *Under the Flags of Freedom: Slave Soldiers and the Wars of Independence in Spanish South America*, Pittsburgh: University of Pittsburgh Press, 2008, 38–45, 143–148.

18. Street, *Artigas*, 193–201; Katra, *José Artigas*, 24–25, 147–53. Artigas and Rondeau had had an earlier falling out, and so the level of trust between the two was very limited. Alex Borucki, *From Shipmates to Soldiers: Emerging Black Identities in the Río de la Plata*, Albuquerque: University of New Mexico, 2015, 118–121; Thomas B. Davis, *Carlos de Alvear, Man of Revolution*, Durham: Duke University Press, 1955, 10–12.

19. Street *Artigas*, 193–213; Acevedo Vásquez, *Anales Históricos*, I, 133–38. For Otorgués testimony about his daughter, see Street, *Artigas*, 207, note 1. Halperín-Donghi, *Politics, Economics, and Society*, 275–77; Lynch, *Spanish American Revolutions*, 98.

20. Street, *Artigas*, 218–27, Katra, *José Artigas*, 28.

21. Katra, *José Artigas*, x–xi; J. P. Robertson and W. P. Robertson, *Letters on South America: Travels on the Banks of the Paraná and the Río de la Plata*, Vol. III, London: John Murray, 1839, 101–3.

22. Street, *Artigas*, 218–24; Katra, *José Artigas*, 28–29; López-Alves, *State Formation*, 75–77; Much after the fact, travel writer William Henry Koebel, *Uruguay*, London: 1912, 71 said "no man in Uruguay possessed less of the lamb in his disposition than Otorgués." For the "waistcoat," see 90.

23. Street, *Artigas*, 174–78; Katra, *José Artigas*, 23–24. Nicolas Shumway, *The Invention of Argentina*, Berkeley: University of California Press, 1991, 48–57, 62. E. Bradford Burns, *The Poverty of Progress: Latin America in the Nineteenth Century*, Berkeley: University of California

Press, 1983, 67,92, referred to leaders like Artigas and others as folk *caudillos* because of their promotion of democracy and social reform. Street, *Artigas*, 174–79; Katra. *José Artigas*, 20–24.

24. Street, *Artigas*, 179–88.

25. Street, *Artigas*, 225–26.

26. For works discussing popular republicanism and popular liberalism in other nations, see James Sanders, *Contentious Republicans: Popular Politics, Race, and Class in Nineteenth Century Colombia*, Durham: Duke University Press, 2004, and Peter Guardino, *The Time of Liberty: Popular Political Culture in Oaxaca, 1750–1850*, Palo Alto: Stanford University Press, 2005.

27. Katra, *José Artigas*, 32–34; Street, *Artigas* 227–42; Shumway, *Invention*, 59–63. Halperín-Donghi, *Politics, Economics, and Society*, 283–85.

28. Street, *Artigas*, 214–16; Katra, *José Artigas*, 29–32.

29. Katra, *José Artigas*, 32–35; López-Alves, *State Formation*, 75–76. Halperín-Donghi, *Politics, Economics, and Society*, 283–85.

30. Street, *Artigas*, 212–21; Katra, *José Artigas*, 28, 41–64, 69–126, 244–79.

31. Street, *Artigas*, 311–22.

32. Ricardo Goldaracena, *Juan Manuel Blanes*, Montevideo: Editorial Arca, 1978.

33. Street, *Artigas*, 297–98; Katra, *José Artigas*, 128; Barbara Ganson, *The Guaranis under Spanish Rule in the Río de la Plata*, Palo Alto: Stanford University Press, 2014, 160–62.

34. Street, *Artigas*, 293–294; Katra, *José Artigas*, 128–29.

35. Street, *Artigas*, 295–307; Katra, *José Artigas*, 128–29. Lynch, *South American Revolutions*, 100–101; Borucki, *Shipmates to Soldiers*, 121–23. India Muerte got its name from the legend of an indigenous female ghost who guided coaches onto the correct road through the swampy terrain.

36. Katra, *José Artigas*, 132–34.

37. Katra, *José Artigas*, 168–69; Street, *Artigas*, 321–326; Halperín-Donghi, *Politics, Economics, and Society*, 332–36.

38. Katra, *José Artigas*, 179; Street, *José Artigas*, 326–33. Lynch, *Spanish American Revolutions*, 101–2; and Enrique de Gandía, *Los treinte y tres orientales y la independencia del Uruguay*, Buenos Aires: Espasa-Calpe Argentina, S.A., 1939, 148–57. Washington Lockhart, *Rivera, tal cual era*, Montevideo: Impreso en impresara, Dolores, 1996. Lockhart's revisionist biography disparages Rivera's military abilities and highlights his moral failings. Lockhart notes Rivera's opposition to Artigas's land reform (14) and alleges that Lecor paid him 10,000 pesos to redeem his gambling debts, 17–21.

39. Street, *Artigas*, 327–28, 370–74. The second reason for Artigas's decision to remain in exile is discussed in Goran Lundahl, *Uruguay's New Path: A Study in Politics during the First Colegiado, 1919–1933*, Stockholm: Library and Institute of Ibero-American Studies, 1962, p. 9. Pedemonte, *Hombres con dueño*, 39. For the quote, see Gandía, *Treinte y tres orientales*, 133–34.

40. Street, *Artigas*, 329–36.

41. Gandía, *Treinte y tres orientales*, 148–70. Lavalleja also managed a *saladero* in Buenos Aires during his time in exile.

42. Ferns, *Great Britain and Argentina*, 33, 147–48. Street, *Artigas*, 338–341; Diggs, "The Negro," 299; Gandía, *Trente y tres orientales*, 173–205.

43. José M. Fernández Soldaña, *Diccionario Uruguayo de Biografías, 1810–1940*, Montevideo: Editorial Amerendía, 1945. Lavalleja's biography is on pages 727–32, Rivera's is at 1089–95. Gandía. *Treinte y tres orientales*, 207.

44. Street, *José Artigas*, 338–43. Ferns, *Great Britain and Argentina*, 148, does not have a high opinion of Rivera, this "bird of ill omen" who "displayed his genius for desertion" on more than one occasion. Lockhart, *Rivera*, 22–32. Lockhart reproduces several letters as well as Rivera's signed statement saying that he had surrendered. Gandía, *Treinte y tres orientales*, 208–25.

45. Street, *Artigas*, 341–48. Ferns, *Great Britain and Argentina*, 150–53. Fernando Otorgués, who had been imprisoned by Lecor in 1819, had the misfortune of being captured and imprisoned again by the Brazilians. He eventually escaped and fought briefly for Lavalleja, but because of his injuries played no role in the political life of the country after independence, see José M. Fernández Saldaña, *Diccionario Uruguayo de biografías, 1810-1940*, Montevideo: Editorial Amerindia, 1945, 945–47. Gandía, *Treinte y tres orientales*, 226–43; Ron Seckinger, *The Brazilian Monarchy and the South American Republics, 1822–1831*, Baton Rouge: Louisiana State University Press, 1984, 68–73.

46. Ferns, *Great Britain and Argentina*, 156–60; Gandía, *Treinte y tres orientales*, 243–45. For details about the naval conflict, see Brian Vale, *A War betwixt Englishmen: Brazil against Argentina on the River Plate, 1825–1830*, London: I. B. Tauris, Publishers, 2000, 137–48.

47. Street, *Artigas*, 348–51; Gandía, *Treinte y tres orientales*, 244–52; Acevedo Díaz, *Anales Históricos*, I, 323–48, esp. 338–43; Vale, *Betwixt*, 170–71.

48. Ferns, *Great Britain and Argentina*, 190–91; Street, *Artigas*, 357–365; Lynch, *Spanish American Revolutions*, 103. Gandía, *Treinte y tres orientales*, 262–72; Lockhart, *Rivera*, 33–35. For a full description, see Alcides Cruz, *Incursión del General Fructuoso Rivera a los Misiones*, Montevideo: Claudio García, ed. 1916, 48–79.

49. Ferns, *Great Britain and Argentina*, 169–76; Vale, *Betwixt*, 166–69, 213–15.

50. Ferns, *Great Britain and Argentina*, 180–88. Seckinger, *Brazilian Monarchy Diplomacy*, 96–98, mentioned that Minister of Foreign Affairs Fructuoso Rivera carefully watched the discussion about the border, but that it remained unsettled. The quote is from David McLean, *War, Diplomacy and Informal Empire: Britain and the Republics of La Plata, 1836–1853*, London: British Academic Press 11; Martin, "Founder of Uruguayan Nationality, 14–15; Gandía, *Trente y Tres Orientales*, 373–4.

Three

The Near-Death of the Republic, 1828–1875

Following independence, Uruguay, like other Spanish American republics, found its path to nationhood strewn with obstacles. Only imperial Brazil, with an emperor vested with political legitimacy because of his lineage, and Chile, because of its compact geography and centralized government, experienced a relatively smooth transition from colony to independent state. Of all South American countries, Uruguay had one of the roughest and longest transitions. With the least experience with governance during the colonial period, and as the continent's smallest and most militarily vulnerable country, it became the battleground for Brazilian and Argentine imperialistic ambitions as well as for regional warlords and their supporting cast of civilian politicians. This chapter examines Uruguay's political and military struggles to overcome these challenges, as well as to secure its borders and build a viable economy between 1830 and 1875.

THE CONSTITUTION OF 1830

Uruguay's Constitution of 1830 became a symbol of national identity. It proved to be the third most durable national charter in Latin American history. After Brazil and Argentina signed the treaty guaranteeing Uruguay's independence in 1828, Governor Rondeau organized an election in the Banda Oriental's cities and towns to choose delegates for a Constituent Assembly. He then presided over the civilians who met between February and April 1829 at La Aguada Church, the forerunner of the Basílica de Nuestra Señora del Carmen, not far from the present location of the Legislative Palace in Montevideo.

The delegates replaced the country's geographical label, the Banda Oriental, with a new name, the *República Oriental del Uruguay*. With the U.S. Constitution and the Spanish Constitution of Cádiz of 1812 as models, the document featured three branches of government, each of which enjoyed separate powers. The constitution created a strong executive, a weaker bicameral legislature, and an independent judiciary. Given Uruguay's small size and its history as a single entity, Assembly members favored a centralized state (repudiating Artigas's federalism) with the national government dominating the nine departments (the French nomenclature for province or states). The centralized state existed in theory rather than reality until the 1870s because Montevideo lacked the muscle to impose its will on distant departments. The draft document established Roman Catholicism as Uruguay's sole religion.

The president served as the commander in chief of the military, directed diplomatic relations, oversaw the national budget, and appointed the *jefes políticos* (police chiefs) who administered the nine departments and preserved law and order. Although the constitution prohibited the president from immediate reelection, he could serve a second term following a four-year interval. The president selected three cabinet members who served at his pleasure. In the instance of "unacceptable conduct," the Senate could impeach a cabinet member, but not the president. The executive could initiate legislation and enjoyed limited veto power. He could authorize a state of emergency and suspend individual liberties in the event of a foreign invasion or a domestic uprising.

The constitution provided for one senator for each of the departments and one member of the Chamber of Deputies for every three thousand inhabitants of a department, chosen at large. Because at least one third of eligible voters lived in Montevideo, the city had a disproportionate influence in the chamber. Only wealthy male property owners could vote (about 5 percent of the population); poor rural transients (gauchos), women, illiterates, drunks, enslaved persons, peons, criminals, servants, and soldiers could not. The legislature could pass statutes and object to presidential actions, including his authorization of a state of emergency. Legislators in the early years reviewed budgets, but that practice quickly ended. Strong presidents habitually ran roughshod over the legislature's attempts to impose restraints on executive authority. The Senate and the deputies met together as the general Assembly (each legislator having one vote) every four years to choose the next president by simple majority, a practice that lasted into the early twentieth century. The General Assembly also selected members of the Supreme Court, who, with the advice and consent of the Senate, chose the lower-levels of the judiciary.

Most importantly, the delegates made it virtually impossible to amend the constitution by requiring that any proposed change be approved by three consecutive legislative sessions (chapter 3, articles 152–159). Because of the discontinuity of membership in the Assembly, constitutional amendments almost never occurred. The long-lasting Constitution of 1830 that created a republican form of government and a narrow definition of citizenship also became a symbol of Uruguayan national identity.

In September, the Assembly sent printed versions of the constitution to towns and cities throughout the republic. During the interval between authorship and official approval of the document, quarrels erupted between Fructuoso Rivera and Juan Antonio Lavalleja, each positioning himself to become president. By April of 1830, the Assembly thought it unseemly that an Argentine should serve as interim governor, and Rondeau resigned. Lavalleja, who had his army nearby, took over as president of the Assembly. On June 18, both Argentina and Brazil found the language of the Constitution acceptable, and Lavalleja and Rivera agreed to abide by the Assembly's choice as to which of them would become Uruguay's first president. On July 18, 1830, the government's principals approved the document in the *cabildo*'s main room that housed the legislature until the 1920s. In an excellent example of popular republicanism at work, whereby the people expressed their opinions, an orator read the document to the assembled crowd in the Plaza Matriz (now Plaza

Figure 3.1 "Sketch for the People's Oath to the Constitution of 1830," by Pedro Blanes Viale. Pedro Blanes Viale's "Sketch for the People's Oath" is an unfinished work depicting the moment of popular republicanism when the people of Montevideo swore an oath of allegiance to the Constitution of 1830. Blanes Viale, no relation to Juan Manuel Blanes, depicts the dramatic scene on the Plaza Matriz on July 18, 1830, that followed the Assembly's formal adoption of the document. Four flags flew outside the *cabildo*: the Uruguayan, the Argentine, the Brazilian, and the British, the latter because of its decisive role in securing full independence. Source: Legislative Palace, Montevideo.

Constitución) where the gathered public enthusiastically cheered and swore their oaths to uphold the Constitution of 1830.[1]

INDEPENDENCE HEROES: CAUDILLO PRESIDENTS AND THEIR PARTIES, 1830–1839

As routinely occurred in post-independence Latin America, the presidential electors in the Assembly turned to military heroes for political leadership. In 1830 the Assembly chose Rivera, in part because Lavalleja's brief dictatorship in 1827 flew in the face of the republican sentiments of the constitution, but also because Rivera's bold invasion of Misiones had forced Brazil to agree to Uruguay's independence. A charismatic leader with an aptitude for politics, Rivera served from 1830 to 1834. Like Artigas, Rivera enjoyed considerable popularity with the gauchos, Indigenous people, and Afro-Uruguayan troops who constituted his followers because of his interests in popular republican beliefs. Both Rivera and Lavalleja also attracted influential members of the civilian elite, the *patriciado*. The *patriciado* came from different walks of life (*estancieros*, merchants, businessmen, intellectuals, and military men) but shared social ties and a belief in public service. They would play a dominant role as cabinet members for the next twenty years.[2]

Once president, Rivera promoted his military friends and opened additional ports to international commerce, putting him at odds with Argentina's Juan Manuel de Rosas, who aspired to dominate trade in the La Plata region. Like the infamous Mexican *caudillo*, Antonio López de Santa Anna, Rivera enjoyed the glory of being president, but demonstrated little interest in actually governing, spending much of his term in his palatial home (Paso del Molino) in Durazno. Rivera had founded Durazno in 1821 on the banks of the River Yí. He even hoped to move the seat of government there, because, like Artigas, he disliked Montevideo, despite owning a stately home there (now the National Museum of History). Governing from Durazno made practical sense because he spent much of his term in the saddle fending off three Lavalleja inspired cross-border invasions as well as trying to "pacify" the northern territory.

Rivera's popularity rested in part on his advocacy for the popular classes. Shortly after independence, the Assembly had issued a decree evicting individuals who had occupied small parcels of land pursuant to Artigas's agrarian reform program. Rivera, who sympathized with them, urged the Assembly to pass the Law of 1833 that allowed people to lease abandoned public lands with minimal rental payments under a system called emphyteusis. Those tenants who claimed emphyteusis land were required ultimately to purchase the property, which most could not afford to do. (Argentina in the 1830s adopted a similar policy that also resulted in wealthy estancieros ultimately purchasing most of the land.) Nevertheless, rural people remembered Rivera's advocacy, which explains his ability to easily raise new armies during the ensuing civil wars.

Lavalleja's 1832 rebellion began with his supporters breaking into Rivera's Durazno *quinta* and attempting to assassinate him. Hearing the ruckus, Rivera jumped out the window of his office, ran to the Yí, and swam to safety. Meanwhile, Lavalleja attempted to suborn the capital's Afro-Uruguayan unit, which remained loyal to Rivera. When Rivera arrived, Lavalleja fled to Argentina. A year later, he organized two more unsuccessful rebellions with assistance from Argentina's Rosas. Cumulatively, responding to the three rebellions and Rivera's casual spending habits exhausted Uruguay's national treasury. Meanwhile, civilians created some of the building blocks of national identity. In 1828, influential politician Joaquín Suárez designed the nation's flag and an illustrator created the national coat-of arms. In 1833, poet Francisco Acuña de Figueroa completed the package of national identity tools when he composed the lyrics for the national anthem.[3]

BOX 3.1: MASSACRE OF THE CHARRÚA

In the republic's first days, Rivera, Lavalleja, and other influential politicians decided that the nomadic Charrúa presented a threat to peaceful settlement in northwestern Uruguay. During the wars for independence, Rivera, like his commander Artigas, had befriended Indigenous allies, a number of whom had participated in Rivera's conquest of Misiones in 1828. As a result, they agreed to meet Don Fructuoso in a small glen, later nicknamed Salsipuedes ("get out if you can") on April 11, 1831, ostensibly to plan a joint attack on Brazil. After plying them with liquor, Rivera betrayed them and shot one chief, the signal for the massacre to begin. Rivera, his nephew Bernabé, and their soldiers slaughtered forty Charrúa men and sent three hundred women and children to Montevideo as servants. Bernabé continued the campaign near Bella Unión, killing many men and enslaving women and children before himself being captured, tortured, and executed. Four adults, later referred to as the last Charrúa, attracted the attention of a French scientist, who displayed them like circus animals in Paris before they died. Although the Charrúa culture disappeared, the bloodline remained. Generations later, Uruguayans repudiated Rivera's actions. Today, demographers agree that as many as 6 percent of Uruguayans have some Indigenous ancestry, many of whom belong to the Association of the Descendants of the Charrúa Nation.[4]

In 1835, Rivera threw his influence behind Manuel Oribe's presidential candidacy. Oribe had proven his loyalty by fighting alongside Rivera in the three campaigns against Lavalleja. Rivera promoted him to general and made him minister of war. Rivera believed that he could dominate Oribe, describing him as a "simple lieutenant" who would do the *caudillo*'s bidding. Most of the *patriciado* concurred with the choice of Oribe because he had merchant and *estanciero* friends and because he promised fiscal integrity and stability. In exchange for endorsing Oribe, Rivera received the title of inspector general of the army with a generous salary and also continuing influence over the military.

As soon as possible, Oribe shook off Rivera's handcuffs, stripping Rivera of his post. The president launched an investigation into the propriety of his predecessor's expenses and allowed Lavalleja to return from Argentina and regain his property. Finally, Oribe rekindled his friendship with Rosas who hoped to reincorporate Uruguay into Argentina. When on March 5, 1836, Oribe mailed Rivera a letter informing him about these decisions, the latter was outraged. Hostile letters soon degenerated into armed hostilities as their collaboration ended.[5]

The civil war in 1836 led to the beginnings of Uruguay's two-party system and divided the *patriciado*. Because neither gaucho army had official uniforms, both sides looked identical on the battlefield. To distinguish his followers from the enemy, Oribe took the advice of Rosas and required his soldiers to wear a *divisa* (badge), pinned to a hat or lapel, or alternatively, worn as an armband or hatband to identify his soldiers. Oribe chose a white *divisa*, one of the colors of the flag. Rivera, seeing the efficacy of such insignia, selected blue (the other color in Uruguay's flag) for his partisans' *divisas*, but when exposure to Uruguay's bright sun bleached the blue *divisas* white, Rivera exchanged the blue for red. Thereafter, Lavalleja's and Oribe's party became known as the Blancos, while Rivera's, the Colorados. Most significantly, party identity became generational: "A man is born . . . a Blanco or a Colorado."[6]

Rivera's forces received a thrashing at the hands of Lavalleja and Oribe's brother Ignacio in September 1836 at the battle of Carpintería (the first battle in which both sides wore *divisas*), forcing Rivera to flee across the border to Brazil. Rivera's

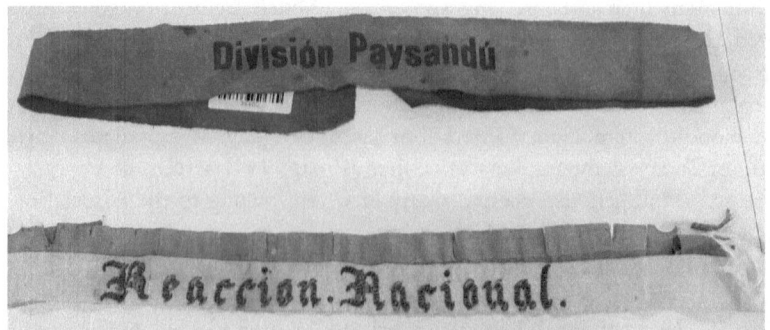

Figure 3.2 *Divisas* from the Battle of Carpintería. In the absence of formal uniforms, the Blancos' white *divisa* and the Colorados' red *divisa* enabled gaucho cavalrymen to differentiate their friends from their enemies. This battle marked the first time both factions used *divisas*. With few exceptions, families have handed down party loyalties from generation to generation right up to the present. *Source*: Museo Histórico, Paysandú, Uruguay.

reorganized Colorado forces invaded Uruguay the following year with the assistance of Argentine general Juan Galo Lavalle, who enjoyed a significant following among the anti-Rosas exiles in Montevideo. When France blockaded Buenos Aires harbor in March 1838, it prevented Rosas from assisting Oribe. As a result, Rivera decisively defeated Ignacio Oribe's Blanco forces at Palmar. In October, Oribe admitted defeat, resigned his presidency with four months remaining in the term, and with Lavalleja, fled to Argentina. Rivera declared war on the troublemaker Rosas, urged to do so by the anti-Rosas Argentine Unitarian party exiles. Rosas's reputation for ruthlessness induced his childhood friend, Mariquita Sánchez, to flee to Montevideo because she was afraid of him. Oribe had hoped that the elite's desire for order would prove decisive, but his inability to accommodate the popular Rivera cost him his presidency.[7]

THE GUERRA GRANDE (GREAT WAR): 1839 (OR 1843)–1845

Caudillo-inspired instability not only encouraged vitriolic domestic politics, but also Argentine, Brazilian, British, and French intervention between 1839 and 1851. As a result, Uruguay's Guerra Grande represented the longest transnational conflict in South America during the nineteenth century. Because of the duration of the Great War, its brutality, and its negative economic effects, Uruguayans today find little praiseworthy about these years. For some historians, the Guerra Grande began with Rivera's declaration of war against Rosas at the urging of the Argentine Unitarians in 1839. Others who prefer the later date of 1843 see the first four years as a "phony war" and therefore argue that the Great War began when the Blancos initiated the siege of Montevideo.

Once exiled in 1838, Oribe regrouped the Blancos and accepted Rosas's offer to command the Auxiliary Force of the Republic of the Orient. After almost a year of preparation, Oribe's army crossed the Río Uruguay and marched toward Montevideo. When the Blanco forces met the Colorados at Cagancha on December 10, 1839, Rivera inflicted a decisive defeat on Oribe, Lavalleja, and their Argentine allies just a short distance from the capital. The Blanco forces scattered, retreating across the river. Oribe blamed the loss on Lavalleja's incompetence and diminished his role thereafter. By 1851, Lavalleja had retired to his *chacra* (small farm) in Miguelete near Montevideo.

After Cagancha, France's blockade of Buenos Aires harbor secured its diplomatic objective: the grant of most-favored-nation trade status (like Great Britain enjoyed); and the right to arbitrate its citizens' claims. Rosas, however, proved the big winner in the negotiations. Not only did the French lift their blockade, but Rosas merely conceded a vague promise to respect Uruguay's independence "so long as the rights, honor, and security of the Argentine Confederation" went unendangered, which essentially gave him a free hand to meddle in Uruguayan affairs whenever he chose to do so. Rosas celebrated his diplomatic triumph while the sizable French colony in Montevideo felt betrayed.[8]

Figure 3.3 "President Fructuoso Rivera," by Juan Manuel Blanes. General Fructuoso Rivera served as the first and third president of Uruguay and led the Colorado party until 1846. A typical *caudillo*, he had no formal military training and relied on his bravado and innate skill to lead his gauchos in battle. He had played a decisive role in the war against Pedro I in 1826 and led the Colorado military effort in the Guerra Grande until his transactional behavior forced the civilian leadership to exile him. *Source*: Museo Casa de Rivera, Durazno.

After Cagancha, the battlefield shifted to the Argentine interior. Rivera's ally, General Lavalle, launched an offensive from Uruguay in August 1840 with the encouragement of the thousands of anti-Rosas exiles in Montevideo. Lavalle found less popular support than anticipated and as his fortunes declined, Oribe proved his military mettle by defeating Lavalle and changing the momentum of the Argentine *caudillo* wars. An increasingly vengeful Oribe willingly complied with Rosas's terror campaign, encapsulated in his *lema* (slogan) "Oribe: Law or Death, Death to the Savage Unitarios." He executed large numbers of captives, thereby earning the nickname, "the throat slitter."[9]

Rivera took command of the anti-Rosas forces in Entre Ríos, apparently with vain hopes of creating the expanded Uruguayan nation he had dreamed about in 1828. He suffered a stunning defeat at the battle of Arroyo Grande in Entre Ríos on December 6, 1842, however, where Oribe, his auxiliary forces and pro-Rosas caudillos annihilated the Colorado army. Captured officers had their throats cut while Oribe's men ran enemy rank-and-file gauchos through with lances. As the battle waned, Rivera and approximately one hundred surviving gauchos swam with their mounts across the Uruguay River and disappeared into the interior. Returning to Montevideo in March 1843 with fresh volunteers, a testament to his popular following, Rivera assumed the title of commander in chief of the Colorado army, now dominated by foreigners. As one Uruguayan wrote, "The battle of Arroyo Grande destroyed Rivera's army, but not his prestige as a caudillo."[10]

Days before his term ended, Rivera resigned the presidency in favor of Joaquín Suárez, the president of the Senate (and according to the Constitution of 1830, the vice president). The Assembly delayed the 1843 presidential election until the conclusion of the civil war; as a result, Suárez held the interim presidency until 1852, the longest serving chief executive in Uruguayan history. Alone among the founders of the republic, Joaquín Suárez received respect from both Blancos and Colorados, uniformly praised by both parties as a man of integrity and civic virtue.

While Oribe and his army wasted time taking vengeance on the survivors of Arroyo Grande, General José María Paz directed the construction of two stout lines of fortifications around Montevideo's Old City. By the time Oribe arrived on February 16, 1843, the capital was well defended by the foreign legions (French, Spanish, and Italian mostly) and several thousand formerly enslaved Afro-Uruguayans, promised emancipation if they defended the capital. (The Blancos would make similar overtures to enslaved persons in 1846.) Although Rosas ordered Admiral Guillermo Brown to bottle up Montevideo harbor to halt the flow of supplies and bombard the city, British and French pressure prevented Rosas from implementing this plan.[11]

Oribe's forces encamped at Los Cerritos, just east of the capital. He recalled the members of his 1838 legislature to legitimize his government, proclaimed himself president, and opened a customs' house at nearby Buceo (the present-day location of Montevideo's yacht club) to collect customs' duties. Oribe pledged Rosas that Uruguay would join the United Provinces. In April, the Blanco leader issued a manifesto decreeing that Europeans serving in Colorado ranks would be executed after capture. Great Britain's and France's envoys protested and forced Oribe to rescind the order. The siege of Montevideo lasted from 1843 to 1851, giving the city the nickname of the "New Troy," coined by famed French author Alexandre Dumas.[12]

The foreign legions comprised the core of the Colorado forces. The French Legion consisted of about 3,500 men, the Spanish Legion was slightly smaller, the Italian Legion numbered around eight hundred with the British Legion smaller still. The most famous member of the Italian Legion, Giuseppe Garibaldi, following his South American adventures, would lead the Italian unification movement in the 1860s. After serving as the admiral of the *Farroupilha*'s (popularly called the Ragamuffins) rebel forces in southern Brazil, Garibaldi, his girlfriend Anita, and their baby abandoned Río Grande do Sul for Montevideo, where he found work teaching mathematics and history and worked on the docks. They lived in poverty, renting one room in a tiny four-room house near the waterfront. Because of his international reputation, Garibaldi quickly became the leading figure in the foreign legions. While the Colorados styled themselves "the Defenders of the Nation" because of their battle against Rosas, the Blancos renamed their faction the "National Party" because of the presence of so many foreigners in the Colorados' military.[13]

Meanwhile, Rivera's recently acquired gaucho recruits won several skirmishes in the interior. Oribe begged Rosas for assistance, who asked his most powerful provincial governor, Justo José de Urquiza, to fight Rivera. Oribe and Urquiza enjoyed superior numbers when they confronted Rivera on the morning of March 27, 1845, at India Muerta in eastern Uruguay. Rivera's poorly armed forces had only spears fashioned from their knives (*facóns*) attached to lances because the rifles from Montevideo never arrived. After a hot two-hour battle, Rivera fled across India Muerta Creek in a hail of bullets. Oribe reported that he had taken 350 prisoners and killed over a thousand Colorados. Shocked witnesses decried the brutality of the victors on the day after the battle, when Urquiza allegedly ordered some five hundred captives to be beheaded. After India Muerta, only Montevideo and Maldonado remained in Colorado hands as Rivera took refuge in Brazil where the imperial government placed him under house arrest.[14]

THE FAILED CORONADO COUNTEROFFENSIVE AND PEACE, 1845–1851

After India Muerta, the British and French ministers informed Rosas that their governments would not allow Oribe to take Montevideo, nor could Argentine admiral Guillermo Brown continue his blockade of the port. Their joint fleets captured the Argentine navy, removed all British and French sailors (a sizable number) from his crews and in turn blockaded Buenos Aires. The British and French even stationed troops in Montevideo to help to protect the city, which now had only 3,500 Colorado defenders. Then the allies launched a counteroffensive as their combined fleets, assisted by the Colorado ships, bombarded and occupied coastal towns once in Oribe's possession, including Colonia (August 30, 1846) and Martín García island. Garibaldi's Italian Legion sacked the Argentine town of Gualeguaychú but suffered defeat at Paysandú before taking Salto, while the British and French fleets continued up the Paraná. These victories breathed life into the Colorados' cause. Garibaldi remained in control of Salto throughout the year, but in early 1847, the Italian Legion abandoned Uruguay to undertake their glorious campaign to liberate Rome.[15]

As the Colorado counteroffensive began, Rivera escaped from house arrest in Río de Janeiro and returned by ship to Montevideo. The provisional government led by Suárez and the Council of Notables, all civilian members of the urban *patriciado*, attempted to prevent Rivera from disembarking. But his wife, Bernadina Fragosa de Rivera, had organized his loyal friends as well as the Afro-Uruguayan troops stationed in the garrison who mutinied and insisted that he be allowed ashore. Their commander, Colonel Venancio Flores, a protégé of Rivera's, negotiated an agreement whereby Rivera resumed his role as military commander in chief while Suárez remained as interim president. For his part, Colonel Flores's role in the affair elevated his status and identified him as the leading *caudillo* of the next generation.[16]

After a few skirmishes in the interior, Rivera, now in Maldonado, began to negotiate directly with Oribe in an attempt to end the war. When the Colorado patriciado government got wind of Rivera's unauthorized actions, it dispatched council member General Lorenzo Batlle to arrest Rivera and force him aboard a ship bound for Brazil. The council formally banished Rivera until the end of the Guerra Grande. Deprived of his salary, Rivera experienced great poverty in Brazil, which contributed to his declining health.[17]

Meanwhile, wiser heads in London and Paris questioned the wisdom of the naval intervention in the La Plata region. Both Britain and France hoped to mediate a solution, but Oribe's recent successes on the battlefield (he retook Maldonado and Colonia in August 1848, leaving only Montevideo in Colorado hands) made Rosas intractable. Rosas preferred to keep the situation roiling because his speeches about foreign intervention proved politically popular at home. The French minister and Interim President Suárez, however, firmly refused to consider Rosas's demand to install Oribe as interim president. Unable to change Rosas's position, Great Britain unilaterally terminated its blockade in the fall of 1849, while the French fleet left the following year. This episode marked the final instance of the British using military force to influence events in the La Plata region.

On Rosas's orders, Oribe agreed to an armistice, and the fighting diminished until 1851. Without foreign assistance, the Colorado government teetered on the brink of surrender until Brazilian entrepreneur Irineu Evangelista de Sousa, the Baron Mauá, offered the Colorados large monthly stipends, arms and munitions to sustain themselves until the war ended. The Brazilian monarchy also assisted the Colorados because it feared Rosas's expansionist plans in the La Plata region.[18]

The final stage of the Guerra Grande began when Entre Ríos's caudillo, José Urquiza, challenged Rosas's "tyranny" over trade in the La Plata area, which severely affected his province's interests. For the first time, Rosas had required all goods shipped from the interior destined for international markets pay taxes in Buenos Aires. After Urquiza secured the cooperation of other provincial caudillos, he crossed the Río Uruguay in July 1851 and defeated Rosas's most potent ally, Oribe and the Blanco government in Cerritos. Meanwhile, Uruguayan diplomat Andrés Lamas negotiated a Brazilian intervention in September. As Oribe's troops melted away in the face of overwhelming odds, he disbanded his army and surrendered on October 8, 1851, entering private life and ending the Great War.[19]

Four days later, Brazilian and Uruguayan diplomats signed five treaties, each of which increased Brazil's influence over Uruguay. First, the treaties resolved Uruguay's disputed northern border in favor of Brazil. The line now ran from the Uruguay River along the Cuareím creek, past the Cuchilla de Santa Ana, along the Río Yaguarón and the Posta del Chuy tollhouse, to just south of Lake Merín on the

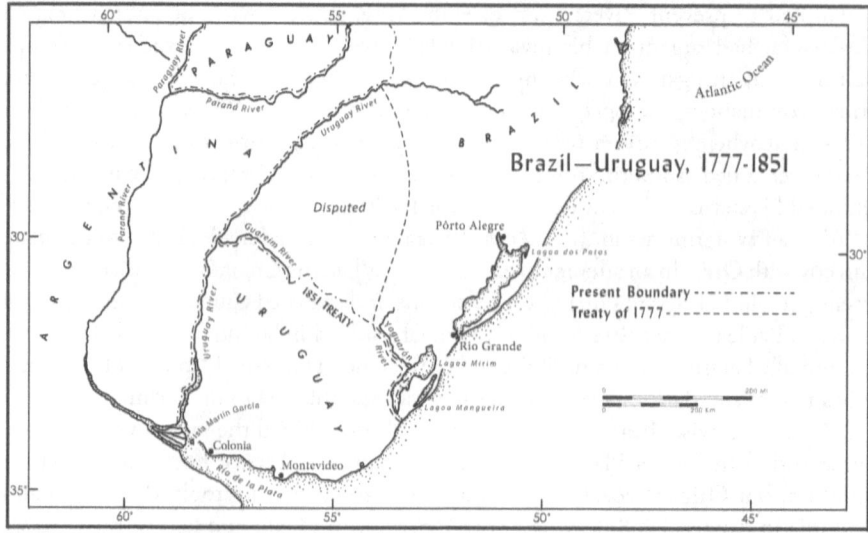

Map 3.1 Map of the Revision of the Brazilian Border in 1851. *Source:* cc Graphics.

Atlantic coast. Thus, Uruguay relinquished its historic claims to Misiones province based on the Treaty of San Ildefonso of 1776. Other treaties also compromised national sovereignty. One treaty permitted Brazil to intervene militarily at its discretion; another required Uruguay to accept a forced loan to pay its debts to Brazil, Great Britain and France. The final treaty required Uruguay to allow Brazilians to bring their slaves into Uruguay and to return fugitive slaves to their owner. These one-sided treaties greatly expanded Brazil's influence for the next twenty years.[20]

BOX 3.2: A CAUDILLO'S WIFE: BERNADINA FRAGOSA DE RIVERA

During the post-independence years, elite women like Bernadina Fragosa de Rivera lived in a world that retained colonial-era rules of patriarchy. She grew up in San José, where her father owned a *pulpería*. In 1816, she met and married the dashing young officer Fructuoso Rivera, Artigas's most-trusted officer. Before having her eight children, only two of whom survived into adulthood, she joined her husband on his military campaign in Misiones. As a *caudillo*'s wife, she shared the good and bad times with her husband: the honors, glory, and fortune after Cagancha and the penury after the Guerra Grande. Like other wives of elite men, she suffered the indignity of his frequent infidelities, including installing his favorite mistress across the plaza from their home in Durazno. Despite his philandering ways, the couple remained devoted to one another. She complied with the expected duties of an elite woman, founding

Figure 3.4 Portrait of Bernadina Fragosa de Rivera, by Amadeo Gras. Elite women played important roles in the early nineteenth century. She and Don Fructo had eight children, only two of whom survived to adulthood. Like many nineteenth-century elite women, Sra. Rivera became heavily involved in charitable causes, the acceptable and admirable role for someone of her social status. *Source:* Museo Nacional de Historia, Casa de Rivera.

"The Philanthropic Society of Uruguayan Women" to provide health care for the poor in Montevideo in 1843. When her husband passed away during his return from exile in 1853, she accompanied his corpse from Melo for burial in the Matriz Church (the Cathedral) in Montevideo. Because her husband had sold most of the 760,000 acres that he owned to support the Colorado cause, she lived in modest circumstances until her death in 1863.[21]

Remarkably, despite the duration and violence of the Guerra Grande, Uruguayans accepted diplomat Andrés Lamas's assessment of the war: "there were no winners and no losers." Thus, on October 8, 1851, Colorados and Blancos formed lines outside Montevideo and embraced each other. Whereas sharp ideological differences marked almost all other nineteenth-century civil wars in Latin America, in Uruguay the differences were superficial. The weak institutional Church did not arouse passions as it did in Mexico, for example. Nor did Domingo Faustino Sarmiento's metaphor of a war between civilization and barbarism seemed inapplicable because the city party's founder (Rivera) held vast *estancia* lands, while Montevideo-born Oribe led the country party. As Uruguayan historian Juan E. Pivel Devoto noted, the city party that espoused liberal principles and abstract rights survived because of the support of the quintessential *caudillo* (Urquiza) and the most powerful defender of the institution of slavery, Brazilian Emperor Pedro II. The economic consequences of the war did force numerous *estancieros* like Fructuoso Rivera (owner of 760,000 acres) and Joaquín Suárez (381,000 acres) to sell land to immigrants, weakening the power of the early landowning class.[22]

THE ABOLITION OF SLAVERY, 1842–1851

By 1830, Uruguay's population included numerous enslaved Africans. Despite the language of the Constitution, that population increased during the 1830s after the Assembly passed a law permitting Brazilians to import "colonists" who had recently arrived in Montevideo from Angola. In 1835 President Oribe attempted to end the fiction of willing African colonists working land owned by wealthy Brazilians voluntarily, and decreed that they be freed when they came of age. Most of the urban Black population resided in Montevideo's Old City. Urban elites and members of the middle class owned enslaved people, most performing artisanal tasks just as they had during the colonial era. Beyond the walls of the Old City, Afro-Uruguayans, both enslaved and free, performed heavier labor in tanneries, saladeros, and brickmaking factories. On a much smaller scale, slavery existed in rural Uruguay on ranches.[23]

Brazil's most important trading partner, Great Britain, used its influence to end the abomination of human bondage. Sometimes, the British employed persuasion based on arguments of humanity; on other occasions it twisted arms through diplomacy (as they did with Brazil) to end the slave trade. Uruguay attempted to end slavery several times. Joaquín Suárez signed abolition legislation on December 12, 1842; and the Blancos concurred four years later. The abolition of slavery in Montevideo enabled Rivera to recruit successfully among the Afro-Uruguayan population there. By 1850, however, Brazilians owned 11.8 million acres of land along the border in Cerro Largo, Rocha, and Tacuarembó. Under the 1851 peace treaty, Uruguayans were required to return fugitive slaves to Brazilian owners. The following year the Brazilian chargé d'affaires in Montevideo reinvented the convenient fiction of Black "colonists" working voluntarily for twenty-five years to earn their emancipation. In short, Brazilian influence trumped Uruguayan legislation aimed to end the abhorrent institution until the 1870s.[24]

THE FUSIONIST MOVEMENT AND POLITICS TO 1864

Taking the conciliatory words "there were no winners and no losers" literally, the two parties agreed to put aside their differences and joined into a fusionist movement. To avoid diving too deeply into the weeds, between 1852 and 1855 Uruguay experienced two constitutionally elected presidents, three provisional governments, and two brief interim regimes. Desperate politicians thought that a triumvirate of the old Colorado and Blanco heroes, Fructuoso Rivera and Juan Antonio Lavalleja, and Rivera's protégé Venancio Flores, might accomplish their objective. Before the triumvirate took office, however, Lavalleja died of apoplexy at his ranch in 1853, and Rivera, riding south from Brazilian exile, passed away in Melo three months later. The days of the independence-era warriors had passed. Even the senior members of the patriciado now played lesser roles.[25]

The youngest member of the triumvirate, Venancio Flores, had fought alongside Rivera in 1825 and throughout the Guerra Grande before joining Urquiza in 1851 during the war's final campaign. A genuine believer in the Fusionist movement, Flores signed the Pact of Union with Manuel Oribe on November 11, 1855, whereby the two *caudillos* agreed to collaborate to seek a national reconciliation, but Oribe passed away shortly thereafter, and the agreement died with him.[26]

From 1856 and 1864, civilian Colorados and Blancos cooperated in this power sharing Fusionist agreement. Under this arrangement, two Blanco politicians, served full terms as presidents. Despite the compromise, minor rebellions against fusionism occurred. At the end of an uprising in 1858, for example, government commanders received an order to execute all prisoners, including one of the few surviving members of the Immortal Thirty-Three. The new government's budget ran a deficit, and Brazil in particular continued to impinge on Uruguay's sovereignty. International tensions by 1864 would ultimately cause the Fusionist government to collapse.[27]

The Fusionist governments survived that long because Uruguay's wealthiest part-time resident, the Baron Mauá, viewed the La Plata region as a more hospitable investment environment than his own slaveholding Brazil. Because of Mauá's financial assistance, the government authorized him to establish a private bank, the *Banco Mauá y Compañía*. While earlier banks were required to retain gold equivalent to the nominal value of the paper money it issued, Mauá's bank adopted a newer banking principle: that a bank should issue more paper money or loans (in Mauá's case three times) more than the value of the gold it held. This allowed Mauá's bank to offer investment funds to businesses that would produce new wealth, expand the economy, and generate profits for the bank. Thus, the Mauá Bank provided the capital that underwrote the first railroad, Montevideo's municipal gas service, and improved port facilities. The bank also lent the Bernardo Berro government 6 million pesos so it could meet its obligations on the foreign debt owed to Brazil.[28]

THE PASTORAL INDUSTRIES IN THE MID-NINETEENTH CENTURY, 1840–1875

Two significant changes: the development of an industrial style *saladero* and the emergence of a wool industry, marked Uruguay's transition toward a modern pastoral industry between 1840 and 1875. Before these changes could happen, Uruguay's herds of cattle (an estimated 7.5 million head in 1840 reduced by two-thirds to 2.5 million by 1852) had to recover from the decimation of the Great War. Marching gaucho armies gorged themselves on free beef to the point that many *estancieros* abandoned their ranches. During the war each faction confiscated *estancias* owned by their enemies, but now agreed to return them; however, this agreement excluded property that immigrants had purchased during the Guerra Grande when prices fell dramatically.[29]

The Great War disrupted rural society. As landowning families fled, the interior looked deserted. Without beef to process, *saladeros* closed. Although the Great War had seriously damaged Uruguay's economy, it rebounded in the late 1850s because the country's rich prairie grasses favored the natural propagation of cattle. With nature taking its course, by 1858 over 4 million creole cattle roamed the range.[30]

As the cattle industry revived, ranchers rejected calls to import pedigreed cattle like Herefords as Argentine stockmen were doing, for three reasons. First, the omnipresent ticks in the Uruguayan prairie drove thin-skinned Herefords to madness. Second, the thick hides of *criollo* cattle produced better leather. Finally, the stringy flesh of *criollo* cattle tasted better than fattier Hereford meat when processed into beef jerky, the principal source of protein fed to enslaved people in Brazil and Cuba. Jerky's repulsive taste, however, kept it off the tables of even the poorest Europeans.

The mechanized *saladero* (called *charqueadores* in eastern Uruguay) enabled greater production. As Uruguay's most valuable industrial sites until the twentieth century, *saladeros* produced hides, tallow, and *tasajo*, but in much greater quantities than previously. A modern *saladero* could process up to 1,200 cows a day. Workers removed the hides and stacked them in sheds for shipment. Steam-powered boilers rendered fat into tallow. Workers sliced the meat into thin strips, placed it in brine pans for four to six days, and left it to dry in the sunshine. Baron Mauá operated one of the nation's largest *estancias* near Mercedes, where he raised over one hundred thousand animals for processing.[31]

Slow transportation of pastoral products limited Uruguay's ability to export during the post–Guerra Grande years. Moving hides, tallow, or *tasajo* to market could be done by oxcart, but it took time. Stagecoach lines for passengers developed in the 1850s, but the trip from Montevideo to Durazno took four to five days to cover roughly two hundred miles. Shipping along the navigable rivers remained slow until 1860 when a steamship connected Salto to Montevideo in three days. The lack of rapid means of transportation not only hindered commerce but also hampered the government's response to rebellions.[32]

The introduction of large numbers of sheep by British and French immigrants into southwestern and western Uruguay at the conclusion of the Great War marked the second important transition in the pastoral industry. Initially, sheep farmers raised *criollo* sheep that produced low-quality wool useful only for mattress stuffing or carpet manufacture. Because of favorable land prices during and after the Great War, numerous immigrants purchased the relatively small parcels (compared to a cattle ranch) necessary to enter the sheep raising business. Sheep farmers could earn as much as a cattle rancher on one-fifth the land and in general earned twice as much income as cattlemen.

By the 1860s immigrant British, German, Basque, and French sheep farmers introduced flocks of Merino and Lincoln sheep that produced wool suitable for clothing. By the end of the decade, 18 million sheep roamed Uruguay's pastures. Eventually Uruguayan wool won prizes at international competitions in London and Paris. Because sheep owners wanted to protect their purebreds, they built stone walls and large barns. In addition, sheep farmers dedicated a portion of their spread to space for a chemical bath that cured the mange that ruined their wool.[33]

While Uruguay had exported 6 million pounds of wool in 1862, that quantity and its price tripled by 1875. By then, the wool industry provided about 24 percent of the country's exports while beef jerky slumped to 13 percent as slavery in Cuba and Brazil neared its end. (Hides remained the largest export.) British mills accepted the upgraded Uruguay wool as equal in quality to wool from Australia, New Zealand, and Argentina. When Napoleon III (1851–1871) embarked upon a program of industrialization, France also purchased large quantities of Uruguayan wool.[34]

Immigrant sheep ranchers embodied the entrepreneurial spirit of the new rural middle class. Many arrived in Uruguay with little capital and initially worked as herders. In exchange for their labor, they received a portion of the newborn lambs, and they eventually earned enough cash in addition to rent or purchase their own spreads. Because of the nature of the enterprise, a sheep ranch required a larger and more skilled permanent work force than did the cattle *estancia*. Hands tended the flocks, oversaw the lambing, and drove sheep through baths of sheep dip. The highest paid worker, the sheepshearer, eventually used a mechanical shear to remove the wool from the animal. Sheep farms contributed to the demise of the fabled careers of roaming gauchos of early lore because they required a permanent workforce with specific skills.[35]

BOX 3.3: GAUCHESCA LITERATURE AND NATIONAL IDENTITY

Between 1830 and 1870, the peripatetic lifestyle of the gaucho became a symbol of freedom and the most popular subject of Uruguayan literature and popular theater. *Gauchesca* literature originated from ballads that troubadours sang in pulperías about love, courage, loyalty, freedom, and rural life. Gauchesca writers expropriated these songs and the popular idiom of the gauchos that mixed Spanish and Guaraní words. The literature took multiple forms: poetry, dialogues, and plays that exalted the heroic deeds of patriots like Artigas, Fructuoso Rivera, Juan Lavalleja, and Manuel Oribe and their gauchos during independence and the Guerra Grande. Bartolomé Hidalgo (1788–1823), a close friend of Artigas and arguably the Zane Gray of Uruguay, founded the genre. Hidalgo and his successors viewed gauchos as Romantic outlaws and freedom fighters: the authentic Uruguayans. In the early twentieth century, writers like Javier de Viana rekindled this nostalgic view and portrayed the gaucho's tragic end as the modernizing cattle business and the growing importance of sheep ranching transformed them from independent cowboys into poverty-ridden peons. Even today, many Uruguayans consider the *gauchesca* as Uruguay's quintessential literature because of its themes that clash with the reality of modern Montevideo.[36]

THE WAR OF THE TRIPLE ALLIANCE AND ITS CONSEQUENCES, 1864–1870

Turbulent politics in Uruguay, intertwined with larger transnational issues in the Southern Cone, precipitated South America's bloodiest war, the War of the Triple Alliance. Aggravated by President Bernardo Berro's partisan straying from fusionism, in 1863 Venancio Flores sought to restore Colorado dominance. While in exile in Argentina, he and his subordinates assisted *porteño* general Bartolomé Mitre in defeating Urquiza's Confederation. With Mitre's blessing and weaponry, Flores's small army and Argentine volunteers invaded Uruguay in mid-April, crossing the river near Paysandú where they met an unenthusiastic response. Because his revolt sputtered, Flores avoided direct confrontation with the Blanco National Guard, instead relying on small skirmishes to keep his cause viable for the next year.[37]

Fortunately for Flores, President Berro's inept handling of the crisis enhanced the likelihood of Colorado success. Berro's deep roots in the Blanco Party and his bitter hatred of Rivera's friends sullied his claim to be a fusionist. Although honest, Berro alienated his colleagues because he refused to listen to advice. Soon Colorados abandoned him as did some Blancos. Berro's policy mistakes also weakened his administration. By encouraging Uruguayan settlement in the north, he antagonized Brazil, which already resented his attempts to free enslaved people there in violation of the Treaty of 1851. Berro quarreled with his generals and alienated the officer corps, some of whom joined Flores. Finally, Berro allied Uruguay with Paraguayan President Francisco Solano López, who had expansionist ambitions and desperately needed Berro's support. Berro's decision to assist López gave Pedro II the excuse to invade Cerro Largo in October 1864 under the terms of the Treaty of 1851.[38]

In turn, Berro's pact also provided Argentina and Brazil with a reason to assist Flores. After army officers defected to Flores, the Blancos relied heavily on their National Guard (local militia). Late in 1864, Flores and the Brazilian navy besieged the Blanco stronghold of Paysandú. Its commander, General Leandro Gómez, despite being outnumbered and outgunned, fought valiantly for thirty-three days, sleeping on a bench in the plaza wrapped in his vicuña poncho in order to be ready for any attack. Brazilian bombardments eventually eviscerated the city center so General Gómez surrendered on January 2, 1865. Flores's subordinates shot Gómez and two of his officers after they surrendered, making him a Blanco hero and ironically, an icon of the national army. The battle for Paysandú cost more Uruguayan lives than any other during the War of the Triple Alliance.[39]

While the battle for Paysandú raged, Emperor Pedro II's army invaded southern Uruguay, besieging Montevideo, which surrendered on February 20, 1865. Flores claimed the presidency, initiating the succession of Colorado presidents that lasted until 1958. Brazilian troops occupied Montevideo during Flores's term (1865–1868). In May, Flores signed the Triple Alliance treaty with Pedro II and Mitre, and led some five thousand troops northward to join the invasion of Paraguay.

Initially, Paraguay's army outnumbered those of the three allies combined. But Solano López's ill-devised strategy and poor luck squandered that potential advantage. Flores and his troops contributed to early Allied victories that introduced the world to the horrors of trench warfare. They acquitted themselves particularly well at Tuyutí, the bloodiest battle ever fought on South American soil. Flores returned to Montevideo at the end of 1866 to take up the reins of government while the remainder of the Uruguayan forces remained in the field. Although Uruguay's army played a lesser role, it fought well, but lost approximately 1,100 soldiers, many due to the horrendous diseases and infections in Paraguayan swamps. During the conflict, the Uruguayan military experienced its first taste of battle in years which helped to professionalize the army. In the end, Uruguay gained nothing tangible from its participation in the war except a short-lived economic boom that hardened public opinion against Brazil.[40]

Uruguayan merchants profited from their role as the "meat larder," supplying necessities to the Brazilian forces. Pedro II spent millions on butchered Uruguayan beef for his soldiers as exports nearly doubled during the war. The prospering merchants and other middle-class residents of Montevideo engaged in an orgy of conspicuous consumption, importing French wine, clothing, fashionable shoes, porcelain, and jewelry. Europeans no longer needed to militarily conquer the Plata region; instead, they had gained an informal trade empire at no cost in lives! Uruguay's newly enriched merchants constructed elegant homes in the suburb of Pocitos where they enjoyed their sumptuous lifestyle. They also speculated heavily, assuming that prosperity would continue. The first glimmerings of technology appeared with the construction of a short rail line and an underwater cable to Buenos Aires.[41]

For Uruguayans, the War of the Triple Alliance and the events of February 19, 1868, reminded them of the dangers of courting international alliances as well as the frailties of their own democracy. Four days earlier, Flores had resigned his dictatorship and angled to have the Assembly elect him for a full term as president. Berro, seeking revenge for his ouster from office, plotted to prevent this eventuality and seized the cabildo where the Assembly met. British traveler J. H. Murray, in Montevideo at that moment, reported that when Flores heard this news, he rushed from his

Figure 3.5 "The Assassination of Venancio Flores," by Juan Manuel Blanes. In 1867, Flores hoped to finagle his way into a second successive presidential term because of a technicality. Seeking to frustrate his ambitions, Blanco opponents arranged for a riot near the *cabildo*, knowing that Flores would leave the safety of his lodgings to try and restore order. The assassins waylaid him en route and stabbed him to death. Enraged, Colorados then assassinated the leader of the Blancos, former president Bernardo Berro. *Source*: Museo Municipal de Bellas Artes, Juan Manuel Blanes.

hotel toward the cabildo. Meanwhile, the Blancos had stationed assassins along the route, shot Flores's coachman, and stabbed the former president to death. Shortly thereafter, Berro and his friends took the ancient fort in Zabala Plaza. Flores's son, once Berro's friend, pretended to congratulate him on the coup, but when he got in close range, shot Berro dead. Even by nineteenth-century Latin American standards, the murder of two former presidents on the same day was extraordinary![42]

THE REVOLUTION OF THE SPEARS AND THE ECONOMIC DOLDRUMS, 1870–1875

In the aftermath of the assassinations, the Assembly chose Lorenzo Batlle as president. The son of the owner of Montevideo's first flour mill, the French-educated Batlle had been a prominent member of the Colorado patriciado during the Guerra Grande. He served ably as Joaquín Suárez's Minister of War and carried out the delicate mission of persuading Fructuoso Rivera to accept exile in 1847. Now Batlle united the Colorados by promising to establish a *gobierno de partido* (single party regime) rather than a fusionist government. Completely ignoring the Blancos caused immediate friction.[43]

Batlle's attempt to replace Blanco *jefes políticos* and muster out the National Guard led to a serious rebellion. Thousands of Blancos fled to Argentina where they found willing collaborators. On March 5, 1870, the exiles, led by Colonel Timoteo Aparicio, crossed the Uruguay River and initiated the War of the Spears, so called because most gauchos resorted to homemade weapons, called *tacuara* (spear or lance), made by tying sheep shears to a bamboo shaft. Some historians refer to this conflict as the Second Guerra Grande because of its numerous casualties as well as the devastation done to the cattle industry. Partisanship reached a fever pitch. When a British immigrant inadvertently wandered into a Colorado encampment, "they surrounded me, gesticulating wildly, and pointed to the white covering of my cap," which they grabbed, shot full of bullet holes, and returned minus the white band.[44]

Aparicio had served in the Uruguayan military for thirty years, gaining fame defending the Berro government. In the early stages of the War of the Spears, Aparicio and his gaucho fighters controlled the interior from Florida to Tacuarembó. Because Aparicio and his sizable cavalry force even captured the Cerrito, but could not take Montevideo, the War of the Spears resembled the Guerra Grande. Facing a larger Colorado army, Aparicio and his Blancos lost the battle of the Arroyo de Sauce on Christmas Day in 1870 after which the Colorado general executed numerous prisoners. The defeat made the rebels' long-term hopes untenable.[45]

But President Batlle refused to negotiate, so the war continued for another two years. His successor achieved peace one month after taking over by offering the Blancos a reasonable compromise. The settlement of April 6, 1872, gave the Blancos the right to appoint *jefes políticos* in four Blanco majority departments. Because *jefes políticos* controlled local elections, this arrangement, called co-participation (essentially a variation of fusionism), allowed the Blancos to pick the deputies for these four departments and hence gave them a voice in national government.[46]

In addition to extending the War of the Spears unnecessarily, Batlle was blamed for the Depression of 1868: prices for beef and wool plummeted, leading to the most serious financial crisis in many years and the failure of the Mauá Bank. Batlle, who despised Mauá because of his Brazilian citizenship, purposefully helped to bankrupt him. By the end of Batlle's term, many contemporaries considered him Uruguay's least successful president, or certainly its unluckiest. Intermittent cholera and yellow fever epidemics also cast a pall on his presidency.[47]

Batlle was the last independence-era patriot to wear the presidential sash. By 1872, youthful idealistic intellectuals known as the *principistas*, who wanted to lead "parties of ideas" (principles) in both parties and reject *caudillismo*, gained influence. These newcomers distrusted the state and advocated for greater personal liberties. Two prominent members of the group included José Pedro Varela, later known as the founder of Uruguay's public education system, and Julio Obes y Herrera, elected president later in the nineteenth century. Blanco principistas believed in upholding the rights of the minority party to representation.[48]

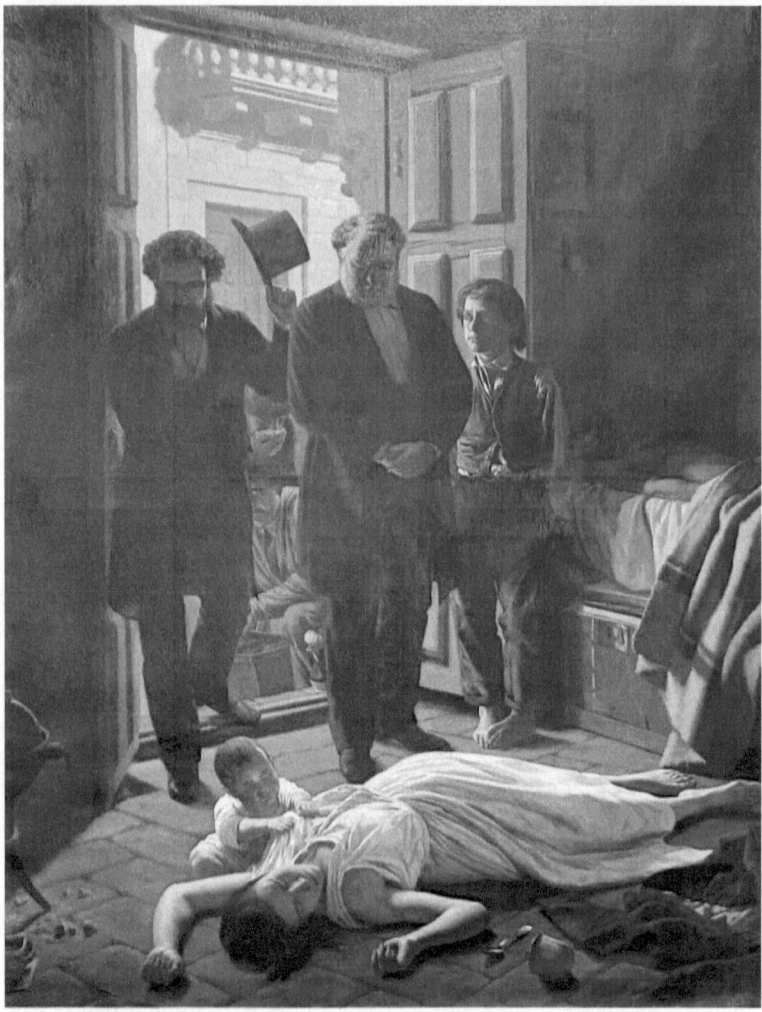

Figure 3.6 "The Yellow Fever Epidemic," by Juan Manuel Blanes. This famous Blanes painting depicts the tragic death of an overwise healthy young woman because of the yellow fever epidemic of 1875. In these days before doctors realized that mosquitoes breeding in standing water infected people with the yellow fever virus, epidemics were common in the Southern Cone. This cycle of disease compounded the miseries of 1875. *Source*: Museo Nacional de Artes Visuales, Montevideo.

Because both parties had split into factions, in 1873, the Assembly chose a nondescript compromise as president. The principistas, however, won several seats in the Chamber of Deputies and introduced legislation calling for significant electoral, administrative, and judicial reforms. Although none of these measures passed, some would reappear on the Colorados' twentieth-century platform. The *principistas*' opponents, who represented ranchers and Montevideo businessmen and wanted political stability and a stronger central government, preferred the government that seized control in 1876.⁴⁹

Because the president had minimal personal support, he could not solve the ongoing economic crisis. The vice-like grasp of the Panic (Depression) of 1873 that crippled European and U.S. economies diminished British and French demand for hides, wool, and cattle (by 25 percent, 30 percent, and 40 percent, respectively) and contributed to what Uruguayans called "the terrible year of 1875." The future looked bleak.⁵⁰

CONCLUSION

Superficially, the Uruguay of 1875 closely resembled the country of 1830 with its discordant politics, its boom-and bust export economy, and its uncertain sense of national identity. Beneath the surface, however, subtle changes had occurred. The political debate had matured to a discussion about co-participation between urban Colorados and rural Blancos versus single party domination. None of the issues that divided Latin Americans elsewhere—not military dictators, not the Catholic Church, not large landowners—dominated Uruguayan politics and economics. Although still exporters of pastoral products, immigrants and their sheep diversified the economy and enabled the country to participate more broadly in global trade. Perhaps most importantly, no political figure now advocated for the incorporation of the "buffer state" into one of its larger neighbors. Because of the rapid changes occurring after 1876, the final years of the century would see remarkable progress, as chapter 4 will demonstrate.

NOTES

1. Héctor Gros Espiell (ed.), *Las constituciones del Uruguay (exposición, crítica y textos)*, Madrid: Ediciones Cultura Hispánica, 1956. Frank Safford, "Politics, Ideology, and Society," in Leslie Bethel, ed. *Spanish America after Independence, c. 1820–c. 1870*, Cambridge: Cambridge University Press, 1987, 62; Eduardo Acevedo Vásquez, *Anales Históricos del Uruguay*, I of 6 Vols, Montevideo: Casa Barreiro y Ramos, 1933–1934, 328–30, 338–45. Uruguay's first historian, was an eyewitness to these events, see Isidoro Demaria, *Montevideo Antiguo: Tradiciones y Recuerdos*, 2 Vols., II, 342–45, Montevideo: El Siglo Ilustrado, 1888.

2. Fernández Saldaña, *Diccionario Uruguayo*, entry for Juan Antonio Lavalleja, 727–33; For a scholarly look at the members of the patriciado, see Carlos Real de Azúa, *El Patriciado uruguayo*, Montevideo: Ediciones Asir, 1961, 11–12, 19, 24–25. For Rivera's personality, see Juan A. Pivel Devoto, *Historia de los partidos y las ideas políticas en el Uruguay: La definición de los bandos, 1829–1838*, Vol. II, Montevideo: Medina, 1956, 76–80.

3. Pivel Devoto, *Los partidos*, 71–118. For another discussion of the first Rivera presidency, see Alejandro Martori Orguet, *El Brigadier General Don Fructuoso Rivera y su sistema*, Montevideo: Universidad de la República, 1980. See also Alex Borucki, *From Shipmates to Soldiers:*

Emerging Black Identities in the Río de la Plata, Albuquerque: University of New Mexico Press, 2015, 126–29; Acevedo, *Anales*, I, 384–89, 390–97, 400–401. Christopher Conway, *Nineteenth Century Spanish America: A Cultural History*, Nashville: Vanderbilt University Press, 2015, 187–88. The anthem has eleven verses, the longest in Latin America. The music changed over the years with the present tune, based on an Italian opera, being written in the 1840s.

4. Pi Hugarte. *Los indios*, 214–18; Acevedo, *Anales*, I, 383–87; Real de Azúa, *Patriciado*, 36–38; Pivel Devoto, *Los partidos*, 116–18.

5. Manuel Oribe to Fructuoso Rivera, March 5, 1836, in which Oribe responds to Rivera's concerns, framed letter, Casa de Fructuoso Rivera Museum, Durazno, Uruguay, Room 1; David McLean, *War, Diplomacy, and Informal Empire: Britain and the Republics of La Plata*, London: British Academic Press, 1995, 19–20; Acevedo, *Anales*, I, 456–60, 463–72; Real de Azúa, *Patriciado*, 90–92; Pivel Devoto, *Los partidos*, 127–49.

6. Pivel Devoto, *Los partidos*, 151–62. Luis Alberto de Herrera, *Por la verdad histórica (cómo se han adulterado los hechos)*, Montevideo: Private Printing, 1946, p. 616. Herrera, the long-time head of the Blanco party provides a favorable view of Oribe and the party's early politics. Acevedo, *Anales*, I, 473–76. Real de Azúa, *Patriciado*, 92–96. A British traveler reported that because Oribe rode a white horse and the gauchos tipped their spears with white pennons (emblems), the Blancos chose white *divisas* while Rivera rode a roan horse and his gauchos had red pennons; see James Bryce, *South America: Observations and Impressions*, New York: The Macmillan Company, 1913, 357; Koebel, *Uruguay*, 32.

7. José M. Fernández Saldaña, *Diccionario Uruguayo de biografías, 1810–1940*, Montevideo: Editorial Amerindia, 1945, Manuel Oribe entry, 930–36; John Lynch, *Argentine Dictator: Juan Manuel de Rosas, 1829–1852*: Oxford: Clarendon Press, 1981, 26–32, for a biography of Lavalle. Iwan Morgan, "Orleanist Diplomacy and the French Colony in Uruguay," *The International Historical Review*, Vol. 5, No. 2 (May, 1983), 201–28, esp. 202–5. Ferns, *Britain and Argentina*, 240–47; McLean, *War, Diplomacy*, 12–21. Winn, "British Informal Empire," 100, 105. The term "informal empire" suggests that the British refrained from conquering new colonies in South America, thereby avoiding the costs of government and military occupation, while reaping the benefits of trade. Acevedo, *Anales*, I, 476–91; Pivel Devoto, *Los partidos*, 130, 163–74. Jeffrey M. Shumway, *A Woman, a Man, a Nation: Mariquita Sánchez, Juan Manuel de Rosas, and the Beginnings of Argentina*, Albuquerque: University of New Mexico Press, 2019, 181–200.

8. Acevedo, *Anales*, I, 381, 391–93, 407–8, 464–69, 472–77; John F. Cady, *Foreign Intervention in the Río de la Plata, 1838–50*, Philadelphia: University of Pennsylvania Press, 1929, 15–17, 44–53.

9. Lynch, *Rosas*, 203–46. McLean, *War, Diplomacy*, 25; Morgan, "Orleanist Diplomacy," 202–11; Winn, "British Informal Empire" 105; Cady, *Foreign Intervention*, 15–91.

10. McLean, *War, Diplomacy*, 25–27, 34–36; Ferns, *Britain and Argentina*, 249–63; Cady, *Foreign Intervention*, 89, 103–4; Acevedo, *Anales*, II, 78–97. When the Blanco government in 1860 decided to reduce all pensions because of dire financial straits, they made an exception in favor of Suárez "because of his forty years of service which cost him his fortune." Acevedo, *Anales*, III, 177. For Suárez's biography, see Isidoro Demaria, *Rasgos biográficos de Don Joaquín Suárez*, Montevideo: Imprenta a vapor de El Ferrocarril, 1881.

11. Borucki, *Shipmates to Soldiers*, 40–46; Acevedo, *Anales*, II, 105–7; Pedemonte, *Hombres con Dueño*, 128–33.

12. Juan E. Pivel Devoto and Ranieri de Pivel Devoto, *La Guerra Grande, 1839–1851*, Montevideo: Editorial Medina, 1971, 12–15; Ferns, *Britain and Argentina*, 272–80; Cady,

Foreign Intervention, 104–26; Acevedo, *Anales*, II, 97–102; 124–29. Alexandre Dumas, *Montevideo, ou une nouvelle Troie*, Paris: Imprimiere Central de Napoleón Chaix et cie, 1850. Dumas received the story from French emigrees. He praised Rivera's character but criticized his military mistakes.

13. Richard Bourne, *Garibaldi in South America: An Exploration*, London: Hurst & Company, 2020, 7–37, 121. Lynch, *Juan Manuel de Rosas*, 203, 234–36, 305–7; Borucki, *Shipmates to Soldiers*, 130–35, 142–46. For more details see his *Abolucionismo y tráfico de esclavos en Montevideo tras la fundación repúblicana, 1829–1853*, Montevideo: Biblioteca Nacional, 2009; Pivel Devoto, *Guerra Grande*, 107–8; Acevedo, *Anales*, II, 102–3.

14. Bourne, *Garibaldi*, 37–38; Ferns, *Britain and Argentine*, 263; Cady, *Foreign Intervention*, 129–47; Acevedo, *Anales*, II, 130–33, 195–96. The historical monument at India Muerta claims that Rivera suffered four hundred dead and five hundred taken prisoner. Blanco historians have attempted to portray Oribe in a softer light, see Luis Alberto de Herrera, *Origines de la Guerra Grande*, 2 Vols., Montevideo: Impreso en los talleres de A. Monteverde y cia., 1941. Rivera lost a battle in November, 1816 against the Portuguese general Lecor at this same location. The site contains several small indigenous *cerritos* (see chapter 1).

15. Ferns, *Britain and Argentina*, 268–74; McLean, *War, Diplomacy*, 63–65; Winn, "Informal Empire," 106–7; Morgan, "Orleanist Diplomacy," 216–25; Pivel Devoto, *Guerra Grande*, 19–22, 28–32; Cady, *Foreign Intervention*, 147–56; Acevedo, *Anales*, II, 134–38; Lynch, *Rosas*, 243, 277–86; Fernández Saldaña, *Diccionario Uruguayo*, Fructuoso Rivera entry, 1093.

16. Mclean, *War, Diplomacy*, 37, 70–86. Although in the long run inconsequential, the British and French blockade continued the pattern of international involvement in the La Plata region. See Pivel Devoto and Pivel Devoto, *Guerra Grande*, 51–85. Ferns, *Britain and Argentina*, 263 supplied the quotation. The pro-Rosas British minister thought Oribe should have launched an attack and taken the city; Cady, *Foreign Intervention*, 205–7.

17. Bourne, *Garibaldi*, 46–60; Acevedo, *Anales*, II, 134–42, 178–83. Fernández Saldaña, *Diccionario Uruguayo*, biography of Lorenzo Batlle, 143–47.

18. Pivel Devoto, *Guerra Grande*, 29–32. Cady, *Foreign Intervention*, 207–39, 255–63; McLean, *Informal Empire*, 121–58. Morgan, *Orleanist Diplomacy*, 223–28. Ferns, *Britain and Argentina*, 281–89. Several prominent Colorados sold some or all of their estancias to finance the Great War: Rivera sold his property north of the Río Negro, and Joaquín Suárez sold everything, see Real de Azúa, *Patriciado*, 44, 46–48, 54, 60. For Mauá, see Anyda Marchant, *Viscount Mauá and the Empire of Brazil: A Biography of Irineu Evangelista de Sousa (1813–1889)*, Berkeley: University of California Press, 1965, 145–49.

19. Pivel Devoto, *Guerra Grande*, 85–104; Winn, "Informal Empire," 108–9, Cady, *Foreign Intervention*, 265–6; Acevedo, *Anales*, II, 335–42. Colorado diplomats had tried to turn Urquiza against Rosas since 1847.

20. Pivel Devoto, *Guerra Grande*, 104–6; Lynch, *Juan Manuel de Rosas*, 313–20; Acevedo, *Anales*, II, 341–48. For many years two French brothers who built the stone bridge collected the fees and maintained the small bridge over the stream that marked the frontier.

21. Fernández Saldaña, *Diccionario Uruguayo*, biography of Bernadina Fragoso de Rivera, 1087–89.

22. Lynch, *Juan Manuel de Rosas*, 311–12; Pivel Devoto, *Guerra Grande*, 84–106; Acevedo, *Anales*, Vol. I, 352–74, 497–547 and Vol. II, 7–9, 18–19; Carlos Rama, *La Religión en el Uruguay*, Montevideo: Ediciones Nuestro Tiempo, 1964, 18–19; McLean, *War, Diplomacy*, 12; José P. Barrán and Benjamin Nahum, *Historia rural del Uruguay moderno*, I., Montevideo:

Ediciones de la Banda Oriental, 1967–1978, 15–17; Washington Reyes Abadie, *Latorre: La forja del estado*, Montevideo: Ediciones de la Banda Oriental, 1977, 6, is the source of the Sarmiento quote; Fernando López-Alves, *State Formation and Democracy in Latin America*, Durham: Duke University Press, 2000, 54, 61, 83; Aldo Solari, *El Desarrollo social del Uruguay en la postguerra*, Montevideo: Editorial Alfa, 1967, 58–59, notes that many estancieros sold land to immigrants at this time.

23. John Hoyt Williams, "Observations on Blacks and Bondage in Uruguay, 1810–1836," *The Americas*, Vol. 43, No. 4 (April 1987), 411–27; Pivel Devoto, *Los partidos*, 254–56; Pedemonte, *Hombres con dueño*, 39–41.

24. Pedemonte, *Hombres con dueño*, 117–56; Acevedo, *Anales*, II, 607–8, Acevedo, *Anales*, III, 121–122; Borucki, "Trans-Local Black Communities," in Pedro Cameselle-Pesce and Debbie Sharnak (eds.), *Uruguay in Transitional Perspective*, New York: Routledge, 2024, 58, 64–66; Borucki, *Shipmates to Soldiers*, 147–82.

25. Fernández Saldaña, *Diccionario Uruguayo*, biography of Venancio Flores, 489–94.

26. John Lynch, "The River Plate Republics, in Leslie Bethel (ed.), *Latin America after Independence*, c. 1820–c1870, Cambridge: Cambridge University Press, 1987, 314–75, at 360–61. Fernández Saldaña, *Diccionario Uruguayo*, biography of Venancio Flores, 489–94.

27. For a thorough description of the Pereyra presidency, see Acevedo, *Anales*, II, 538–72, 597–663, and for Berro's term, see Acevedo, *Anales*, III, 8–255. López-Alves, *State Formation*, 71–72; Fernández Soldana, *Diccionario Uruguayo*, biography of Bernardo Berro, 192–97.

28. Marchant, *Mauá*, 118–30, 152–53, 168.

29. José P. Barrán and Benjamín Nahum, *Historia rural del Uruguay moderno*, 7 Vols. Montevideo: Ediciones de la Banda Oriental, I, 16–31. Their conclusions are summarized in volume 7, and synthesized in José Pedro Barrán and Benjamín Nahum, "Uruguayan Rural History, *Hispanic American Historical Review*, Vol. 64, No. 4 (November 1984), 655–73. Real de Azúa, *Patriciado*, 113–14, estimates that as much as three quarters of Uruguayan real and personal property was foreign owned. This sounds high, but certainly immigrants had bought considerable amounts of land.

30. Barrán and Nahum, *Historia Rural*, I, 36–46.

31. Barrán and Nahum, *Historia Rural*, I. 98–116; Koebel, *Uruguay*, 259–64. Marchant, *Mauá*, 154–55, 229. By 1861, Mauá had become the greatest landowner, banker, and industrialist in the La Plata region. Today his estate outside Mercedes houses a modern vineyard as well as the Alejandro Berro Paleontology Museum. Urban saladeros were a blight in neighborhoods as British traveler Richard Seymour noted, "The smell from the saladero is not very nice." Richard A. Seymour, *Pioneering in the Pampas: The First Four Years of a Settler's Experience in the La Plata Camps*, London: Longman, Green, 1869.

32. Barrán and Nahum, *Historia Rural*, I, 68–72, 88–90, 94–104. For a masterful discussion of Argentine developments, see James R. Scobie, *Revolution on the Pampas: A Social History of Argentine Wheat, 1860–1910*, Austin: University of Texas Press, 43.

33. Barrán and Nahum, *Historia Rural*, I, 53–54, 296–97. Uruguay's rural history has many similarities to that of Argentina in the nineteenth century. Scobie, *Revolution on the Pampas*, 46, 118–21, and 131–32.

34. Barrán and Nahum, *Historia Rural*, I, 141–73; López-Alves, *State Formation*, 89–90.

35. Barrán and Nahum, *Historia Rural*, I, 159–76; J. H. Murray, *Travels in Uruguay, South America: Together with an Account of the State of Sheep-farming and Emigration to That Country*, London: Longmans & Co., 1871, 161–234. Murray traveled some four thousand miles in Argentina and Uruguay compiling data for prospective emigrants.

36. Domingo A. Caillava, *Historia de la literatura Gauchesca en el Uruguay: Resumen histórico, 1810–1940*, Montevideo: Claudio García & Cia., 1945, 13–27, 193–210; Shumway, *Invention*, 67–30; Nichols, *Gaucho*, 58–63, William G. Acree, *Everyday Reading: Print Culture and Collective Identity in the Río de la Plata, 1780–1910*, Nashville: Vanderbilt University Press, 2009, 43–83. See also John F. Garganigo, *Javier de Viana*, New York: Twayne Publishers, Inc., 1972.

37. Fernández Saldaña, *Diccionario Uruguayo*, biography of Venancio Flores, 489–94.

38. Fernández Saldaña, *Diccionario Uruguayo*, biography of Bernardo Berro, 192–97. Lynch, in Bethell (ed)., *The River Plate Republics*, 358–65; Acevedo, *Anales*, III, 42–57. For two different interpretations of the war, see Charles J. Kolinski, *Independence or Death: The Story of the Paraguayan War*, Gainesville: University of Florida Press, 1965; and Thomas L. Whigham, *The Paraguayan War: Causes and Early Conduct*, Vol. I, Lincoln: University of Nebraska Press, 2002, which contains more information about Uruguay's role.

39. Alfredo Castellanos, *Timoteo Aparicio; el ocaso de las lanzas*, Montevideo: Ediciones de la Banda Oriental, 18–24; 46–52; Fernández Saldaña, *Diccionario Uruguayo*, biography of José María Leandro Gómez, 578–82.

40. Fernández Saldaña, *Diccionario Uruguayo*, biography of Venancio Flores, 488–94; Gabriele Esposito, *Armies of the War of the Triple Alliance 1864–1870, Paraguay, Brazil, Uruguay, and Argentina*, Oxford: Osprey Press, 2015, 8–16; Acevedo, *Anales*, III, 263–85.

41. Esposito, *Armies*, 22–23; Acevedo, *Anales*, III, 289–98, 356–402; Barrán and Nahum, *Historia Rural*, I, 221–25. Acevedo, *Anales*, III, 434–63; Castellanos, *Timoteo Aparicio*, 56–57.

42. Fernández Saldaña, *Diccionario Uruguayo*, biography of Venancio Flores, 488–94; and biography of Bernardo Berro, 192–97; Acevedo, *Anales*, III, 418–25; Murray, *Travels in Uruguay*, 44–48. The Colorados wanted to give Flores a state funeral, but they could not find an embalmer to prepare the body, so they gave the job to a taxidermist. When his work failed, they tried a vat of alcohol, but that too failed, so they buried Flores without ceremony. Murray, *Travels in Uruguay*, 48.

43. Milton Vanger, *José Batlle y Ordóñez: The Creator of His Times, 1902–1907*, Cambridge: Harvard University Press, 1963, 12–15, provides a brief biography of Lorenzo Batlle. See also Fernández Saldaña, *Diccionario Uruguayo*, biography of Lorenzo Batlle, 143–47. Juan Antonio Oddone, *El principismo del setenta: Una experiencia liberal en el Uruguay*, Montevideo: Universidad de la República Oriental del Uruguay, 1956, 17–18, 25–36.

44. Acevedo, *Anales*, III, 509–16; Castellanos, *Timoteo Aparicio*, 52–62; William C. Tetley, *Blanco y Colorado; Old Days among the Gauchos of Uruguay*, London: Simpkin, Marshall, Hamilton, Kent & Co., LTD, 1921, 20–21.

45. Castellanos, *Timoteo Aparicio*, 61–69, 138–39; Acevedo, *Anales*, III, 517–32.

46. Castellanos, *Timoteo Aparicio*, 75–80; Acevedo, *Anales*, III, 531–47, 647–50. López-Alves, *State Formation*, 85–87, 91–94.

47. Griffin, "Land Use Patterns," 25; Barrón and Nahum, *Historia Rural*, I, 245–56; Tetley, *Blanco y Colorado*, 30, 35–39, describe Colorado and Blanco thefts of horses, cattle, and sheep. W. H. Hudson, *The Purple Land*, second ed., New York: Grossett & Dunlap, probably the best-known English language novel about Uruguay, offers a similar portrayal of the futile effort of ranchers to protect their herds from scavenging armies on both sides. Acevedo, *Anales*, III, 579–98; Marchant, *Mauá*, 186–203. For the epidemics, see Koebel, *Uruguay*, 124; Murray. *Travels in Uruguay*, 43, estimates four thousand people died in Montevideo alone.

48. Oddone, *Principismo*, 94–101, 121–56; Acevedo, *Anales*, III, 634–37; Juan Oddone, "Uruguay: 1870–1930" in Leslie Bethel, ed. *Cambridge History of Latin America*, V, 453–74, at 457; López-Alves, *State Formation*, 57, 86.

49. Acevedo, *Anales*, III, 647–64. López-Alves, *State Formation*, 86, 91–94; Fernández Saldaña, entry for José Ellauri, *Diccionario Uruguayo*, 430–34; Juan Pedemonte, *El año terrible: Latorre, Santos, Tajes: Hombres y hechos de su tiempo*, Montevideo: Barreira & Ramos, 1956, 17–21.

50. Barrán and Nahum, *Historia Rural*, I, 248–57; Acevedo, *Anales*, III, 714–30. Imports also decreased by 50 percent between 1873 and 1875, Michael Mulhall, *The English in South America*, New York: Arno Press (reprint) 1977, originally published in 1878, 587.

Four

Forming the Nation

Progress and Order, 1876–1903

For certain Latin American nations (Mexico, Argentina, Brazil, Uruguay, and Chile), the final twenty-five years of the nineteenth century marked a great leap forward, an era of progress. Their evolution followed a recognizable pattern based upon the new European brand of developmental liberalism called positivism. These pragmatic changes included the achievement of political stability (either a long-term dictatorship or a republic led by aristocratic notables); the acquisition of foreign capital to finance infrastructure; the arrival of European immigrants (at least in the Southern Cone); and the transfer of western technology to improve transportation and communication, often (but not always) to deliver profitable, high-demand export products to ports. As a result of the developing economy, people moved from rural areas to cities where they shared space with the new European arrivals. Urbanization and the thriving economy resulted in an expanding middle class that demanded public education for its children and broader rights of suffrage. Uruguay followed a variation of this pattern.

POSITIVISM AND THE RURAL ASSOCIATION, 1871–1885

The ideas behind the state's renovation came primarily from positivism, the brainchild of Auguste Compte, the Father of Sociology. Compte applied Charles Darwin's theory of evolution to society, arguing that human society, like a biological organism, passed through several stages of development. By applying the scientific principles of developmental liberalism (positivism), national leaders could achieve social and material progress and lead their nation to the stage of development enjoyed by Western Europe and the United States. Positivism measured progress by the achievement of material wealth, the emergence of a more modern society, and a stronger state. After 1870, positivism captivated many Latin American intellectuals, eager to move forward from the doldrums of the post-independence era.

Positivism gained a foothold in Uruguay's *Associación Rural* (Rural Association), made up of upper- and middle-class cattle and sheep ranchers eager to challenge the political influence of the traditional elite. The association's principal spokesperson, Domingo Ordoñana, a Basque immigrant, argued that national development required ranchers to rethink their production methods. He believed that ranchers could use innovative scientific and technological practices to improve the quality of sheep and cattle, opening new market possibilities in Europe. Most of the members of the Rural Association resided in the south and west of the country, and roughly a third were immigrants or children of immigrants. The members of the Rural Association wielded political influence with the military and civilian regimes that dominated politics between 1876 and 1903. Such ranchers found kindred spirits among the wealthy merchants and entrepreneurial members of the middle class who created industries and businesses in Montevideo, often dedicated to processing products from cattle and sheep.[1]

Ordoñana and other contributors to the association's publication also hoped to assist the plight of the impoverished gauchos. The association favored offering the technical education necessary to teach gauchos to work with pedigreed cattle and sheep. This never happened, and the rural poor remained a nagging problem for generations. In addition, the Rural Association naively believed that promoting religion and family values would uplift the rural poor.[2]

Some policies of the Rural Association conflicted with the interests of urban industrialists. Ranchers and farmers wanted free trade or at least minimal tariffs for select technological products needed for improving pastoral and agricultural production. On the other hand, their urban middle-class manufacturing allies wanted selective tariffs to protect their products from competition. In fact, domestic manufacturers of comestibles had unrealized advantages in the local market. The new generation of ranchers also begged for the establishment of rural banks and access to credit.[3]

THE (RELATIVE) STABILIZATION OF THE STATE, 1876–1894

The country's transition to a stronger state, which some Uruguayan historians refer to as the second founding of the nation, began when the military ended the decade-long political and economic chaos that culminated in the high inflation and unrest caused by the "terrible year of 1875." On March 10, 1876, thirty-seven-year-old Colonel Lorenzo Latorre, the minister of war, overthrew the civilian government and established a brief dictatorship. The son of a Spanish immigrant and small business owner, Latorre sought a more adventurous life and joined Colorado party leader Venancio Flores's army in 1863. He suffered a near fatal wound fighting in the War of the Triple Alliance. After leading government troops and defeating Aparicio's gauchu army, Latorre became the senior figure in the military. His coup in 1876 enjoyed considerable popular support. As a self-made, middle-class man, Colonel Latorre declared that his dictatorship stood for "honest administration, liberty and order, respect for the law and rights guaranteed by the Constitution" as well as the positivist ideas of the reformers of the Rural Association.[4]

During his presidency (1876 to 1880), Latorre strengthened the national government and restored law and order. Modern military equipment enabled the national army to gain the upper hand against those who conspired against the government. The dictatorship purchased brand-new 1874 model Remington rifles, Mausers, Krupp artillery, and Gatling guns, while gaucho caudillos continued to rely on cavalry charges with men wielding homemade lances. Such disparities in equipment provided the army with a near-monopoly of lethal force and minimized uprisings. Latorre also reformed the army by eliminating the *leva* (draft of the urban poor; there was no draft in rural areas) because it discriminated against Afro-Uruguayans. (After Latorre's time, the mandate was ignored at times.)

Latorre committed his administration to protecting private property. Thus, he authorized the use of private armies in rural areas, allowing estancieros to patrol their own properties. As Domingo Ordoñana (who served a dual role as Latorre's personal secretary) stated, "To make rural life livable, we must restore security." Following Ordañana's recommendation, Latorre encouraged each department to organize a rural police force. To assist them in their work, he granted new authority to the national army allowing it to pursue rustlers and bandits across departmental boundaries and bring them to quick justice. Allegedly, he turned a blind eye to the use of the *Ley Fuga* that allowed police to shoot prisoners "while attempting to escape," which apparently, a remarkably large number attempted to do.[5]

Latorre's positivist measures included the first codification of national laws in Uruguay's history, resulting in the Code of Criminal Procedure, the Code of Civil Procedure, the Commercial Code, the Mining Code, and, most importantly, the Rural Code. These statutes provided uniform justice. Sentences for rustling and vagrancy stiffened. New bureaucratic agencies such as the Office of Agronomy heightened the government's visibility and taught improved farming methods to assist immigrants. Like the other Latin American nations pursuing progress, Latorre's dictatorship used technology, especially railroads and telegraph lines, that increased the capital's control over the departments and would within decades eliminate the possibility of a successful provincial rebellion.[6]

After Latorre voluntarily relinquished his dictatorship in 1878, the Assembly elected him president because of his achievements. Only one year into his elected term (1879–1882), Latorre abruptly resigned, claiming fatigue after five years of service and constant criticism about his personal friends, the handcuffs he had placed on the press, and his "unconstitutional" rule. A man of few words, he said, "I retire to private life believing our country is ungovernable." While contemporaries described Latorre as modest and bashful, General Máximo Santos, who harbored designs on the presidency, appeared more comfortable in the public sphere, and impressed people initially as intelligent but lacking a sense of restraint.[7]

After an interim completed Latorre's term, Minister of War Santos muscled himself into the presidency. From modest social beginnings, Santos had served under Latorre's command during the Timoteo Aparicio revolt, and they had become good friends. Santos claimed he had received battlefield promotions for valor although he could never produce documentation other than a suspicious-looking certificate. Before the election of 1882, his toughs beat opponents and closed opposition newspapers to ensure that the Assembly, which under the Constitution of 1830 elected the president, contained a majority friendly to Santos's candidacy.

Once president, Santos strengthened his following. Whereas Latorre had reduced the size of the military and the bureaucracy to balance the budget, Santos doubled their numbers. The three short-lived rebellions that occurred after he assumed office added weight to Santos's argument for the firm hand. Like other progressing Latin American nations (Mexico, Chile, Brazil, and Argentina), Santos revived the military academy in 1885 to create a professional force that would further strengthen the state, deter internal rebellions and (hopefully) remain aloof from politics. Santos, through astute promotions, strengthened the linkage between the Colorado party and the majority of regular army officers.[8]

A booming economy in the early 1880s, as well as the British loan of 1883, provided funding for projects like more railroads and telegraph lines that strengthened the state. But prosperity also increased Santos's thirst for corruption. By the end of his term, the venal Santos had acquired over a million pesos in cash as well as two opulent homes in Montevideo. No wonder he schemed to retain the presidency in 1886! To do so, he resigned the presidency, took a seat in the Senate, and argued that the appointment of an interim president made him eligible for election. Santos's successful shenanigans set off fireworks. Emerging political leader and journalist José Batlle y Ordóñez, liberal *principistas*, and famed poet Juan Zorrilla de San Martín fled to Argentina to participate in a rebellion. Santos sent General Máximo Tajes and the army to tackle the invaders at Quebracho where the professional army easily crushed the rebels, taking eight hundred prisoners. Tajes refused to follow Santos's orders to execute the insurgents, riding down the line, shouting, "Death to anyone who attacks a prisoner." Tajes instead sent the captives to Montevideo.[9]

For many, Santos's efforts to establish a long-term dictatorship (he was only thirty-nine in 1886) constituted a threat to the country's democratic tradition. Perhaps not surprisingly, in August, a young lieutenant who claimed descent from one of the Immortal Thirty-Three, approached the president's carriage and shot Santos twice in the face with bullets laced with mercury. Badly burned, Santos gamely continued to govern, but eventually resigned and left the country seeking treatment in Europe. Because Tajes had acted with such moderation at Quebracho and agreed to a democratic election in 1890, the Assembly chose him to finish the remainder of Santos's term.[10]

Tajes, like Latorre, had won his spurs as a battled-tested officer in the War of the Triple Alliance. He proclaimed himself a transitional figure who would return Uruguay to its two-party electoral system. When Santos asked to return home, Tajes denied his request, fired Santos's friends from the cabinet, and dissolved his personal

Figure 4.1 "Machero of General Santos," by J. M. Correa. Black men continued to enlist in (or be impressed into) the army even after Latorre's proclamation ending the practice. Once any individual, regardless of race, obtained the rank of officer, this elevated his status in society. Although ordinary recruits experienced a very difficult life in the barracks, serving as a soldier did provide meals, clothing and a place to sleep.
Source: National Museum of History, Casa de Rivera.

military escort. Tajes appointed civilians to lead his "National Conciliation" government, led by Colorado Julio Herrera y Obes, the minister of the interior. Herrera y Obes promised to reconcile all factions to facilitate the transition to civilian rule. In 1890 Tajes happily retired. His decision established the principle of military subordination to civilian rule. An unsung hero, Tajes thus proved himself the most moderate of the military presidents.[11] Nevertheless, altogether the generals provided political stability for fifteen years and laid the foundation for national progress.

THE EMERGENCE OF NATIONAL IDENTITY

The golden anniversary of the culmination of the independence movement (1825–1828) inspired spirited discussions about national identity and expanded the basic "tool-kit" (the flag, coat of arms, national anthem). During the anniversary celebrations, the works of an artist, a poet, and a novelist constructed Uruguay's historical identity as a project defined by the coda for the Charrúa and gauchos. Artist Juan Manuel Blanes, whose paintings have illustrated several pages of this book, produced his monumental masterpiece "The Oath of the Immortal Thirty-Three" to celebrate the landing of the liberators in April 1825. Residing on an estate near the Playa de Agraciado, he visited the beach daily to visualize details about the scene and even brought home grains of sand to capture its texture. The flag in the center of the painting served to viewers the ideals of the liberators. When the painting opened to the public viewing at Blanes's home in 1878, 6,200 people came to see it in a single month. Thereafter, he donated it to the National Museum of Art (today the Juan Manuel Blanes Municipal Museum of Fine Arts).

The patriotic celebration that took place in Florida (the city) in 1879, where the declaration of independence from Brazil had been signed, also brought about the first recognition of the genius of poet Juan Zorrilla de San Martín, whose flowery and Romantic poem "The Fatherland Legend" described the battles for independence and especially the moment that the Thirty-Three took the oath to fight for liberty or suffer death. Zorrilla de San Martín's moving recitation of the 413-verse poem earned him such applause that the official prize winners, who had written poems within the prescribed stanza limits, gave their first and second place medals to Zorrilla de San Martín, soon hailed as the "Poet of the Fatherland." Eduardo Acevedo Díaz penned a quartet of novels detailing the events of the independence era, the third of which, *Cry of Glory*, depicted the deeds of the Immortal Thirty-Three. Acevedo Díaz portrayed the Thirty-Three as heroic and valiant patriots resisting the Brazilian occupation, offering a patriotic teaching moment to his readers.[12]

The nationalistic themes of the artwork, poetry, and statuary in these years raised the thorny question about which independence-era figure should be identified as Uruguay's national hero: Artigas, Lavalleja, Rivera, or Oribe. Each had flaws. Members of the patriciado had denigrated Artigas's contributions for years. He fought for a greater Federal League rather than an independent Uruguayan state; he favored radical agrarian reform; his gauchos personified Sarmiento's barbarians; he did not take part in the struggle against Brazil; and he rejected an invitation to return to his homeland thereafter.

The other three had first earned their reputations as Artigas's officers. Lavalleja did lead the Immortal Thirty-Three, but post-independence, his multiple rebellions and lack of battlefield success tarnished his luster. Oribe had risen to the presidency, but during the Guerra Grande, had meekly done Rosas's bidding. Uruguay's most successful caudillo, Rivera, ultimately proved himself an untrustworthy transactional leader. Exiled journalist Juan Carlos Gómez discussed the problems of identifying any of them as the father of independence, and sarcastically added that Emperor Pedro I and Argentine president Manuel Dorrego should be recognized as such because they had signed off on the treaty prepared by British diplomat Viscount John Ponsonby.[13]

A British contemporary commentated, "For generations the feathers of Artigas's remained of undisputed black, now. . . . Uruguayans have initiated a cleansing process to change the plumes to too blinding a white." As another observer stated, "Artigas . . . whose memory not so long ago rivaled that of the most traditionally cruel old-world potentates, is now become the Savior and National Hero of Uruguay. The apostle of the democratic principle." Two contemporary historians, each of whom had inked a textbook, laid out the debate. Artigas's ultimate appeal rested not only in the fact that he won the first important battle of the wars for independence, but that he led the Exodus of 1811 that personified the wishes of the Uruguayan people, and that during the chaotic Guerra Grande, he did not take sides.

By the early 1880s, public opinion settled on Artigas, but not without opposition. To commemorate the Exodus, Santos commissioned the enormous bronze equestrian statue of Artigas that graces the Plaza de Independencia in Montevideo. A hot debate arose about the inscription for the monument. The Chamber of Deputies proposed "Thanks to José Artigas, the founder of Uruguayan Nationality." The Senate rejected these words and successfully insisted that no more than his name be inscribed on the statue. Ever the politician, Santos also commissioned statues of Lavalleja and Rivera to adorn different plazas. Finally, the president removed the textbook that painted Artigas in dark hues from the list approved for use in primary schools. Zorrilla de San Martín's "The Epic of Artigas (1910) also whitewashed the hero. During the early twentieth century, the expansion of democracy and legislation of social reforms, cemented Artigas's identification as Uruguay's national hero. Only in 1919, however, did politicians resolve the issue of the date of celebrate independence (August 25) by providing a second holiday, Constitution Day (July 18) to satisfy the Colorados.[14]

FOREIGN INVESTMENT, 1870–1903

After the War of the Triple Alliance, Great Britain asserted its informal empire in Uruguay by making direct loans and encouraging British entrepreneurs to invest in Uruguayan utilities. Although the Batlle government in 1871 defaulted on its British

Figure 4.2 "Artigas's Remains Being Repatriated," by Domingo Rois. Rois's painting of the repatriation of Artigas's remains in 1860 provides clear evidence of the relative disinterest in the independence figure. The absence of huge crowds awaiting the arrival of the coffin of the person who would ultimately become Uruguay's national hero indicates the ambivalence with which Uruguayans viewed Artigas at this moment. *Source*: National History Museum, Casa de Rivera.

loan, Latorre and his finance minister, future president Juan Lindolfo Cuestas, understood the importance of regaining British bankers' confidence in the nation's fiscal trustworthiness, and repaid the overdue loans. Contrasting himself with his predecessors, Latorre stated, "Mine will be an honorable government, not one of thieves." To keep his promise, he returned Uruguay to the gold standard, made debt payments in specie, and signed a treaty agreeing to pay off outstanding claims, even that of Baron Mauá. With repayment issues settled, British capital again flowed into Uruguay, which became the fourth largest recipient of pounds sterling in South America.[15]

Because only Uruguay and Argentina of all the Latin American debtors had resumed payments, British entrepreneurs and banks, flush with capital, saw the La Plata nations as excellent credit risks and felt confident funding public works projects. British investors also offered low interest rates to Argentina and Uruguay because they supplied Britain's demand for grain, meat, and wool caused by a series of European bad harvests. By 1883 this aura of confidence, fiscal reforms, as well as rising prices for pastoral products enabled Santos to negotiate further loans and arrange further direct investments that totaled over 25 million pounds by the end of the decade.

The first British-owned enterprise, the Montevideo Water Works Company, began pumping fresh water (not necessarily potable), forty miles from the Santa

Lucia River to the Plaza Matriz in Montevideo. British capital also constructed railroads, tramways, flour mills, urban utilities (gas, electric and telephone), and opened banks and insurance companies. At the same time, British land companies shrank away from purchasing large tracts because the risks and low profit margins of ranching paled in comparison to their more secure and profitable investments in public works. As a result, land ownership and its bovine occupants (cattle and sheep), the nation's source of wealth, remained in the hands of Uruguayans and immigrant families.[16]

After the Assembly authorized the *Banco Nacional de la República Oriental*, Emilio Reus, who had made his fortune in Argentina, persuaded a group of his countrymen to invest 20 million pesos in the bank. The bank provided a line of credit to the Tajes government and lent money to ranchers and farmers. Unfortunately, Reus gambled on speculative urban construction projects in Montevideo. In 1890, the failure of the British Baring Brothers Bank, the guarantor of the Banco Nacional, forced the latter's closure resulting in Reus's personal bankruptcy. Despite trepidations because of this experience, Uruguay needed a sound financial institution. Six years later the government authorized the *Banco de la República Oriental del Uruguay* (Bank of the Republic), also funded with British capital. The Bank of the Republic followed safer banking practices and only issued twice as much paper currency as it held in gold, but it remained a commercial rather than an investment bank.[17]

By 1893, British financiers had poured over 40 million pounds sterling into the country, the third most in Latin America. Despite its small size, Uruguay, like Argentina, had become a profitable and secure repository for investors. So dominant had the presence of British capital become that President Julio Herrera y Obes in 1890 remarked that he felt like "the manager of a huge ranch whose board of directors lived in London." By the end of the nineteenth century, with high profits from public works flowing out of the country, Uruguayan officials began to regulate British investment. An 1888 statute required strict accounting by the British railroad company. Britain's foreign investments returned higher profits than could be generated at home, but the funds also made possible Uruguay's stability and civilian rule.[18]

IMMIGRATION, 1840–1903

Immigrants from France, Spain, and Italy had first arrived in the 1830s, and by 1891, immigrants represented roughly 30 percent of Uruguay's population. Native-born Uruguayans contributed to population growth because the nation had a very high birth rate and a low infant mortality rate compared to most Latin American countries. Argentina and southern Brazil attracted more European immigrants than did Uruguay, as some who arrived in Uruguay moved on to Argentina for various reasons. Because cattle and sheep ranchers controlled much of the land, disappointed would-be farmers often left the provinces to seek their fortunes in Montevideo.[19]

There, the absence of a language barrier allowed Spanish and Italian immigrants to assimilate easily. By 1900, several successful immigrants had become wealthy

Figure 4.3   Aguas Corrientes Water Works. Museo del Agua. Aguas Corrientes. In 1871, British entrepreneurs, later incorporated as the Montevideo Waterworks Company, constructed a facility in the town of Aguas Corrientes to bring water to Montevideo. The main facility housed British manufactured pumps that took clean water from the Santa Lucia River and pumped it thirty-five miles to the Plaza de la Constitución in the heart of the Old City. This project enabled households in Montevideo to enjoy clean water for household use. Only in 1923 did the plant add a purification process that made the water potable. When World War II diminished the amount of oil Uruguay could import, the company burned wood to power the pumps. *Source:* Author photo.

members of society. Italians made up about 20 percent of the city's population and Spaniards about 15 percent. Other immigrants, particularly the British in the south and west, and the Brazilians in the north, settled in the countryside. When progressive ranchers founded the Rural Association in the 1870s, roughly one-third of its members were immigrants or descendants of an immigrant.[20]

Elites and racist nation-builders throughout Latin America concocted various theories to prove the need for European immigrants. Some argued that they already possessed agricultural or technological skills as well as the "strong arms, knowledge, and capital" that could develop a country's resources. Others claimed that European immigrants possessed the work ethic, thrift, and morality that would uplift the impoverished, unemployed gauchos. Immigrants allegedly promoted democracy, a goal that reformers advocated. Argentina, Uruguay, and southern Brazil also benefited because of the similarity of the climate and soil to that of southern Europe. Many immigrant families became the backbone of Uruguay's middle class.[21]

BOX 4.1: AN IMMIGRANT SUCCESS STORY

In 1862, a German, August Tidemann, purchased a 38,500-acre *estancia* in San José department and sent his younger brother Hugo to administer it. He and his hired hands constructed two dwelling places; one for the owner and the other for the workers. The *estancia*'s prior owner had built traditional corrals with stone walls and wooden fences. Tidemann pioneered the use of revolutionary barbed wire to fence more of the land while also increasing the size of each pasture, thereby lessening the likelihood that mange would spread. Although primarily dedicated to sheep, the *estancia* also ran a few cattle and horses. Hugo Tidemann's duties kept him place-bound except for his annual business trip to Montevideo that took eight days by diligence (stagecoach) from Durazno. Train service (which carried his wool to market) reduced his trip to four hours. The estate remained profitable well into the twentieth century.[22]

TECHNOLOGY, 1875–1903

Technological innovations after 1875 transformed the countryside. Barbed-wire fencing, railroads, Remington rifles, the telegraph, and postal system helped to create the modern state. The first and foremost of them, barbed-wire fencing, allowed estancias to expand. The Rural Code of 1879, proposed by the Rural Association, required ranchers to perfect their titles by recording written deeds and marking ranch boundaries with barbed-wire fences. Despite the code, ranchers in the north neither purchased nor fenced their open range grazing lands (*tierras fiscales*) over which they enjoyed color of title (rights by occupation) to avoid paying property taxes. Latorre also required the Office of Brands to collect data from each department and publish a nationwide catalog of brands to discourage rustling.[23]

For ranchers running pedigreed breeds, the importation of barbed-wire fencing after 1874 had enormous social and economic consequences. Invented in Great Britain by a farmer who noticed that thorny hedges effectively contained livestock, Uruguayan ranchers strung thousands of miles of duty-free barbed wire onto wooden posts transported from Argentina (the hollow wood of the native *ombú* tree was useless for posts) over the next decade, closing the open range in the south, west, and central portions of the country. Ranchers fenced their land to protect their pedigreed sheep and cattle from breeding with creole livestock, which would have reduced the quality of beef and wool. Uruguayan landlords likened fencing their range to the English eighteenth-century enclosure movement that made farming more efficient while evicting tenants to urban slums. The fencing of the prairie and even its communally held woodlands, public roads, and sources of water, trumpeted the triumph of private property over the open range and confined Uruguay's equivalent of sodbusters to small plots.[24]

Figure 4.4 Tool for Installing Barbed-Wire Fence. As the Rural Association noted, fencing was critical for Uruguay's pastoral development. Prior to the invention of barbed wire in the 1860s, ranchers, particularly in northern Uruguay, built stone walls to contain herds of animals. Stone walls required an immense quantity of stones and considerable labor. The arrival of barbed wire and tools to construct fences of that material reduced costs and effectively enclosed much of the countryside. *Source*: Gaucho Museum, Tacuarembó, Uruguay.

Fencing reduced rustling, limited stampedes, and allowed for easier feeding and caring for stock within confined spaces. It also lessened *estancia* employment, eliminating the jobs of many stable boys and itinerant gauchos. By the end of the century, cattle ranchers needed only a single hand to manage around 2,500 acres of land, although sheep farming required larger numbers of workers. Although costly (ranchers spent between an estimated 5 million and 7.5 million pesos on fencing between

1874 and 1882), the prosperity of the 1880s enabled most ranchers to finance the enclosure project themselves. Landlords in the north avoided these expenses by controlling the lightly inhabited open range to graze their creole cattle.[25]

Railroads, a second imported technology, sped up the transport of certain bulk goods and allowed the military to respond quickly to *caudillo* rebellions. After Uruguayan investors could only raise enough revenue to construct eleven miles of track by 1875, Latorre allowed British capital and technological expertise to design a national railway system. The British investors received their concession for the Central Uruguay Railroad Company and completed the line from Montevideo to Durazno by January 1, 1878. When more capital became available during the Santos years, the Assembly enacted the Railway General Routes Law of 1884 that established the parameters of further projects. Like Argentina, Uruguay adopted a radial network system with six lines: the Central to Salto, Paysandú, and Rivera; the Western to Carmelo, Nueva Palmira and Mercedes; the Northeast to Treinte y Tres and later Melo; the Eastern to Maldonado, Rocha, and Laguna Merim; a line to Santa Rosa, Cuareim, and Artigas (a branch of the Central); and another to northeastern Colonia.

Santos awarded the British entrepreneurs a favorable contract; a government-guaranteed dividend of 7 percent per kilometer of track laid, twice the profit typically earned in Great Britain. In addition, the government paid ten thousand pounds per mile of track laid. (Although complaints about costs quickly emerged, Uruguay paid two-thirds the rate that other South American countries paid because of its flat terrain.) The "per mile" provision encouraged contractors to design a winding track that avoided hills and ridges. Because of Uruguay's gentle terrain, each line could use standard gauge track, which eliminated extra labor costs that occurred in mountainous Andean nations. Each line terminated in Montevideo, which facilitated the export of bulk pastoral products and the transport of passengers to the capital. In all, the British built over 1,700 miles of railway lines with a spiderweb of trunk lines reaching many small towns. The construction of the railroad included bridges, including one that spanned the Río Negro, physically uniting the otherwise bifurcated country.[26]

The railroads' high freight rates meant that only bulk cargo (leather and wool) made money when transported by rail; live beef proved too costly to market in that manner. As a result, ranchers and farmers continued to use rough roads and wagons to move animals to stockyards well into the twentieth century. European technology also allowed for the long-delayed overhaul of the port of Montevideo, making it again competitive with Buenos Aires. President Juan Lindolfo Cuestas hired French and German engineers to plan the project; the French Allard Compagnie completed the work in 1901. Rather than seeking foreign funding, the government raised custom revenues to pay for the improvements.[27]

Almost as significant as railroads, communication networks helped to unify the country as well as connect it to the outside world. As with railroads, British financiers took the lead stringing telegraph lines, first from Montevideo to Río Grande do Sul on the Brazilian border and then from Montevideo to Durazno along the railroad right-of way. Later, telephone lines allowed for quick transmission of messages for commercial or military purposes. The interoceanic cable linked Uruguay with Europe and its markets. British technology installed Montevideo's natural gas lines, telephones, electric lighting, and ultimately the electric tram system that made travel within the city much easier. A modern postal system also contributed to improved communications.[28]

Finally, foreign technology provided innovations that diversified Uruguay's export economy, particularly in the meat preservation industry (extracts, canning, and ultimately refrigeration). For example, the Liebig's Extract of Meat Company, established in Great Britain in 1865, built a factory at Fray Bentos (formerly Villa Independencia) with an investment of 150,000 British pound sterling (roughly $27 million in today's money) as discussed in the next section.[29]

PRODUCTS: CATTLE AND SHEEP, 1860–1903

During the late nineteenth century, Uruguay remained beholden to its traditional source of wealth: pastoral products. Although the economy suffered periodic hiccups between 1876 and 1903, generally the country harvested the fruits of peace that the military presidents brought to the countryside. Peace allowed cattle to multiply from 5 million to 8 million head between 1875 and 1885, while the sheep population doubled from 8 million to 16 million during the same decade. As herds proliferated, the newly constructed railroads enabled ranchers to move record quantities of leather and wool to Montevideo for shipment abroad (Great Britain, France, Belgium, and Germany), thereby deepening Uruguay's relationship with the global economy. Despite stiff competition from Argentina, Australia, and New Zealand, after the Second Industrial Revolution European demand for the necessities of life (food, footwear, and clothing) derived from cattle and sheep brought record prosperity.[30]

In the 1860s, a new product, meat extract derived from creole cattle, found an eager market among poor British and French workers who yearned for the taste of meat but could ill afford the price of freshly butchered beef. The British-owned Liebig's "Extract of Meat" factory in Fray Bentos began marketing Oxo meat extracts and Oxo beef stock cubes (like bouillon cubes) under the LEMCO brand. A Germany chemist, Justus von Liebig (his statue stands in the town's plaza), had invented beef extract in 1847 by cutting beef into small pieces, boiling it in water, reducing the product to a paste, and bottling it in a jar. Because valuable European cattle were too costly to use for this purpose, von Liebig and his British investors based their company in Uruguay, where they could obtain the cheap and preferable lean meat of creole cattle simultaneously slaughtered for hides. By 1864, the factory at Fray Bentos exported fifty thousand pounds of the meat extract. Although initially marketed as a nutritious meat substitute for butchered beef, testing soon revealed that the extract only flavored food. By 1875, Liebig's had sold nearly half a million tons of the jarred substance. Sales remained strong through the early 1920s.[31]

Liebig's second innovation, canned corned beef (salt-cured beef packed in a tin), joined its product line in 1873. Again, scrawny creole cattle were perfectly suited

Figure 4.5 Advertisement for LEMCO Meat Extract. The Liebig's plant in Fray Bentos produced meat products derived from creole cattle. Extract became quite popular with poor Britons because it provided meat flavor to an otherwise bland diet even though it did not offer positive nutrition as originally advertised. By the 1880s, corned beef supplemented and at times replaced extract as a popular and inexpensive source of meat. Because the tins preserved corned beef well, European armies used LEMCO products in the hot climates of Africa and Asia. *Source*: Anglo Museum, Fray Bentos, Uruguay.

for corned beef and other canned meat products (tongue as well as steak and kidney pie, both British favorites). Corned beef's name comes from the large-grained rock salt (corns) used to preserve the beef. Liebig's added other spices as well as nitrates that reduced the chances of botulism and allowed for safe storage for months or even years. To make both extract and corned beef, the plant required modern technology in order to salt and flavor the meat, as well as to package it in colorful tins for marketing. Fray Bentos's corned beef outsold all other brands through World War II.[32]

The Fray Bentos plant required as many as six hundred workers to prepare corned beef. The largest machine steam cooked the meat. Workers mixed in spices and compressed the product into tins. Corned beef quickly surpassed sales of extract and became a staple for European working-class families. Like the old *saladeros*, the Fray Bentos factory also sold the residual parts of the carcass (dried blood and bones) as fertilizer, and made soap from the fat. Great Britain and France purchased large quantities of corned beef to feed their imperial armies undertaking conquests in Africa and Asia. The Liebig plant at Fray Bentos purchased enormous numbers of cattle, but many ranchers resented the British company because it paid less than did the few remaining *saladeros*. By the 1880s, the Fray Bentos plant had become one of the largest industrial sites in all of South America, and its jobs attracted immigrants. During World War I, Great Britain and France relied upon corned beef as a staple food on the front lines.[33]

Domingo Ordoñana, the Rural Association, and cattle ranchers committed to upgrading their product, looked across the La Plata in 1876 and saw the future unfolding. As the leading economic historians have argued, "The era marked the struggle between the old Uruguay that refused to die and the new Uruguay determined to the born." The arrival of two refrigerator ships, *Le Frigorique* and the *Paraguay*, foretold a day when ammonia refrigeration technology would revolutionize the meatpacking industry by preparing frozen and chilled beef for shipment to Europe. But scrawny creole cattle lacked sufficient fat content to be tasty as fresh meat, and as a result, the 36 percent of the ranchers who foresaw the future began upgrading their herds with pedigreed British bulls like Durhams and Herefords that produced mixed offspring with creole cows. These ranchers also supplemented prairie grass with feed of alfalfa and oats to fatten cattle before slaughter. These ranchers, mostly immigrants, owned 55 percent of the live cattle destined for the Atlantic market.[34]

Wool remained Uruguay's leading export during the 1880s, as sheep farmers sold vast quantities of fine Merino wool to Great Britain, the United States, France, and Belgium for textile manufacturing. Even as the quantity of sheep doubled, ranchers could not breed enough animals to satisfy the demand for wool. Progressive middle-class immigrants embraced the protection of barbed-wire fences that allowed for the careful breeding of expensive Merino sheep.[35]

Unlike their counterparts in the United States where sheep ranchers and cattlemen fought range wars, Uruguayan pastoralists often raised both cattle and sheep together as a hedge against bad times caused by drought or floods. While sheep died from the parasites that multiplied during rainy years, cattle thrived on the abundant grass. In dry years, such as between 1890 and 1893, sheep prospered because they foraged closer to the ground, while cattle died of thirst. Uruguay's wool met strong competition in the British market, which required longer fibers like those of Australian sheep for manufacturing fine clothing. Nevertheless, France and Belgium, the leading makers of carpets and other products, proved eager consumers of Uruguayan wool.[36]

SOCIAL CHANGE: THE DEMISE OF THE GAUCHO, URBANIZATION, INDUSTRY, AND LABOR

The imposition of political order, the influx of investment capital, immigrants, and modern technology wrought enormous changes to Uruguayan society. Like Argentina, Uruguay experienced a "Revolution on the Pampas," as one scholar dubbed the transformative effects of the pastoral economy. The enclosure of land, the end of the open range and the reduction of cattle *estancias*' workforce ended the gauchos' independent lifestyle. Many resettled in small towns in the interior, the *pueblos de ratas*, "rat towns," where they faced hunger and poverty. Others migrated to Montevideo to find jobs, but found clocking in and out of work a difficult cultural adjustment. Thus, the age of the gaucho became only a nostalgic remembrance, celebrated on holidays in the interior.[37]

Agriculture remained backward. The Swiss and Russian immigrant colonies along the Río Uruguay fared well because of better soil and because they could afford the new farm technology: steel plows and eventually harvesters. Elsewhere poor families struggled to survive on *chacras* (individual plots) where they paid high rents and in good years barely scratched out a living. Uruguay's thin soil, in contrast to the rich farmland of Buenos Aires province, yielded poor results. To make matters worse, cheap Argentine grain drove down food prices. Farmers in the departments near the capital (Canelones, San José, and Colonia) who raised corn and wheat, could compete because of their proximity to Montevideo's mills. Their fruits and vegetables sold well because of their freshness. These departments became the breadbasket of the capital and also initiated a profitable wine industry.[38]

As immigrants tripled Montevideo's population to 350,000 by 1900, residents spread eastward from narrow streets of the "Old City" (the port and the historic district) to a glamorous "New Town" (the *Centro*) with wide, tree-lined boulevards, beginning at the Plaza Independencia (the site of the Artigas statue), including the Teatro Solís, through the Plaza de Libertad along Avenida 18 de Julio as far as Ejido Street. New Town became the city's commercial area with a multitude of shops, governmental offices, and elite social clubs like the Jockey Club and the Uruguay Club where leaders of commerce and high finance met their European friends. Already, horse-powered and electrified tramways allowed the elite and middle class to reside in eastern suburbs (sometimes called Newest Town) like Pocitos and Carrasco. By 1904, the first automobiles appeared on the streets of New Town.[39]

BOX 4.2: THE TEATRO SOLÍS: OPERA AND ORCHESTRAL PERFORMANCES IN THE GOLDEN AGE

The Teatro Solís, named for the discoverer of the La Plata River, operated as the center of Montevideo's culture during the Gilded Age (1880s–1910). Completed in 1856, the building held 2,500 patrons and boasted perfect acoustics. Furnished with artwork and chandeliers from France, during its heyday the Solís Theater attracted some of the world's most famous opera singers and orchestral conductors. For all social classes, Italian opera was the popular music of the day and the Solís Theater had the wealthy patrons to attract some of Europe's most important stars. Adelina Patti, the highest-paid singer in the world, performed *La Traviata* in 1888, and after the turn of the century, Enrico Caruso, arguably the greatest tenor ever, sang with an orchestra directed by Arturo Toscanini, the world's most renown conductor at the time. The latter, a temperamental man, hated autograph seekers. One ingenious fan, however, disguised himself as a waiter bringing Toscanini coffee, and chatted him up before requesting his signature. The quality of performers who starred at the Teatro Solís exemplified Montevideo's growing sophistication and prosperity.[40]

Montevideo grew rapidly because immigrants and some rural migrants found meaningful employment in "factories." Larger factories (like the one in Fray Bentos and several in the Cerro district in Montevideo) processed beef or refined "wool tops" for export. Smaller factories and artisanal workshops manufactured "light" industrial goods (processed food and household items) sold for domestic consumption. Latin American businessmen understood that diversifying their economy with industry offered them an escape from their historic role as suppliers of raw materials. By the 1870s, Uruguayans began to produce certain consumables like flour, woolen textiles, shoes and sandals, soap, candles, wine, and furniture from domestically available raw materials. These products enjoyed a comparative advantage over European manufactures because of low shipment costs of the raw materials and the compatibility of products with local tastes.

To nurture these businesses further, Latorre adopted a policy of protectionism, raising existing import duties to 30 percent on certain imports. Small factories offered urban dwellers many of their consumer needs, such as canned fruits and vegetables, soft drinks (Vitícola Uruguaya), beer (Cervecería Montevideana), matches (Fábrica de Fósforos de Villemur), paper, and, to cater to new immigrants, spaghetti. By 1887, 2,682 such businesses had opened in Montevideo, employing over twenty-two thousand individuals. So successful had the tariff regime been that the business community convinced Santos in 1884 and Tajes in 1888 to increase tariff rates. Declining imports directly assisted light industry. At the same time, imports necessary for the growth of the pastoral economy (barbed wire) and machinery (tractors, harvesters, looms) entered duty-free.[41]

As industry emerged and grew prosperous, the working class unionized. The country's first such organization, a printers' mutual benefit society founded in 1865, created a fund that paid benefits to a member's family in the case of a debilitating injury or death. By the 1880s craft or trade unions emerged, where all members in a given industry paid dues and occasionally went on strike. Because Italian and Spanish working-class immigrants brought with them radical European ideologies such as socialism, anarchism, and syndicalism, trade unions sometimes resorted to violence. The spaghetti workers' union conducted the first trade union strike in August of 1884, followed later in the decade by larger unions such as the trolley workers. By 1890 Montevideo's workers had formed nearly six hundred such organizations, most of which primarily demanded a reduction of work hours—part of the worldwide eight-hour a day movement—and better working conditions. To strengthen their position, numerous trade unions joined together to form a national organization, the *Federación Obrera Regional Uruguaya* (FORU).[42]

THE RISING MIDDLE CLASS, 1876–1903

Because of Uruguay's growing economy, the middle class, disproportionately made up of immigrants and the children of immigrants, increased significantly in size. By the 1870s, progressive middle-class sheep ranchers owned more than half of the property in the southern and western departments. Members of the Swiss Colony and other prosperous farmers in the departments near Montevideo joined the rural middle class. Middle class immigrants or their children owned more than half of Montevideo's real estate. There they enjoyed honorable employment that relied on their skills as literate persons: clerks in department stores; *empleados* (employees) in the expanding government bureaucracy; telegraph operators; shopkeepers; and teachers. Entrepreneurial members of the middle class opened new businesses. By using their brains on the job, middle-class people distinguished themselves from *obreros* (workers) who used their brawn to perform manual labor.[43]

Upper-middle-class people owned larger industrial and commercial enterprises. Emilio Reus and Francisco Piria played the leading roles in the business sector and speculated in urban development. In an age when Montevideo burst its traditional borders, Piria's *La Compañía Industrial* constructed numerous buildings in New Town, where in the *Barrio Reus*, Piria regularly employed two thousand workers. Entrepreneurs opened department stores in the New Town that catered to middle-class and elite consumers.[44]

By the early 1890s, Uruguay had the second largest middle class in Latin America after Argentina. The middle class, however, did not content itself with merely accumulating wealth. Increasingly, influential middle-class citizens made demands for expanded educational opportunities for their children and a broadening of suffrage. Although educational reform laws passed during these years and opened new opportunities for many, extending the vote to all citizens would be delayed.[45]

Women also joined the middle class at the end of the nineteenth century because the educational reforms enacted during the Latorre administration provided them with opportunities to teach. As normal schools (teachers' colleges) opened in the 1890s, they appealed almost exclusively to young women, whom elites believed would be particularly suited to careers as primary school teachers because of their "natural roles" as nurturers of children. Soon, other "nurturing" professions, such as nursing, also became available to young women. The lives of middle-class housewives improved, too, as they availed themselves of the newest labor-saving devices, such as washing machines.[46]

EDUCATION, SECULARISM, POSITIVISM, AND ANTI-POSITIVISM

In Artigas's time, the Catholic Church operated the few educational institutions in the Banda Oriental. Post-independence leaders planned a secular education system, but civil wars and shaky finances doomed the project. In 1855, the country had only thirty primary schools that enrolled fewer than nine hundred students. Two decades later, José Pedro Varela revolutionized public education, which resulted in Uruguay having the second highest literacy rate in Latin America by 1930. While in the United States during the 1860s, he befriended Domingo Sarmiento (later known as Argentina's schoolmaster president) and Horace Mann, the founder of public education in the United States, both of whom influenced Varela to join their transnational public education movement. In 1869 he founded the *Amigos de Educación Popular* (the Society of Friends of Public Education) and thereafter wrote an influential book, *La Educación del pueblo* (1874).[47]

Varela shared President Latorre and Rural Association president Domingo Ordoñana's positivist beliefs. The president asked Varela to head the committee that drafted the Law of Public Education in 1877. He persuaded Latorre and others that the wealth and prosperity of the nation depended upon a free, compulsory, and secular public educational system open to all children and adults regardless of gender, race, or class. Whereas in other Latin American nations conservatives battled to keep religion in the classroom, Varela easily won that struggle in secular Uruguay. Appointed the first National Inspector of Education, Varela's tenure ended abruptly when he unexpectedly died in 1879 at age thirty-four. Over twenty thousand people attended his funeral. For his role, Varela received the nickname "the sower of the alphabet." Today his portrait hangs in every schoolhouse.[48]

The Education Law also proposed creating normal schools to educate teachers about the latest methods of instruction, which emphasized experimentation and observation rather than mere memorization. Varela hoped that education would increase the number of upwardly mobile Uruguayans. He also believed that young women deserved the opportunity to hold a dignified, professional and socially respected job like teaching. The government founded the Normal School in 1889 but as enrollments increased, soon moved it to a larger structure. Normal school instructors taught prospective teachers uniform methods and curriculum in order to transmit identical patriotic messages and appropriate values to all students. Normal school students, usually age thirteen or fourteen, paid no tuition, but they were obliged to return to their home town to teach for two years, which allowed poor rural communities to open schools at minimal cost.

The creation of public education unleashed a wave of textbooks and workbooks written about national history, geography, and science. Students received these books and workbooks (over a million copies) free of charge. The richly illustrated workbooks and well-written texts encouraged young students to share the contents with their families. The works of history told stories about Uruguayan heroes like Artigas, Rivera, Oribe, and Lavalleja. Students learned a common national identity at the same time that schools inculcated suitable values for patriotic, hard-working, and well-behaved citizens (in contrast to unruly gauchos). Raising the flag and singing the national anthem every day reinforced national identity. The curriculum also included Spanish grammar, reading, writing, mathematics, and civics. Girls received additional lessons in home economics, hygiene, and the proper behavior for women as future mothers. Schools emphasized discipline, repressing children's natural "barbaric" instincts, while offering recreation and orderly play. By 1910, 60 percent of school-aged children attended coeducational primary schools, the highest percentage in Latin America. Latorre insisted that every military recruit become literate and acquire the skills they needed to function in the army. Adults benefited too as elementary school libraries served the community as well.[49]

Post-secondary education also expanded. Founded in 1849, the University of the Republic initially offered only a law degree, the traditional credential taken by young men aspiring for a political career. In 1884, the university's positivist-influenced rector reformed the curriculum by adding a degree in medicine and acquiring laboratories where students could gain practical experience. Shortly thereafter, the College of Engineering opened, offering degrees in practical subjects like architecture, surveying, and engineering, preparing young Uruguayans to contribute to national development. The government also organized a School of Arts and Trades for artisans and artists.[50]

The university became the arena of contentious philosophical debates at the end of the nineteenth century. Positivism, which preached the scientific evolution of society and was embraced by influential politicians and intellectuals, dominated until the end of the century. Positivists pointed out that Uruguay's prosperity began once the military presidents had established order, encouraged foreign investment, technology, light industry, and immigration, and more fully opened European marketplaces to the country's pastoral products.

Dissenters emerged. Uruguay's most outstanding intellectual of the era, José Enrique Rodó, decried positivism in his famous essay "Ariel." He asserted that Latin Americans had erred in following the materialistic doctrine of positivism and its formula for progress. Using an analogy to William Shakespeare's "The Tempest," Rodó

Figure 4.6 Female Students at the Normal School. Young women enrolled in large numbers in Montevideo's new Normal School. The methods' curriculum that prospective teachers learned downplayed rote memorization. In particular, the new curriculum featured experimentation and observation, with the objective of making learning interesting. As the first profession open to middle-class women, teaching had a great deal of appeal. Because of his interactions with Sarmiento and Horace Mann, Varela knew a great deal about how normal schools functioned and thus he was able to lay the foundations for Uruguay's normal school in Montevideo. *Source*: Museo Pedagógico, Montevideo.

likened the pursuit of materialism to the character of Caliban, who led the villains of the play in a misguided attempt to seduce magician Prospero's daughter and steal his magic, only to be foiled by Prospero's spirit, Ariel. In essence, Rodó urged his country to reclaim its cultural heritage and reject materialism. President Herrera y Obes (1890–1894) agreed, telling the Assembly that by continuing to embrace positivism, the university would create "a generation of infidels and ambitious egotists who would deny greater ideals."[51]

Along with secularizing the educational system, the government further reduced the powers of the weak institutional Catholic Church. The military governments approved a mandatory civil registry for births, marriages, and deaths in each department, removing these functions from church officials. In 1886, the government made civil marriage mandatory, further diminishing the influence of the Catholic Church. The state regulated convents and allowed Protestant sects (Methodists mostly) to open churches.[52]

ELITE POLITICS: CIVILIANS TAKE OVER THE NATION STATE, 1890–1903

Because General Tajes and Colorado politicians had signed the Conciliation Agreement, civilian rule returned in 1890. Julio Herrera y Obes, the Colorado who served as Tajes's minister of the interior, won the contested election. A member of the elite, Herrera y Obes originally belonged to the Generation of 1873 principistas that Latorre had ousted in 1876. By the time of his presidency, however, Herrera y Obes no longer believed in extending personal liberties but rather favored a strong state like the military presidents had imposed. During his campaign, the candidate announced that he intended to end caudillismo and administer a centralized government with enhanced presidential powers as the Constitution of 1830 literally stated.

To strengthen the national government's influence, he appointed loyal Colorados as departmental *jefes políticos* in fifteen departments, thereby reducing the number of departments that the minority Blancos (who now preferred to be called Nationalists) controlled from four to three. Because Herrera y Obes believed in restricting suffrage to members of the country's *gente decente*, the elite and members of the upper middle class, he stripped recent immigrants of their right to vote. His Colorado opponents, like newspaper editor José Batlle y Ordóñez, who advocated for middle-class objectives such as education, an end to dictatorship, and the expansion of suffrage, complained about Herrera y Obes's "dictatorial" measures. The Baring Bank financial crisis of 1890 and the resulting depression added to Herrera y Obes's woes.[53]

With no hope of victory in the 1894 elections, the Nationalists, now led by Luis Alberto de Herrera, abstained. The Colorados remained divided between the oligarchical faction dominated by Herrera y Obes and the reformers led by Batlle y Ordóñez. After forty ballots, the Assembly chose Herrera y Obes's preferred successor, Juan Idiarte Borda. The new president stubbornly ignored Batlle's Colorado faction and ran roughshod over the Blancos' insistence on returning to the co-participation agreement of 1872. In addition, he was patently corrupt. When Idiarte refused to cooperate with the Nationalists, Blanco gauchos crossed the border into Argentina, the prelude to a *caudillo* uprising.[54]

Aparicio Saravia, the son of a Brazilian-born Uruguayan *estanciero* from Cerro Largo, owned land in both countries and had become a beloved leader of the Nationalists. In March, 1897, Saravia led about five thousand men back across the Uruguay River and took up positions near the Río Negro. In response, President Idiarte Borda drafted Uruguayans as well as foreigners into the army, an unpopular decision. Saravia's smaller army, with limited weaponry, mostly lances, had no realistic chance against the well-equipped national army. The Blancos suffered defeat after defeat before seeking negotiations in July. Like earlier *caudillo* rebellions, Saravia's troops controlled much of the countryside, his army swollen by impoverished, unemployed gauchos. He declared that he would surrender if Idiarte Borda accepted proportional party representation and resigned. The president refused to negotiate.

As the rebellion unnecessarily dragged on, a grocery clerk shot the president at point-blank range as he left the Cathedral on August 25, the only assassination of a sitting president in Uruguay's history. So unpopular had Idiarte Borda become that not only did the jury acquit the assassin at trial, but also some citizens urged that a street be renamed for him. Once Juan Lindolfo Cuestas, the Senate president, replaced Idiarte Borda, negotiations proceeded rapidly. Cuestas's decision to compromise reinforced the idea that although the Colorados held an electoral majority, they could only govern with the co-participation of the Blancos.[55]

The Blancos influence grew as a result of the Pact of the Cross of September 18, 1897. In exchange for the Blanco army mustering out, Cuestas agreed to electoral reform, allowing free elections of jefes políticos in all nineteen departments. The pact gave the Blancos control over six departments: Rivera, Treinte y Tres, Maldonado, Cerro Largo, Flores, and San José, their strongholds. Some Colorados, particularly Herrera y Obes, believed Cuestas's concessions too generous, especially the additional agreement that federal troops would not enter these departments without seeking permission from local authorities.[56]

Thereafter, Cuestas remained as interim president and because of the good feelings generated by the Pact of the Cross, won a full four-year term in his own right in 1899. A skillful politician, he abided by his word not to interfere in department elections, but the division within Colorado ranks allowed Nationalists to gain seats in Congress. In 1900, they gained control of the Senate. In the meantime, Saravia continued to have tremendous influence within his party as the Blancos' presence in the legislature increased. Saravia and the Blancos anticipated having a strong voice in the selection of Uruguay's next president in November 1903.[57]

CONCLUSION

In 1903, Uruguay looked radically different from the dispirited nation of 1875. The three military presidents followed the positivists' playbook by strengthening the state before returning it to civilian hands. The stronger state thwarted Argentine and Brazilian interference into Uruguayan affairs. More importantly, stable government encouraged the flow of British capital and technology bringing great prosperity to ranchers as the high demand for its processed beef and fine wool integrated the nation further into European markets. Uruguay's newfound maturity also encouraged swelling numbers of Spanish and Italian immigrants who as sheep ranchers or urban industrialists became important members of the expanding middle class.

Without the extremes of wealth and poverty found in most Latin American countries, these new Uruguayans pressed for further reforms. The government agreed with their request for free, compulsory, and secular education and as a result, Uruguay enjoyed the second highest literacy rate and the second highest per capita income in Latin America by 1900, roughly equivalent to that of Canada, the United States, and Australia. The stronger state now played a greater role in its own economy as evidenced by its ownership of the port facilities in Montevideo harbor.

Yet much remained to be done. The changes of the late nineteenth century created a solid foundation upon which Uruguay could implement the great changes that would make it the envy of its neighbors between 1903 and 1929, the subject of the next chapter.

NOTES

1. 1. José P. Barrán and Benjamin Nahum, *Historia rural del Uruguay moderno*, I, Montevideo: Ediciones de la Banda Oriental, 1967–1978, 330–45; Alan Knight, *Bandits and Liberals, Rebels and Saints: Latin America since Independence*, Lincoln: University of Nebraska Press, 2022, 57–60, 155–62; Enrique Méndez Vives, *El Uruguay de la Modernación*, Montevideo: Ediciones de la Banda Oriental, 1977, 16. Fernando López-Alves, *State Formation and Democracy in Latin America*, Durham: Duke University Press, 2000, 88–91.

2. Barrán and Nahum, *Historia Rural*, I, 85–88, 374–407. Many of the Revista's articles that form the basis for Barrán and Nahum's arguments are contained in their *Historia Rural del Uruguay Moderno (1851–1885): Apendice Documental*, Montevideo: Ediciones de la Banda Oriental, 1967. López-Alves, *State Formation*, 91.

3. Barrán and Nahum, *Historia Rural*, I, 452–65.

4. Méndez Vives, *Modernación*, 10–11. Méndez Vives is unabashedly a proponent of the dependency school of history popular in the 1970s. See also Barrán and Nahum, *Historia Rural*, I, 479–84. A full biography of Latorre is Washington Reyes Abadie, *Latorre: La forja del estado*, Montevideo: Ediciones de la Banda Oriental, 1977. His early career is described in Reyes Abadie, *Latorre*, 8–49. The quote is on page 64. Acevedo, *Anales*, III, 784–93. For Juan Pedemonte, the "terrible year" referred to the overthrow of the constitutional government, the military government's tyrannical repression, and the decade-long suppression of the opposition press. See Pedemonte, *Año Terrible*, 11–15, 59–157.

5. Reyes Abadie, *Latorre*, 73–74; Acevedo, *Anales*, IV, 17–20, 142–43; López-Alves, *State Formation*, 93.

6. Acevedo, *Anales*, IV, 49–52, 237–38; Reyes Abadie, *Latorre*, 79–81; Méndez Vives, *Modernación*, 13.

7. Méndez Vives, *Modernación*, 22; Reyes Abadie, *Latorre*, 120–23; Acevedo, *Anales*, IV, 27–32. Unlike Santos, whom the Assembly banned from ever returning to Uruguay, Latorre was allowed come to Montevideo to attend his wife's funeral before returning to exile in Buenos Aires. José M. Fernández Saldaña, *Diccionario Uruguayo de biografías, 1810–1940*, Montevideo: Editorial Amerindia, 1945, Latorre entry, 720–25 offers a very different portrayal, describing the dictator as cunning, cold, and calculating, and a man who preferred to hang around with buffoons, jokesters, and vulgar friends rather than the *principistas*.

8. Méndez Vives, *Modernación*, 23, 32–35, 67; Reyes Abadie, *Latorre*, 71–72, 78; Acevedo, *Anales*, IV, 83, 177–85, 253–60, 606. Fernández Saldaña, *Diccionario Uruguayo*, entry for Máximo Santos, 1155–60. The records detailing Santos's battlefield promotions disappeared, forcing him to obtain a certificate to mark his achievements. His detractors claimed he never actually earned those promotions. López-Alves, *State Formation*, 94–95.

9. Méndez Vives, *Modernación*. 67–69; Acevedo, *Anales*, IV, 271–78. Pedemonte, *Año Terrible*, 171–80. Famously, Mexican General Antonio López de Santa Anna had the same "a deguello" played at the Alamo before he massacred all of its defenders.

10. Acevedo, *Anales*, IV, 278–86. Fernández Saldaña, *Diccionario Uruguayo*, entry for Santos, 159, credits Santos with the decision to step down. This seems unlikely, especially because the Assembly passed legislation forbidding Santos's return to Uruguay. See also Pedemonte, *Año Terrible*, 183–86, 191–97, 206.

11. Méndez Vives, *Modernación*, 67–73; Acevedo, *Anales*, IV, 379–89; Fernández Saldaño, *Diccionario Uruguayo*, entry for Máximo Tajes, 1218–22; Pedemonte, *Año Terrible*, 198–203, 206–11.

12. Carolina González Laurino, *La construcción de la idendidad uruguaya*, Montevideo: Universidad Católica, 2001, 73–79. She refers to this initial phase of national identity as ethno-culturalism or orientalism dating to the resistance of the Charrúa to Spanish settlement.

13. Hugo Achugar, "Foundational Images of the Nation in Latin America," in William Acree and Juan Carlos González Espitia (eds.), *Building Nineteenth-Century Latin America: Re-Rooted Cultures, Identities, and Nations*, Nashville: Vanderbilt University Press, 2009, 11–31. Acevedo, *Anales*, II, 7–9, 18–19; Acevedo, *Anales*, IV, 125–27; González Laurino, *Idendidad uruguayo*, 49–50, 76–78; Pivel Devoto, *Guerra Grande*, 5–7; Fernández Saldaña, *Diccionario Uruguayo*, 732.

14. Méndez Vives, *Modernación*, 46. Acevedo, *Anales*, IV, 358, 363–64; Gordon Ross, *Argentina and Uruguay*, London: Methuen & Co., LTD, 1911, 31, 71. Koebel, *Uruguay*, 80. González Laurino, *Idendidad uruguayo*, 78–82, 145–47, 200.

15. Barrán and Nahum, *Historia Rural*, I, 290–97; Méndez Vives, *Modernación*, 21–27; Reyes Abadie, *Latorre*, 77–79, 98–100; Acevedo, *Anales*, IV, 72, 91–93; Carlos Marischal, *A Century of Debt Crises in Latin America: From Independence to the Great Depression, 1820–1930*, Princeton: Princeton University Press, 1989, 107–22.

16. Nahum and Barrán, *Historia Rural*, II, 531–37. See their "Uruguayan Rural History," 663. As followers of the dependency school, Nahum and Barrán find that the railroads benefited British investors far more than Uruguayans. Acevedo, *Anales*, IV, 68–69; Méndez Vives, *Modernación*, 39. Winn, "British Informal Empire," 110–12; and his chapter "British Economic Expansion and Informal Empire in Uruguay during the Nineteenth Century," in Pedro Cameselle-Pasce and Debbie Sharnak, *Uruguay in Transnational Perspective*, New York: Routledge, 2024, 81–88.

17. Méndez Vives, *Modernación*, 31–32, 59–61, 103–5. Barrán and Nahum, *Historia Rural*, II, 448–504. Fernández Saldaña, *Diccionario Uruguayo*, entry about Emilio Reus, 1067–69; Acevedo, *Anales*, IV, 319–21, 437–41; Marischal, *Debt Crises*, 127–31, 142–52.

18. Méndez Vives, *Modernación*, 9; Barrán and Nahum, *Historia Rural*, II, 78–80. The Herrera y Obes quote is from Luis C. Benvenuto, *Breve Historia del Uruguay: Economía y Sociedad*, Buenos Aires: Editorial Universitaria de Buenos Aires, 1967, 88–90. Koebel, *Uruguay*, 276–79, Winn, "Informal Empire," in *Transnational*, 88–90.

19. Unknown, *Uruguay*, Washington, DC Bureau of the American Republics, No. 61, 1892, 53–54, provides the larger number. Simon G. Hanson, *Utopia in Uruguay: Chapters in the Economic History of Uruguay*, New York: Oxford University Press, 1938, 9–10, cites evidence stating that 37 percent of Montevideo's population was either first- or second-generation immigrants. Pendle, *Uruguay*, 7–8 estimates over eighty thousand in the years treated in this chapter. Méndez Vives, *Modernación*, 75, claims that Montevideo's population is half immigrant by 1890; later he reduces the number to 40 percent (107). Internal migrants could account for the discrepancy. The difficulty migrants had acquiring land is mentioned in Méndez Vives, *Modernación*, 79, and Barrán and Nahum, *Historia Rural*, II, 386–92, 594–98.

20. Barrán and Nahum, *Historia Rural*, I, 330–33, 469–73; Griffin, "Causal Factors," 22, 24; M. H. J. Finch, *A Political Economy of Uruguay since 1870*, New York: St. Martin's Press, 1981, 35–36; Méndez Vives, *Modernación*, 37; Roque Faraone, *El Uruguay en que vivimos (1900–1968)*, Montevideo: ARCA Editorial, 1968, 9–10. Juan Oddone, "The Formation of Modern Uruguay, c. 1870–1930," 454–74 at 460 in Leslie Bethel (ed). *Cambridge History of Latin America, c. 1870–1930*, Cambridge: Cambridge University Press, 1989. Oddone estimates the number of immigrants between 1887 and 1889 at forty-five thousand.

21. Barrán and Nahum, *Historia Rural*, I, 381–407, 414–31; Méndez Vives, *Modernación*, 75–76, 108; López-Alves, *State Formation*, 63–66.

22. Johanna Inés Quincke Walden, *Estancia "Santa Matilde": Raiz y fruto de un inmigrante innovador*, Montevideo: Ediciones del Concurso Humboldt, 1993.

23. Barrán and Nahum, *Historia Rural*, I, 486–89; 493–504; Méndez Vives, *Modernación*, 12–16. Reyes Abadie, *Latorre*, 72, López-Alves, *State Formation*, 92–93; Acevedo, *Anales*, IV, 59, 431–32.

24. Barrán and Nahum, *Historia Rural*, I, 502–3, 525–49; Méndez Vives, *Modernación*, 13–15. Walter Prescott Webb's classic pioneering study, *The Great Plains*, second ed., Lincoln: University of Nebraska Press, 1981 demonstrates the similarity of the process in Texas and the U.S. plains, see 239–56. Acevedo, *Anales*, IV, 53–54.

25. Barrán and Nahum, *Historia Rural*, I, 531–57. Reyes Abadie, *Latorre*, 105–6. Oddone, "Uruguay, c1870–1930" at 463.

26. Barrán and Nahum, *Historia Rural*, I, 290–97; Méndez Vives, *Modernación*, 62–63; Nahum and Barrán, *Historia Rural*, II, 534–68; Finch, *Political Economy*, 195–202; Acevedo, *Anales*, IV, 414–24, 518–28; Michael G. Mulhall, *The English in South America*, New York: Arno Press 1977 (originally published in 1878), 503–5.

27. Méndez Vives, *Modernación*, 56, 63–67, 100–103; Nahum and Barrán, *Historia Rural*, II, 590–619; López-Alves, *State Formation*, 88–89; Griffin, "Causal Factors," 25; Winn, "Informal Empire in Uruguay," 117–19.

28. Winn, "Informal Empire in Uruguay," 110–13; Acevedo, *Anales*, IV, 532–33; Mulhall, *The English*, 506–9. The original cable went underwater from Buenos Aires to Colonia and then overland to Montevideo, but because during civil wars both sides cut the land portion, the British eventually strung the entire cable underwater.

29. Barrán and Nahum, *Historia Rural*, I, 115–17, 625–26. One of Uruguay's most interesting museums is the *Museo de la Revolución Industrial* in Fray Bentos in the El Anglo plant, formerly owned by Leibig's. Displays feature both the meat extract operation, examples of canned products and the later refrigerated meat slaughterhouse.

30. Nahum and Barrán, *Historia Rural*, I, 597–602, 541–603; II, 20–44, 137; Méndez Vives, *Modernación*, 23–26, 58–59, 100.

31. Barrán and Nahum, *Historia Rural*, I, 614–16.

32. Winn, "Informal Empire," 119–20; Barrán and Nahum, *Historia Rural*, I, 614–23.

33. Barrán and Nahum, *Historia Rural*, II, 118–23; Barrán and Nahum, *Historia Rural*, I, 116–17, 623–29, 641–43.

34. Barrán and Nahum, *Historia Rural*, II, 219–62, 289–300. González Laurino, *Idendidad uruguayo*, 57–59, 180; Méndez Vives, *Modernación*, 100.

35. Barrán and Nahum, *Historia Rural*, I, 141–75, 527–35, 636–47; Nahum and Barrán, *Historia Rural*, II, 27–28, 67–69, 195–214, Méndez Vives, *Modernación*, 25, 96–98.

36. Barrán and Nahum, *Historia Rural*, I, 586; Barrón and Nahum, *Historia Rural*, II, 27–29.

37. James R. Scobie, *Revolution on the Pampas: A Social History of Argentine Wheat*, Austin: University of Texas Press, 1964, makes a similar case for Argentina. Méndez Vives, *Modernación*, 19–20, 28–29, 54–55. Barrón and Nahum, *Historia Rural*, I, 558–82; II, 333–45. For a study of the nostalgic look at gauchos, see John F. Garganigo, *Javier de Viana*, New York: Twayne Publishers Inc., 1972. The Museo Histórico in Paysandú effectively uses the civilization (late nineteenth century) vs. barbarism (early nineteenth century) theme to display its collection.

38. Barrán and Nahum, *Historia Rural*, I, 567–73, 630–35; Méndez Vives, *Modernación*, 28–29, 54–55. Nahum and Barrán, *Historia Rural*, II, 263–87.

39. James R. Scobie, *Buenos Aires: Plaza to Suburb, 1870–1910*, New York: Oxford University Press, 1974, 160–74, traces very similar developments across the estuary; Méndez Vives, *Modernación*, 38–39; Lauren A. Benton, "Reshaping the Urban Core: The Politics of Housing in Authoritarian Uruguay," *Latin American Research Review*, Vol. 21, No. 2 (1996), 33–52, at 35.

40. Susana Salgado, *The Teatro Solís: 150 Years of Opera, Concert, and Ballet in Montevideo*, Middletown, CT.: Wesleyan University Press, 2003, 14–109.

41. Méndez Vives, *Modernación*, 29–31, 61–62. Méndez Vives refers to this law as an early manifestation of import substitution industrialization, but that term did not emerge until the 1930s. Nahum and Barrán, *Historia Rural*, II, 384–92; George Wythe, *Industry in Latin America*, New York: Columbia University Press, 1945, v–10, 122–23, 128; Finch, *Political Economy*, 162–63; Faraone, *Vivimos*, 16–17; Acevedo, *Anales*, IV, 40–44, 65–66, 325–27, 434–35, 446, 516.

42. Robert J. Alexander, *A History of Organized Labor in Uruguay and Paraguay*, Westport, CT: Praeger Publishers, 2005, 9–16, 12–19. Méndez Vives, *Modernación*, 109–110.

43. Méndez Vives, *Modernación*, 20.

44. Méndez Vives, *Modernación*, 77–79. Milton Vanger, *The Model Country: José Batlle y Ordóñez of Uruguay, 1907–1915*, Hanover, NH: University Press of New England, 1980, 3.

45. Méndez Vives, *Modernación*, 99, 109.

46. Christine Ehrich, *The Shield of the Weak: Feminism and the State in Uruguay, 1903–1933*, Albuquerque: University of New Mexico Press, 35–37; William Acree, *Everyday Reading: Print Culture and Collective Identity in the Río de la Plata, 1780-1910*, Nashville: Vanderbilt University Press, 2009, 148–64.

47. Barrán and Nahum, *Historia Rural*, I, 490; Méndez Vives, *Modernación*, 40–42; Reyes Abadie, *Latorre*, 108–13.

48. Reyes Abadie, *Latorre*, 113–16; Acree, *Everyday Reading*, 85–91; Acevedo, *Anales*, IV, 96–99; González Laurino, *Identidad uruguayo*, 241–45.

49. Acevedo, *Anales*, IV, 99–112, 339–43; Acree, *Everyday Reading*, 89–120, 125–47; Méndez Vives, *Modernación*, 40–42, González Laurino, *Identidad uruguaya*, 247–50.

50. Acevedo, *Anales*, IV, 124–25, 233–34, 344–51; Méndez Vives, *Modernación*, 42–43; Reyes Abadie, *Latorre*, 114–16.

51. Acevedo, *Anales*, IV, 588–89; José Enrique Rodó, *Ariel*, Austin: University of Texas Press, 1988, Méndez Vives, *Modernación*, 113–16.

52. Barrán and Nahum, *Historia Rural*, I, 356–68, 489–91; Méndez Vives, *Modernación*, 43–44; Reyes Abadie, *Latorre*, 72–80; López-Alves, *State Formation*, 92–93. Russell H. Fitzgibbon, "The Political Impact on Religious Development in Uruguay," *Church History*, Vol. 22, No. 1 (March, 1953), 21–32, esp. 22–26; Acevedo, *Anales*, IV, 113–15, 147–51, 366–75, 484; González Laurino, *Identidad uruguaya*, 61–62, 236.

53. Méndez Vives, *Modernación*, 69–72. Nahum and Barrán, *Historia Rural*, II, 22–23. Herrera y Obes sent a provocateur to Minas who instigated a brawl in a coffeehouse that resulted in the arrest of two of Minas's five electors. By a margin of two to one, the Colorados triumphed; see Acevedo, *Anales*, IV, 496, 579–83, the quotation is on page 497; Oddone, "Uruguay, 1870–1930," 462–63. Statistics about the economy under Obes y Herrera can be found in Anon., *Uruguay*, 53–86.

54. Méndez Vives, *Modernación*, 87–88.

55. Méndez Vives, *Modernación*, 89–92; López-Alves, *State Formation*, 56–57; Victor Dahl, "Uruguay under Juan Idiarte Borda: An American Diplomat's Observations," *Hispanic American Historical Review*, Vol. 46, No. 1, (1966), 66–77. Minister Granville Stuart was standing beside Idiarte Borda at the time of his assassination. John Chasteen, *Heroes on Horseback: A Life and Times of the Last Gaucho Caudillos,* Albuquerque: University of New Mexico Press, 1995, 153–170; Odonne, "Modern Uruguay," 462–63.

56. Méndez Vives, *Modernación*, 92–95, Chasteen, *Last Gaucho*, 171

57. Méndez Vives, *Modernación*, 165–67; Vanger, Batlle, 3, 13, describes Cuestas as an old, squat fellow who hobbled along the streets supported by his cane.

Five

Uruguay in the Age of Batlle, 1903–1930

By 1931, Uruguayans eagerly embraced the story of their nation's exceptionalism as the "Switzerland of the Americas" because of its broadly based democracy, its sizable and prosperous middle class, its high literacy rate, and its advanced social welfare system. The architect of these latter reforms, José Batlle y Ordóñez, referred to the state as "the shield of the weak," that protected women, children, the aged, the poor, and the working class. Writers have posed several hypotheses for Uruguay's remarkable progress after 1903. Some argued that the absence of strong institutions from the colonial era allowed for the development of a modern progressive state; others pointed to the political alliance of educated, urban middle-class businessmen and entrepreneurial ranchers that dominated politics. Others ascribed Uruguay's success to Batlle y Ordóñez and his progressive colleagues' farsighted policies. Whichever interpretation or interpretations best explains Uruguay's progress, the nation became known during the early twentieth century as "the chief laboratory for social experimentation in the Americas" in marked contrast to its early nineteenth century history, during which time only three presidents out of twenty-five survived their term without facing a serious uprising.[1]

THE ELECTION OF 1903 AND THE FINAL *CAUDILLO* REBELLION

As a young man, José Batlle, the son of former president Lorenzo Batlle (1868–1872), had studied at the University of the Republic, but failed to complete his degree. Like many sons of well-to-do Latin American families, he continued his education in Paris. When he returned to Uruguay in 1886, he founded *El Día* and joined the anti-Santos rebels at Quebracho. His unconventional personal life shocked

Montevideo's high society. After his cousin abandoned his wife, Batlle fathered her remaining four children, only marrying her in 1913 after divorce became legal. Batlle became a powerhouse in the Colorado party, chosen as president of the Senate in 1898. An imposing, burly, gruff gentleman who stood six foot four and weighed well over 280 pounds (his English language biographer described him as "an athlete gone to fat"), Batlle's commanding physical presence, articulate, measured speech, and his vision for Uruguay's future proved valuable assets as his political career evolved.[2]

Despite his relative youth, he launched his campaign for the presidency in 1902. The Colorados had split into three factions, none of which controlled the forty-five Assembly votes necessary to elect their candidate. The *acuerdo* resulting from Aparicio Saravia's rebellion of 1897 provided the Nationalists with thirty-seven votes to use as bargaining chips. During the year preceding the election, Batlle proved his mettle, befriending members of the other two Colorado factions as well as seven moderate-minded Blancos. (Before 1910, legislators were not required to vote for their party's candidate, akin to "unfaithful electors" in the U.S. Electoral College system.) These defectors from the Blanco ranks enabled Batlle to win the election of November 1902 because he promised those Blancos that he would abide by the co-participation agreement of 1897. True to his promise, Batlle appointed two Blancos to his cabinet and Blanco *jefes políticos* to the six departments that the party controlled.[3]

Once inaugurated, Batlle united the Colorado Party and upgraded the military, further strengthening the state. Anticipating another *caudillo* uprising, he purchased additional machine guns and recruited more soldiers. He reorganized the Colorado party from the bottom-up by creating district level political clubs to drum up turnout, and opined about the need for single-party rule and ending *acuerdos*. Although he technically kept his promise to appoint six *jefes políticos* from the Blanco party, two came from the minority faction that had voted for Batlle. These actions aroused the concerns of Blanco *caudillo* Aparicio Saravia. Then in November 1903, Blanco suspicions heightened when Batlle stationed two regiments in Rivera department, bordering Saravia's bailiwick of Cerro Largo, allegedly to prevent Brazilian cross-border incursions. Saravia claimed that this order violated Batlle's promise never to send troops into a Nationalist department. This controversy raised the issue of whether the state could impose its decrees upon a regional *caudillo*, also the spokesperson for the opposition party and the second most powerful man in the country.[4]

In January 1904, Saravia declared war. Early on, he met with success, raising about fifteen thousand gauchos for his army, routing federal troops in early skirmishes and advancing within fifty miles of Montevideo. A charismatic leader and a skilled horseman, Saravia personally led the fighting. Without adequate modern armaments, however, Saravia realized he could not attack the capital; as a result, he retreated to Rivera. Soon reinforcements and munitions arrived from Argentina, bolstering rebel confidence. Saravia hoped to repeat his success of 1897 and force concessions from Batlle, such as control over two additional departments. Blanco civilian leaders demanded Batlle's resignation. Batlle refused to negotiate with the rebels, arguing that any new *acuerdo* would only encourage future rebellions.[5]

Figure 5.1 Poster of Aparicio Saravia. *Caudillo* Aparicio Saravia's unsuccessful revolt in 1904 marked the end of the nineteenth-century gaucho uprisings. With his death, new Nationalist Party leader Luis Alberto de Herrera shifted the Blancos' focus to competing in elections and finding new groups of support among the urban working class. Although the Blancos did not win a presidential election until 1958, the adoption of the Constitution of 1918 granted them coparticipation in government and a proportional division of the patronage for their followers. *Source*: Casa de Fructuoso Rivera, Durazno.

Batlle's modern military enjoyed two advantages: railroads moved men and equipment rapidly to the front while the rebels maneuvered on horseback; and the federal army's modern weaponry proved superior to gaucho charges with lances. The battle at Tupambaé in June saw machine guns decimate Saravia's army with withering fire, forcing him to retreat north and west to the Brazilian border. Despite the defeat, Saravia felt optimistic, having received a second shipment of rifles from Argentina. On September 1, a bloody battle took place at Masoller. As dusk fell after the first day's fighting, General Saravia, wearing his distinctive white poncho, inspected the front lines for the morrow's combat. Federal army sharpshooters fired random shots at the line, one of which mortally wounded Saravia. The rebel lines retreated into Brazil and almost immediately disbanded, as the Revolution of 1904 fizzled.

Despite the disastrous finale, Aparicio Saravia became the Blanco's greatest hero and a symbol for the party. More importantly, civilian party leader Luis Alberto de Herrera hereafter resolved to forgo the miliary option in favor of contesting elections. The annihilation of Saravia's forces strengthened Batlle's argument against co-participation. He refused to utter the slogan that had governed the conclusion of all civil wars since the Guerra Grande: "No victors and no vanquished." Implementing his pledge to end such agreements enabled Batlle to execute a reform agenda.[6]

BATLLE'S FIRST TERM: PRODUCTS, REVENUE, AND REFORMS, 1904–1910

A pragmatic politician rather than an ideologue, Batlle and his allies, a group of moderate social democratic reformers, offered policies over the next two decades that dramatically changed Uruguay. To achieve his objective of single-party rule, in November 1904 Batlle proposed a more equitable reapportionment of seats in the Chamber of Deputies by allocating one seat per five thousand inhabitants of a department rather than one per three thousand. This reform effectively reduced the number of seats allocated to sparsely populated Blanco departments while increasing urban Colorado representation. (British reformers adopted similar measures in the nineteenth century to eliminate so-called rotten boroughs.)

As a consequence of the reform, the results of congressional election of 1905 gave the Colorados fifty-four seats while the Blancos secured only twenty-one. The latter's political strength declined further the following year when the Colorados won six of seven contested Senate seats. As a result, in the presidential election of 1906, Batlle's chosen successor, Claudio Williman (1907–1911), a railroad lawyer, physics professor, and the university rector who did not even bother to campaign, easily won and served as an obliging placeholder until Batlle became eligible for reelection in 1910.[7]

Batlle's first term saw an improving economy that resulted in the country's first ever budget surplus. Prosperity resulted because of the revolution in meat processing. The country's first chilled meat plant, the Uruguayan owned *Frigorífico Uruguaya*, opened in 1904 in Montevideo's Cerro neighborhood; the "mountain" that Magellan spotted as well as the former site of many saladeros. This community had

Figure 5.2 Portrait of José Batlle y Ordoñez. Uruguay's most eminent president, José Batlle y Ordóñez, led a group of like-minded Colorados who built upon late-nineteenth-century progress to lay the foundations of the modern Uruguayan state. He purchased this estate of almost ninety acres on the outskirts of Montevideo in 1904, which he named Piedras Blancas. While in Europe between terms, he refurbished it and filled it with European furniture. He chose it for its relaxed country atmosphere where he could contemplate nature and invite his followers and his opponents to discuss new reformist policies for the model country. *Source*: Quinta de Batlle, Museo Histórico Nacional, Montevideo, Author photo.

long attracted Afro-Uruguayans and recent Italian and Spanish immigrants because most of its jobs required only unskilled workers. After World War I, two hundred thousand new immigrants, mostly East Europeans, would supplement the Cerro's labor force.

The *frigoríficos* revolutionized Uruguay's pastoral industry. European consumers willing to pay high prices for chilled beef demanded quality meat butchered from pedigreed cattle. While Argentine ranchers imported Shorthorns that produced the highest grade of marbled meat, Uruguayan ranchers purchased Herefords that produced leaner and arguably slightly less desirable meat. Uruguayan ranchers chose Herefords because their thicker hides resisted the omnipresent ticks in Uruguayan pastures that drove Shorthorns to madness. The pedigreed cattle rapidly proliferated. By 1916 creole cattle made up only 4 percent of Uruguay's herds. In addition, modernizing ranchers now fed cattle oats and alfalfa to fatten them more rapidly for market.

The Frigorífico Uruguaya and its U.S. rivals, Swift International Company (the Frigorífico Montevideo) and the Armour and Company (Frigorífico Artigas), competed with the Liebig's factory at Fray Bentos, which was converted into a British-owned meat-packing plant (El Anglo) in 1924. Because of the high cost of transport, most *estancieros* still drove their herds to market and fattened them on feedlots near the frigoríficos near El Cerro, the site of the *frigoríficos*. Frozen and chilled beef exports became the mainstay of the Uruguayan economy during Batlle's years. Fresh meat fed the local population. As the common saying went, "In Uruguay, nobody dies of hunger."[8]

As ranchers prospered, Batlle proposed a 10 percent increase in the "mill rate" on rural property (the *contribución inmobiliaria*) because he wanted to increase funding for education and social programs. Politically powerful ranchers protested vehemently. While the "mill rate" increase failed, the Assembly authorized periodic reassessments of property values that essentially accomplished the same objective. As a result, the taxes *estancieros* paid increased by as much as 50 percent during the Batlle years. To appease landowners, Batlle promised he would not require them to purchase the public lands (*tierras fiscales*—called *tierras baldíos* in other Latin American countries) on which they had run cattle since the colonial period.

A moderate reformer, Batlle believed in the sacrosanct right to private property. Thus, he never considered the structural changes in the rural areas that radical Colorados proposed, such as the expropriation of unused *estancia* land for redistribution to displaced gauchos and immigrants. Instead, he provided limited quantities of state-owned land to form agricultural colonies. Batlle accepted the *estancieros*' argument that agrarian reform would severely damage the pastoral industry and reduce the export taxes on which Batlle's reforms partially depended. Batlle also rejected the idea of a personal income tax. While land taxes produced about 10 percent of governmental revenues, Uruguay still relied primarily on the easier to collect import-export duties (roughly 70 percent of the government's revenues). Despite Uruguay's newfound prosperity, the extent of the foreign debt bothered Batlle, so he paid it off and left a surplus in the budget by the end of his term.[9]

Batlle's plan to expand the economic nationalism first invoked in the 1890s proceeded slowly. (Other nations such as Argentina, Brazil, Chile, and Peru would initiate such policies after World War I.) The privately owned electric company in Montevideo charged high rates unaffordable to most potential consumers and provided unreliable service. Batlle purchased the entity, renamed it the *Usina Eléctrica de Montevideo*, gave it monopoly privileges and required it (with a government subsidy) to improve service and lower rates. The monopoly clause required the recently electrified trams to purchase all their power from the state-owned entity. Electric trams changed the face of the capital, enabling middle-class *empleados* (public employees) to build homes even further east.[10]

The tax reassessments and the improved import-export economy boosted government revenue by approximately 350,000 pesos, much of which Batlle spent on education. Because in 1908 roughly 50 percent of the population remained illiterate, he opened new primary schools, particularly in rural areas. He also inaugurated night schools to provide education to workers. Within a generation, Uruguay would have the second most literate population in Latin America with 153,000 children enrolled in primarily schools and a literacy rate of 60 percent, just below that of Argentina.[11]

Batlle also proposed a divorce law, an end to the death penalty, and the formal separation of Church and State. The government forbade reciting the catechism in public schools and proposed progressive labor legislation, but Batlle's term ended before the legislature could act on these measures. Leaving Uruguay for Europe, he served as Uruguay's delegate to the Second Hague Peace Conference of 1907. There, he proposed mandatory arbitration in the event of disputes between nations, a reaction to Uruguay's troubled history with its larger neighbors and later a goal of the League of Nations.

Batlle's successor, the more conservative Claudio Williman did abolish the death penalty (1907), a landmark achievement in Latin America. He also approved the National Public Assistance Law of 1910 that uniquely in Latin America guaranteed a right to universal care for the poor and created an agency, the *Asistencia Pública Nacional* (APN), mostly funded by philanthropic organizations, to oversee its implementation. Work on the divorce bill, labor legislation, and additional social projects would await Batlle's second term. Like many early-twentieth-century administrations, Williman had no patience for labor protests, crushing the railway workers strike in 1908.[12]

University students convinced Williman to consider improvements in higher education. Although historians usually highlight the Argentine University of Córdoba reform of 1918 as the watershed moment of student activism in Latin America, students in Chile, Peru, Argentina, and Uruguay participated in a transnational movement for curricular and administrative reforms as early as 1893. In 1908, the International Conference of American Students met in Montevideo where Uruguay's delegate, future president Baltasar Brum (1919–1923), argued in favor of university autonomy. Thus, a full decade before Córdoba, Williman's government agreed to student representation in university governance and on faculty hiring committees, more student housing and more fellowships.[13]

Just before the presidential election of 1910, the Assembly devised a new voting system designed to maintain party unity while simultaneously recognizing the rights of factions. The complex double-simultaneous system had voters cast their primary election and general election ballot at the same time. With a single ballot voters indicated their choice of candidate (by name) and party (Colorado or Blanco). Thus, the party with the most cumulative votes from its combined factions *sublema* won the election and the candidate from that party whose *sublema* won the most votes became president. Members of the Senate and the Chamber of Deputies were selected similarly. This sweeping electoral victory enabled Batlle and the Colorados to "accelerate" reforms, setting Uruguay on a path that would make it the envy of its Latin American neighbors.[14]

BATLLE'S SECOND TERM: ECONOMIC NATIONALISM AND STATE ENTERPRISE

During the campaign Batlle spoke about transforming Uruguay into the "model country." Over the next two years, he sent a barrage of legislation, one hundred and twelve bills in all, to the Assembly. His dream and those of his Colorado colleagues would result in expanding suffrage to make Uruguay Latin America's most democratic nation, advancing economic nationalism to minimize British influence and initiating social welfare programs. To accomplish the latter two goals, the country needed a budget surplus that, with the exception of the early Depression years, the country enjoyed from 1904 until the mid-1950s. A bonanza began during World War I. After the initial shock of the onset of war passed, shipping resumed in 1915. Prices for primary products rose as the Allies depended on them to meet wartime needs. For the duration of the conflict, British and French soldiers on the Western front subsisted on canned corned beef from the Fray Bentos' plant and wore woolen uniforms. Although a theoretical opportunity existed to expand manufacturing because of the lack of imports, practical difficulties like the inability to import machinery and raw materials limited further industrial development.[15]

Batlle understood that British-owned public utilities, banks, and insurance companies returned huge profits to Great Britain while delivering poor service to customers, and he resolved to remedy the situation. While more radical reformers argued for the expropriation of foreign property (which required compensation to the foreign company), moderates like Batlle preferred forming national corporations sufficiently capitalized to outcompete the foreign monopoly, ultimately driving it from the marketplace.

During his second term, Batlle and the Colorados launched the most extensive program of economic nationalism in Latin America. Economic nationalism rejected the tenets of relatively free trade that had dominated the last quarter of the nineteenth century. In 1912, Batlle expanded the Montevideo Electric Company into a national monopoly called the *Usinas Eléctricas del Estado* purposed to provide power throughout the nation. The electric company became the first of a number of national enterprises (*entes autónomos*) that became a common feature of the Uruguayan economy. The electric company reduced rates and connected most homes in Montevideo to the service. It paid its workers well, yet also yielded excellent profits through 1952. Initially, electrical grids rarely existed in towns outside Montevideo (only twenty-six of seventy-seven towns by 1927), but that slowly changed. In 1931 the monopoly incorporated telephone and telegraph services under its umbrella and today is known as *Usinas Eléctricas y Teléfonos del Estado* (UTE).[16]

Other legislation nationalized the Bank of the Republic that issued currency, held the gold reserves and provided capital for Uruguayan-owned businesses. The bank offered workers and middle-class depositors security for their funds and provided credit for farmers and ranchers in convenient branches in departments. In short, the bank offered comprehensive banking services and generated profits for the treasury. A second bank, the *Banco Hipotecario* (Mortgage Bank), nationalized in 1912, allowed real estate purchasers to acquire mortgages, offered construction loans and savings accounts. Less well-regulated than the Bank of the Republic, the Mortgage Bank fell into arrears in the early 1930s and required a government bailout. The National Insurance Bank founded in 1911 to compete with private British insurers, by 1915 secured a near monopoly fire, life, and workers' compensation policies. It reduced rates for citizens but also earned revenue for the government. In 1926 the government allowed it to cover additional risks. By all accounts the National Insurance Bank proved profitable while delivering insurance to customers at reasonable rates and returning roughly seven hundred thousand pesos annually to the treasury between 1925 and 1934.[17]

BOX 5.1: FRANCISCO PIRIA AND ENTREPRENEURSHIP IN THE BATLLE YEARS

As a firm believer in capitalism, Batlle had no intentions of making Uruguay a socialist state. Francisco Piria's career exemplified that of numerous entrepreneurs who flourished and accumulated fortunes during the Batlle years. Piria speculated in real estate, purchasing large parcels in Montevideo and subdividing them into small lots for sale to prospective homeowners of modest means. After the Depression of 1890, Piria became a real estate mogul on Uruguay's eastern shore where he purchased almost 6,700 acres and developed a beach resort that he modestly named Piriápolis. Granite from the nearby mountain, quarried into building stone and transported to Montevideo, earned him another fortune. Modeling Piriápolis after the French resort of Biarritz, Piria built hotels, including the Hotel Argentino, the largest in South America, spas, and casinos for middle- and upper-class guests. To convey guests to the resort, he built a spur rail line into Piriápolis as well as a port that allowed steamships with Argentine tourists to dock across from the hotel. When Piria died in 1933, a lengthy probate battle took place between his sons and his "adopted daughter," the result of which, like in Charles Dickens's *Bleak House*, concluded with lawyers draining the estate of all the proceeds. Until Punta del Este blossomed after World War II, Piriápolis remained Uruguay's premier beach vacation spot.[18]

Figure 5.3   Photograph of Francisco Piria. After founding the beach resort of Piriápolis, Francisco Piria made another fortune selling house lots and building hotels there. In addition, he used the rural acreage to do truck farming and plant vineyards which supplied the hotel with fresh produce during the tourist season. Despite being an atheist, Piria built a church for his workers, which the bishop refused to consecrate because of the philanthropist's beliefs. It stands unused today. *Source*: Castle of Francisco Piria, Piriápolis, *Source*: Author photo.

Batlle's next nationalistic venture resulted in a new company that manufactured *sarnifugas* (sheep dip—a livestock mange curative) to replace the British supplier whose product had traditionally entered the country tariff free. Batlle argued that since sheep raising constituted one of Uruguay's principal industries, locally made sarnifugas would reduce ranchers' costs, warranting the manufacturing plant's construction as a national priority. The sheep dip plant proved highly successful, made economic sense, and pleased an important constituency.[19] Bringing the railroad and the *frigoríficos* under national auspices, however, was not economically feasible.

Light industries flourished during the Batlle years. Packing plants and factories processing wool regained their market-share in 1915. Local businesses produced greater quantities of consumer items such as clothing, leather goods, paper (*Fábrica Nacional de Papel, S.A.*), chemicals (*Instituto de Química Industrial*), cement, wine, soap, glass, and soft drinks that catered to local taste preferences. In the latter instance, Rómulo Mangini's Paso de los Toros beverages became the country's national soft drink, replacing imported British soft drinks. He experimented with different flavors, and marketed lemon- and grapefruit-flavored beverages so successfully that PepsiCo finally bought him out in 1955. Only after the war when Uruguay could acquire machinery would Uruguay's industrial sector expand. Broadening the economy to a larger industrial sector had important consequences. By 1930, Uruguay had become Latin America's third most highly industrialized nation after Mexico and Argentina.[20]

Figure 5.4 "Processing Beef at the Swift *Frigorífico."* Despite President Batlle y Ordóñez' interest in creating state-owned corporations, the business of meat processing required too much capital for the nation to construct its own plants. Inviting the U.S.-owned Swift and Armour corporations to open *frigoríficos* in the Cerro neighborhood of Montevideo solved two problems. First, the new meat packing plants allowed Uruguayan products to meet the demands of European consumers for high quality beef. In addition, Batlle reduced the British influence in the economy by encouraging U.S. investments. *Source*: Columbus Memorial Library.

Despite Batlle's strong preference for economic nationalism, reality tied his hands when it came to the railroad. High prices and inefficiency limited the British railroads' usefulness. To compensate, Batlle proposed designing a parallel line of government-owned railroads to compete in major service areas. In 1917 the government opened a line that ran from Durazno to Trinidad. Two other short runs followed in the 1920s, but neither earned sufficient profits to justify expansion. Ranchers continued to drive cattle overland or, after 1930, ship them on modern asphalt roads before fattening them at feedlots.[21]

BOX 5.2: THE WORKINGS OF EL ANGLO'S *FRIGORÍFICO*

During its peak years during the 1920s, the El Anglo factory, allegedly the largest meat-packing plant in the world, could process two thousand cattle a day in addition to some sheep, pigs, and chickens. The diesel-powered plant's enormous turbines and steam compressors used ammonia refrigeration to chill or freeze meat for export. Workers drove the fattened cattle up a winding wooden staircase (so they could not anticipate their fate and stampede) where a worker stunned each cow with a sledge hammer (so as not to damage the organs) before his work gang attached the carcass to a hook with pulleys on a gravity-powered conveyor belt. The next group of workers killed the animal by slitting its throat and collected its blood; the next team removed the hide, the third cut off the fat, the next removed the hooves, head, and bones, and finally the last crew severed the carcass in half, washed, and weighed it. This process took between thirty and forty-five minutes per cow.

The blood, bones and hooves became fertilizer, the hide leather, and the fat was rendered into soap. As El Anglo advertised, "We used every part except the moo." Then the conveyor belt carried the carcasses to a separate facility where they were refrigerated or frozen and stored separately until a refrigerated ship arrived at the dock to carry the meat down the Uruguay River to Europe. Because the refrigerated beef had a limited shelf life, El Anglo prearranged its contracts with European buyers who rushed the beef or mutton to market.[22]

SECOND-TERM REFORMS: DEMOCRACY AND LABOR REFORM, 1911–1915

After Batlle's reelection, the Colorados pressed for greater educational expenditures that would elevate Uruguayan society and create a sense of civic belonging to a nation offering greater opportunities. Batlle and his allies extended free, secular public education through the secondary and university levels. Primary school attendance increased from 54,000 in 1904 to 91,000 in 1913, but only 3 percent of these students completed, with most dropping out after the third grade once they acquired sufficient basic skills in reading, writing, and mathematics to hold a decent job. The reformers not only sought improved completion rates but also expanded rural educational opportunities by constructing a new public *liceo* (high school) in each departmental capital. Expanding primary and secondary education required new facilities and hiring additional teachers. Increased funding for the university grew its enrollment, and for the first time significant numbers of women joined male colleagues.[23]

Education also prepared Uruguayans to undertake an important duty of citizenship: voting. Batlle's quest to extend democracy to all citizens provided an example for the democratic left governments of the circum-Caribbean region that emerged in the 1940s and 1950s. As would occur in Costa Rica and Venezuela later, Batlle employed democracy to implement popular social and economic changes. Like the social welfare system, electoral reform came from above but benefited the middle class and workers. The Suffrage Law of 1915 extended the definition of citizenship contained in the Constitution of 1830 to all males—thereby enfranchising servants, day laborers, illiterates, debtors, vagabonds, drunks, immoral people—and women. For various reasons, women did not actually vote until 1937. After 1915, even immigrants with as few as three years residence could cast ballots. Uruguay's law closely resembled Argentina's new suffrage law, passed in 1912. Uruguay's statute also provided for the secret ballot and the direct election of the president.[24]

The law passed with bipartisan support because the Nationalist leadership recognized that given the military strength of the state, they could only gain power through the ballot box. As a result of universal suffrage, both the Colorados and the Nationalists became mass political parties. The Nationalists had reorganized after the 1904 Saravia revolt, as Luis Alberto de Herrera introduced the first labor bill in the Chamber in a pitch to win votes from urban workers. The 1915 statute increased the number of eligible voters from roughly 5 percent of the population to over three hundred thousand.[25]

Batlle understood the political and social benefits for advocating for labor reform as did the Nationalist Party. On May 11, 1911, workers on Montevideo's foreign-owned tram companies struck because of low pay and intolerable working conditions. Forced to work for ten or eleven hours daily without a meal or bathroom break, they demanded a reduction to the eight-hour day that labor unions had successful won in industrialized Europe and the United States. Soon *frigorífico* workers who labored sixteen to eighteen hours daily and flour and paper millworkers who averaged twelve hours, seven days a week, joined them. In contrast to other Latin American governments in this era, Batlle encouraged the strikers and refused to order the police to break up the strikes. The strikes settled peacefully with many workers gaining a reduction in hours. Batlle's decision paid big dividends.

Thereafter, Batlle and bipartisan members of the legislature agreed that legislating the eight-hour day would stave off social unrest. As he said, "We may be a small and little-known republic, but we have big ideas." Large segments of the largest union, the FORU (Uruguayan Regional Workers' Federation) joined forces with the batllistas to pressure the passage in 1915 of the first eight-hour workday bill in Latin America, which excluded agricultural and ranch workers, domestic servants, and children. This peaceful resolution of the eight-hour day controversy had lasting consequences. First, uniquely in Latin America, both political parties favored labor legislation; and second, unions accepted the government's role as mediator between management and labor. Most importantly, Batlle's progressive stance co-opted the unions, rendering them less militant than elsewhere.[26]

Other legislation improved industrial workers' lives. First debated in 1911, a bill protecting laborers from on-the-job accidents passed in 1914. Because businesses disregarded early efforts to assure worker's safety, the Assembly passed and Batlle signed a workers' compensation plan administered by the State Insurance Bank. Injured employees received a portion of their salary while the families of workers killed on the job received an annuity. Benefits increased over time. State corporations and government agencies paid premiums directly into the State Insurance Bank, while most private employers did so voluntarily in order to exempt themselves from further liability. The program remained profitable until the Great Depression and even contributed to the treasury. Despite the statute, enforcement of safety requirements remained spotty, especially in small businesses and in rural areas. Because of the pending bills proposing "radical" reforms such as pensions and social security, as well as the proposed revision of the political system, Batlle's moderate successor in 1916 called "*Alto*" or "Stop," or as one writer said, to put a "brake" on additional reforms for the moment.[27]

REFORMS BENEFITING WOMEN AND CHILDREN

In addition to workers, children, and the elderly, Batlle's "shield of the weak" safeguarded women and opened further opportunities to them. By the late nineteenth century, Uruguayan feminists had moved the needle significantly from the days of Bernadina Fragoso de Rivera. Activists in the 1880s turned their attention to urban social problems: sex workers, the white slave trade (international sex trafficking), and incidents of venereal disease that threatened family life. Uruguay had sanctioned legalized prostitution within specific geographical zones, by registered sex workers who underwent demeaning medical examinations at the hands of male doctors to maintain their licenses. Only painful mercury treatments were available to treat venereal disease. Feminists wanted to help defenseless young women avoid *la mala vida*. Thus, women's organizations provided financial assistance to poor working women and victims of white slavers who enticed young women with promises of money, good jobs, and sometimes passage to the Americas from Europe.[28]

As someone who had lived in and fathered children in an informal relationship, Batlle thought that liberalizing divorce might lessen the stigma of illegitimacy. His desire for a divorce law, the first in Latin America, stemmed both from his liberal anti-clerical opinions and from his own uncomfortable marital situation. Traditionally, the Catholic Church recognized marriage as a sacrament and granted divorce only under limited circumstances. During his first term, Batlle had proposed three grounds for divorce: adultery by the wife (the husband could only be so charged if the offense took place in the marital home), the attempted murder of a spouse, or cruel treatment by the husband. The bill met with stiff opposition from Conservatives and Catholic women, led by the Catholic Ladies League and its president, Margarita Uriarte de Herrera, the wife of Nationalist leader Luis Alberto de Herrera. With an overwhelming Colorado majority, Batlle now proposed and passed an even more liberal law, eliminating the need to provide grounds for divorce by allowing either spouse to sue without the consent of the other.[29]

As previously noted, President Batlle described the Colorado Party as the "shield of the weak," for both married and single women, including those with illegitimate children. In 1914, the government sponsored legislation that allowed single mothers of illegitimate children to receive child support and for those children to have rights of inheritance from their father. Batlle expanded opportunities for women. Although significant numbers had graduated from normal schools, these certificates opened only teaching positions but otherwise were professional dead ends. To expand choice, in 1913 Batlle created a separate Women's University that in addition to the post-secondary curriculum included a school of nursing, a second profession deemed acceptable for women. Conservatives approved of this solution because it separated male and female students, preserving the latter's honor.[30]

Paulina Luisi, the educated, middle-class daughter of immigrants, took the lead in Uruguay's feminist cause. After earning her bachelor's degree, she became the first female medical student, where she faced some harassment from her male teachers and colleagues. On one occasion her classmates placed a severed penis from a cadaver in the pocket of her lab coat. Showing her mettle, at the end of the lecture, she held it up and asked, "Did one of you lose this?" Although she never mentioned this incident publicly and praised the majority of her teachers and classmates for treating her fairly, she found herself practicing gynecology and obstetrics, an acceptable field for female physicians.[31]

As the leader of Uruguay's feminists, Luisi attended her first international women's conference in 1910 and became a firm believer in Pan-American feminism. She founded two feminist organizations, the first of which, the Uruguayan National Women's Council (1916) (Conamu) primarily focused its efforts on social assistance for the poor. Elite and middle-class professional women who viewed their role as primarily philanthropic helped victims of the white slave trade by providing economic assistance to working women. To a lesser degree, the council participated in the struggle for suffrage.[32]

Luisi also formed the Uruguayan Women's Suffrage Alliance (1919). Its membership included younger and more progressive women, who assisted in the quest for implementation of women's suffrage. With the support of President Baltasar Brum (1919–1923), it also demanded greater equality in the workplace, insisting that public employment in the state bureaucracy above the secretarial level be opened to women. Luisi found herself and other Spanish American feminists increasingly alienated from the U.S.-dominated leadership of the Pan-American Women's Conference and Brazilian feminist Bertha Lutz. The Women's Conference chose to pursue political and legal reform while the Latin Americans' more ambitious agenda included economic equality, social justice, and anti-U.S. imperialism.

Although Luisi's voice went unheard at the 1922 meeting, it would become the wave of future Pan-American feminism. Her fame allowed her to serve on various committees at the League of Nations and on international feminist organizations. Although Catholics and Socialists also formed women's organizations, Batlle and Brum favored Luisi's progressive brand of feminism that sought suffrage, increased educational opportunities, and increased equality of employment for people regardless of gender. Despite Luisi's socialist leanings, she refused to join the party, knowing that doing so would alienate her from influential Colorado politicians sympathetic to the feminist cause.[33]

BATLLE AND THE UNITED STATES

President Batlle's growing kinship with the United States resulted from two advantages he perceived from closer ties with the United States. First, he saw salient examples of his vision for Uruguay's "model state" in the United States. Although most of his reform ideas resulted from his European experiences, he felt an affinity for the progressive measures undertaken by U.S. presidents Theodore Roosevelt and Woodrow Wilson, especially their workers' compensation and eight-hour day statutes. Both favored granting suffrage to women. Second, Batlle saw the United States as an effective counterbalance to British economic influence. As a result, he encouraged expanded trade relations between the two countries, especially during World War I.[34]

During Batlle's first term, U.S. secretary of state Elihu Root made a four-day visit as part of a good-will tour of the Southern Cone nations. Crowds in Montevideo gave Root a rousing welcome. President Batlle found two of Root's statements at the recently concluded Pan American Conference particularly comforting: that disputes between nations ought to be resolved by arbitration; and that smaller nations should be treated as equals by their larger neighbors. Batlle feted Root during his stay and introduced him to Uruguay's most famous nineteenth-century poet, Juan Zorilla de San Martín. After Root's auspicious state visit, a direct steamship route shuttled between New York and Montevideo, tourists came to visit the country and businesses like the Kodak Camera Company opened retail stores in the capital.[35]

During World War I, German U-Boats made shipping lanes to Europe treacherous, but the neutral United States filled the void. As a rising global power, the United States flexed its economic muscles in the Southern Cone nations for the first time during the "War to End All Wars." Batlle sold the half-completed Uruguayan frigorífico located in the Cerro to Swift & Company of Chicago in 1913 because he knew U.S. experts skilled in meat-packing could manage it profitably. The Armour Company purchased another *frigorífico* and began exporting frozen beef in 1917. Anglophile traveler and writer William Koebel noted that Great Britain was losing ground as a trading partner to Germany, France, and the United States because the former continued to package products with weights measured in pounds and with useless descriptors like "hardware" while the latter three nations wrote detailed bills of lading in Spanish. U.S. entrepreneur Percival Farquhar constructed the 125 mile-long-railroad line (the Uruguay Railroad Company) that competed with the British. U.S. experts provided information about the latest techniques for dairy farming, commercial fishing, and the manufacture of industrial chemicals.[36]

The war brought the United States and Uruguay closer diplomatically and militarily. Uruguay also remained neutral until 1917 because it feared that the German population in southern Brazil might use the war as an excuse to regain the entire Cisplatine province. Batlle's protégé Baltasar Brum favored closer relations with the United States, particularly after a German U-boat sank a Uruguayan vessel in the South Atlantic. With U-boat attacks increasing, U.S. admiral William Cupperton captured eight German packet ships stranded in Montevideo harbor in September 1917. Uruguay entered the war a month later. At the Versailles Peace Conference, Uruguay's delegates supported Woodrow Wilson's League of Nations and joined almost immediately. World War I proved highly important because the United States replaced Great Britain as the most important supplier of imports (particularly oil and machinery) as well as becoming its new source of investment capital.[37]

Figure 5.5   Baltasar Brum with Robert Lansing. Baltasar Brum was Batlle's closest protégé and served as president from 1920–1924. He led the charge during World War I to replace British influence and form closer relations with the United States. He spent time in Washington, and was warmly received by the Wilson administration. U.S. economic influence grew during the 1920s, especially during Brum's term as president. *Source*: U.S. Library of Congress, LC-DIG-hec-11316.

BOX 5.3: THE LEGALIZATION OF DUELING IN 1920

Notable Uruguayans participated in duels with swords or dueling pistols regularly during the nineteenth century. Most of these challenges resulted from "insults" by politicians from opposing parties or by highly partisan newspaper editors against their political opponents. Although banned, participants in duels rarely faced legal prosecution. That changed in 1920. First, as a modern nation that prided itself on enforcing laws, the practice of ignoring dueling seemed wrong. Second, during his second term, Batlle had received challenges but postponed them because dueling seemed inappropriate while he remained head of state. With his term concluded, ex-President Batlle accepted the challenge of a rising Nationalist Party politician and killed him on April 2, 1920. To protect their hero, Colorado legislators passed the Nationalists' bill that proposed legalizing dueling. Dueling remained legal in Uruguay until 1992 when the Assembly banned the practice.[38]

THE CONSTITUTION OF 1918 CREATES THE FIRST *COLEGIADO*

Batlle's most controversial proposal entailed replacing the Constitution of 1830 with an entirely new governmental structure called the *colegiado* (collegial executive), a plan modeled after Switzerland's plural executive that Batlle came to admire during his European sojourn (1907–1911). By adopting a plural executive and holding frequent elections, he argued, Uruguay would deepen its democracy and prevent the rise of an ambitious dictator (like Santos in the 1880s). His opponents, the Blancos and conservative Colorados, feared the reform as an attempt to perpetuate the Batlle faction in office permanently. The Swiss Confederation's elected Assembly chose seven of its members to serve as the Federal Council; one of whom became president and another, vice president. Both fulfilled purely ceremonial functions, having no greater authority than any other council member. The fact the majority of Swiss citizens with whom he spoke could not name their current president further impressed Batlle.[39]

Batlle believed that the Swiss plural executive system would allow further social reforms. By the end of his second term, however, the new president questioned additional progressive legislation, hence the "Halt." As one of Batlle more conservative Colorado opponents argued, "Are we Colorados or are we Socialists?" The idea of the colegiado splintered the Colorado party into factions. Batlle's proposal envisioned nine council members serving staggered terms, with one being replaced or reelected annually. Both Colorados and Nationalists agreed with two of his other ideas: compulsory voting and the secret ballot. No longer would the old gaucho saying apply: "The police chief's horse always wins the race."[40]

Batlle's plural executive proposal resulted in its opponents winning a majority of the seats (137 to 87) at the constitutional assembly. In January 1917 the deadlocked assembly tasked the drafting of a new document to eight attorneys who proposed a nine-person National Council of Administration, which split executive powers between the president, in charge of the departments of war, interior (the police force) and foreign affairs, and the remaining council members who oversaw education, industry, public works, and the treasury. This bicephalous (divided) executive became its centerpiece.

The Constitution of 1918 included each of the provisions of the Electoral Law of 1915 and made suffrage mandatory. Because of the "Halt," the controversial provision for women's suffrage failed. As a result, Paulina Luisi organized the Uruguayan Women's Suffrage Alliance. The National Council of Administration had proportional representation based upon the electoral strength of each party, with Colorados holding six seats and Blancos three. The lemas remained, guaranteeing the continuance of the two-party system. In essence, the Constitution of 1918 revived the nineteenth-century practice of co-participation in government, the sharing of power and patronage (and the generous benefits that came from government employment), precisely the result Batlle opposed. With the Colorados holding the majority, progressive reforms would continue in the 1920s.[41]

The architects of the Constitution of 1918 formally separated Church and State. The Catholic Church lost all claims to property ownership other than houses of worship. President Brum in 1919 renamed Holy Week as the "the Week of Tourism" and Christmas as the "Day of the Family," although most households continue to celebrate the latter traditionally. Uruguay was clearly the least Catholic of any of the Latin American countries although many Blancos, like Luis Alberto de Herrera, remained devout. Finally, departmental councils and assemblies replaced the once powerful *jefes políticos*.[42]

ADVANCING THE WELFARE STATE IN THE 1920s

With the fray over the constitution settled, Batlle and his protégé Baltasar Brum returned to the business of instituting South America's most progressive social welfare state. Batlle twice served on the Council of Administrators and acted as senior adviser to the Colorado party until his death in 1929. During this decade, the Colorado government enacted a host of social reforms and welfare programs unrealized in other Latin American states. Early on, the government passed the "one day of rest in seven" (six-day work week) statute. Because of Batlle's aversion for the Catholic Church, he hoped to persuade workers to select a day off other than Sunday, their usual holiday. By nearly a four-to-one margin, however, most workers preferred Sunday.[43]

By the 1920s, factory workers' wages had improved significantly. As previously noted, a series of strikes beginning in 1911 had allowed workers to better their financial situation. Employees of state-owned corporations and government workers, allied to the political parties, reached a favorable minimum wage guarantee approved by the National Council of Administration. Batlle even took up the cause of defenseless rural workers who had historically labored for paltry wages as little as nine pesos a month, which the Assembly raised to eighteen pesos in 1923. Two years later urban workers demanded large increases to keep up with inflation, but the rigorous opposition of the railroads, frigoríficos, and other major industries caused the proposal to fail. Observers noted that Uruguay's host of small labor unions with various political affiliations (Socialist, Anarchist, Communist) instead of a big umbrella organization like the AFL in the United States hindered collective bargaining. Nevertheless, Batlle's progressive welfare umbrella and labor legislation blunted the radicalism of the early unions as most workers remained loyal Colorados. The batllista reforms closely resembled the British Liberal Party's social liberal reformism of the early twentieth century, which had the identical effect.[44]

Despite labor's progress, the feminist movement failed to connect with working women. Batlle's reforms had offered only one minor concession to working females, the so-called chair law of 1918 that required factories and stores to offer them a place to sit down for breaks during long hours of toil. The Alianza offered encouragement to telephone operators during their 1922 strike. Although the operators won a small wage increase, they continued to complain unsuccessfully about their working conditions. The upper- and middle-class members of Conamu and the Alianza thought working women insufficiently grateful for their assistance. Likewise, class differences prevented early feminists from sympathizing with domestics who requested a day off every week; this law only passed in 1931. Elite women had difficulty understanding that their domestics held two jobs—as employees and taking care of their own home.[45]

Uruguay developed a more expansive pension system during the 1920s. By the end of the nineteenth century, military men, civil servants, and teachers received modest pensions upon retirement. Flush with profits from sales of meat and wool during World War I and high prices for chilled beef from 1925 to 1929, the government required private employers like the railroads, trams, foreign-owned meat-packing plants, as well as utility companies (telephone, telegraph, waterworks, and gasworks) and their employees to contribute payments to the national pension system. The National Insurance Bank administered the system and distributed funds to workers retiring at age sixty after thirty years of service. (These requirements were quite flexible in practice.) In 1925 bank and stock exchange personnel joined the system. By 1930, nearly all private sector workers except domestic servants had become participants. The retirement system's expansion to include so many beneficiaries, however, exceeded contributions, requiring the government to provide additional funds.[46]

Uruguay established a social security system before any other nation in the hemisphere. This system, inelegantly referred to as "Old Age" pensions during the 1920s, provided moneys to indigent people sixty or older even if they had never contributed to the fund. As Batlle argued, "Every Uruguayan has the right to demand a means of sustenance from the state." "The state cannot say to an old or incapacitated man; you were a wastrel when young—now starve or let the chill of winter take you." Like the retirement system, the government proved overly generous by providing benefits to numerous people who did not qualify and by increasing payouts in excess of available funds.[47] The pension and social security systems both became the third rail of Uruguayan politics by the late 1920s.

By the time of the Great Depression, pensions now vested after relatively few years of service, encouraging workers to retire at age sixty and collect for many years. By the 1930s, even the well-funded and administered workers' compensation fund fell into arrears. Nevertheless, Uruguayans could proudly claim that Batlle and his colleagues had created the most progressive state in South America.[48]

THE ROARING TWENTIES: THE FINAL YEARS OF BATLLISMO

The *lema* statute permitted one Colorado faction or another to hold onto the presidency throughout the 1920s despite the party's divisions. The minority Blancos continued to win proportional seats on the National Council of Administration. In 1925, the Nationalists took control of the Senate and Blanco leader Luis Alberto de Herrera became president of the National Council. The Nationalists' co-participation in government allowed them to slow the pace of reforms and enact changes that benefited their constituents, the ranch owners, and industrialists.[49]

The Colorados most divisive moment occurred during the presidential election of 1926 when Batlle became involved in the fray because of his antipathy for an emerging rival, Gabriel Terra. At this moment the Colorado hero retained sufficient influence to scotch Terra's presidential candidacy. After Batlle's death in 1929, Terra pushed the former's ghost aside, won the election of 1930, and eventually took revenge by undoing some of Batlle's treasured measures (see chapter 6). While orderly electoral processes continued, the divided colegiado governments found themselves hard-pressed to accomplish much legislatively.[50]

University students grew increasingly frustrated and radicalized at the slowing pace of social reforms. They had organized the Ariel Student Center in 1917 to protest the "halt" of social reforms. In line with other transnational student movements, the Ariel Center proposed a university extension division that would offer evening classes to workers at union halls. This evolved into a demand for full-scale "peoples' universities" similar to those that Peruvian populist Victor Raúl Haya de la Torre had originated. By the end of the decade, the student movement insisted upon curricular changes, including new courses studying social questions. The Ariel Center also protested against U.S. imperialism in the hemisphere.[51]

Paulina Luisi also radicalized during the 1920s and urged the transnational feminist movement to press for greater social change. In Uruguay, she advocated for the teaching of sex education in public schools. Because she believed that sexual activity should occur only within the bonds of matrimony, not surprisingly her view of sex education emphasized the prevention of pre-marital sex through a combination of will power, regular physical exercise, and avoiding sexual stimulation. More realistically, her course on health education offered scientifically based discussions about reproduction, anatomy, hygiene and the prevention of venereal disease. The class caused controversy. Some Uruguayans preferred that their children remain ignorant and innocent; others feared that the class would encourage more sexual activity. In 1944, the government endorsed the course as part of the public school curriculum.[52]

Batlle's argument in favor of economic nationalism became bipartisan by the end of the Roaring Twenties. Although prices for cattle on the hoof fell in the latter 1920s, surging demand in Great Britain and the U.S. boycott of Argentine beef allowed the foreign-owned *frigoríficos* to earn huge profits and sell meat at elevated prices in Montevideo. The Rural Association, a bastion of the Nationalist party, suggested that a combination of private investment and government financing could finance Uruguay's own meat-packing plant. Thus, in 1928 the government opened the public-private enterprise known as the *Frigorífico Nacional*, which offered investors profits and consumers high-quality beef at modest prices because it enjoyed a monopoly of meat sales in Montevideo. The *Frigorífico* Nacional proved to be one of the Batlle era's most popular state-owned corporations. By the 1950s, it drove Swift and Armour out of the marketplace and remained profitable until privatized in 1978.[53]

U.S. financial and industrial interests played a crucial role in Uruguay's material progress between 1925 and 1928. The National City Bank of New York established a branch in Montevideo. Its loans led to the "Dance of the Millions," the flurry of spending that spurred new public works' construction in Montevideo, Salto, and Paysandú. Ford Motor Company and General Motors each built assembly plants that offered consumers different models as well as favorable prices because tariffs did not apply. Contractors completed the construction of the Legislative Palace as well as the Palacio Salvo. In addition, U.S. loans allowed the government to expand the highway system from 190 miles in 1923 to 530 miles by 1928 and provided a less expensive means of transport of goods than the British railroads.[54]

The Roaring Twenties temporarily returned Uruguay to prosperity. The export boom in chilled beef and wool lasted from 1924 to 1929. By 1929, however, the foreign debt had grown, and Uruguay's trade balance turned negative. Limited local capital prevented the government from realizing Batlle's dream of nationalizing the British-owned railroads. Even more serious storm clouds soon darkened the horizon.[55]

CONCLUSION

The efforts of Uruguay's most consequential president, José Batlle y Ordóñez, and his Colorado colleagues transformed the nation into Latin America's most progressive state. Building upon the late nineteenth-century foundation, Batlle improved an already prosperous economy that expanded the middle class and redistributed wealth in an egalitarian manner. Politically skillful, Batlle and his broadly based political

Figure 5.6 The Palacio Salvo: Latin America's Tallest Skyscraper in 1928. For several years after its completion in 1928, the Palacio Salvo remained the tallest skyscraper in Latin America. Built on the site of the Confiteria La Giraldo, where the famous tango "La Comparsita" was first performed in 1917, the Palace symbolized Montevideo's prosperity as immigrants flooded into the city and the economy flourished. The Salvi family, Italian immigrants themselves, opened a modest workshop sewing clothing, which blossomed into a major manufacturing operation in the early twentieth century. They used part of their fortune to build the Palacio Salvo as a real estate investment that rented fashionable apartments. Source: Author photo.

party created a fully participatory democracy that enacted progressive legislation for workers and provided a social safety net for the most defenseless members of society. By founding state-owned corporations, Batlle reduced the influence of British capital and generated profits for the treasury, enabling the state to deliver services to consumers at a lower cost. By 1931, with the exception of Argentina, Uruguay enjoyed the highest literacy rate, the largest middle class, and the highest per capita income in Latin America. Even the *colegiado* system had certain advantages; it forced Colorados and Nationalists to compromise, and accept co-participation in government and share patronage. Labor and welfare reforms moderated once radical workers into batllistas negotiating bread-and-butter issues. By the time of his death, Batlle had convinced the vast majority of Uruguayans to identify with the state's ideals: democracy, economic nationalism, and justice for the oppressed. Uruguayans rightfully could claim, "Like Uruguay: there is no other." Whether that reputation could survive the tumult brought on by the Great Depression will be explored in chapter 6.

NOTES

1. Barrán and Nahum, *Batlle, los estancieros, y el imperio británico*, 8. Vols., Montevideo: Ediciones de la Banda Oriental, 1979–1987, esp. volume 4, *Las primeras reformas, 1911–1913*; see 10–12. The idea of the "shield of the weak" is explored in Christine Ehrick, *The Shield of the Weak: Feminism and the State in Uruguay, 1903-1933*, Albuquerque: University of New Mexico Press, 2005, 2, 71–74; Milton Vanger, *The Model Country: José Batlle y Ordóñez of Uruguay, 1907–1915*, Hanover, NH: University Press of New England, 1980, concludes the first volume of three by arguing "Batlle created his times," 274. Pioneering Latin Americanist Percy Alvin Martin opined much the same thing in his early article, "The Career of José Batlle y Ordonez," *Hispanic American Historical Review*, Vol. 10, No. 4 (November 1930), 413–28. The quote is from Simon C. Hanson, *Utopia in Uruguay: Chapters in the Economic History of Uruguay*, New York: Oxford University Press, 1938, v; and Russell H. Fitzgibbon, *Uruguay: Portrait of a Democracy*, New Brunswick: Rutgers University Press, 1954, 92–136. An excellent recent dissertation by Lars Edward Peterson, "In the Shadow of Batlle: Workers, State Officials, and the Creation of the Welfare State in Uruguay, 1900–1916, unpublished PhD dissertation, University of Pittsburgh, 2014, downplays Batlle's individual role and argues that he and his Colorado colleagues created a safety net to mitigate social tensions.

2. Vanger, *Batlle*, 20–26.

3. Vanger, *Batlle*, 25–69.

4. Vanger, *Batlle*, 75–106. Hanson, *Utopia*, 20; Oddone, "Uruguay, 1870–1930," 405.

5. Vanger, *Batlle*, 110–46; John Chasteen, *Heroes on Horseback: A Life and Times of the Last Gaucho Caudillo*, Albuquerque: University of New Mexico Press, 1995, 172–74.

6. Vanger. *Batlle*, 143–66. Chasteen, *Heroes on Horseback*, 174–79.

7. Vanger, *Batlle*, 171–86, 218; M. H. J. Finch, *A Political Economy of Uruguay since 1870*, New York: St. Martin's Press, 1981, p. 13.

8. Hanson, *Utopia*, 215–25; Finch, *Political Economy*, 123–25, 135–37; Oddone, "Uruguay, 1870–1930," 472–73. For U.S. industrial expansion to Uruguay, see Dudley M. Phelps, *Migration of Industry to South America*, New York: McGraw Hill Book Co., 1939, 32–5, 44–46; Solari, *Desarrollo social*, 102.

9. Milton Vanger, *Uruguay's José Batlle y Ordóñez, the Determined Visionary, 1915-1917*, Boulder, CO, Lynne Rienner, 2010, 195, 221–22; Hanson, *Utopia*, 235–37; Finch, *Political Economy*, 91–96; Barrán and Nahum, *Batlle*, IV, 119–28, 141–45. Leftist critics argued that Batlle's failure to divide estancias and instead favor the palliative solution of agricultural colonies was an error, see Carlos Real de Azúa, *El Impulso y su freno: Tres decadas de batllismo y las raices de la Crises Uruguaya*, Montevideo: Ediciones de la Banda Oriental, 1964, 18–19, 50–52. Julio Martínez Lamas's classic, *Riqueza y Pobreza del Uruguay: Estudios de las causes que retardan el progreso nacional*, Montevideo: Palacio del Libro, 1930, triggered the debate about tax policy by arguing that high land-based taxes prevented ranchers from fully modernizing and unduly benefited urban industrialists and recipients of urban social programs. The land tax question gave rise to the *Federación Rural*, which became an influential political pressure group in the 1950s. Milton Vanger, *Uruguay's José Batlle y Ordóñez: The Determined Visionary*, Boulder, CO: Lynne Rienner, 2010, 55–57.

10. Hanson, *Utopia*, 24–25, 70–86; Vanger, *Batlle*, 189–94; Anton Rosenthal, "The Arrival of the Electric Street Car and the Conflict over Progress in Early Twentieth Century Montevideo," *Journal of Latin American Studies*, Vol. 27, No. 2 (May, 1995), 319–41.

11. Hanson, *Utopia*, 242–45; Real de Azúa, *Impulso*, 25–26; Vanger, *Model Country*, 197–204.

12. Vanger, *Model Country*, 190–93, 221–46; Vanger, *Model Country*, 16; Faracone, *Vivimos*, 32–33. For Model Country's impact on the Second Hague Conference, see Uruguayan Institute of International Law, *Uruguay and the United Nations*, Westport, CT: Greenwood Press, 1974, 1–3; Ehrick, *Shield*, 71, 110–11.

13. Mark J. Van Aken, "University Reform before Córdoba," *Hispanic American Historical Review*, Vol. 52, No. 3 (August 1971), 447–62.

14. Vanger, *Model Country*, 68–98.

15. Hanson, *Utopia*, 19–25. Martin, "Batlle," 426; Vanger, *Model Country*, 207–8; Barrán and Nahum, *Model Country*, IV, 18–19; Oddone, "Uruguay, 1970–1930," 469–70; Fernando López-Alves, *State Formation and Democracy in Latin America*, Durham: Duke University Press, 2000, 62–66. Bill Albert, *South America in the First World War: The Impact of the War on Brazil, Argentina, Peru and Chile*, Cambridge: Cambridge University Press, 1988, 67–70; 120–21; 232–35. Although Albert's book does not consider Uruguay specifically, his section on Argentina provides likely parallels. His in-depth research provides the most through explanation of the effects of World War I on Latin America's economies.

16. Hanson, *Utopia*, 40–55, 99–106; Finch, *Political Economy*, 192–95, 207–15; Barrán and Nahum, *Model Country*, IV, 21–23, 29–30, 33–36, 41.

17. Hanson, *Utopia*, 26–37, 71–85; Barrán and Nahum, *Model Country*, IV, 23–26, 38–41; Vanger, *Model Country*, 141–47, Finch, *Political Economy*, 211–13.

18. Fernández Saldaño, *Diccionario Uruguayo*, entry for Piria, 1017–18. The lawsuit arose because Piría's adopted daughter was actually his mistress.

19. Vanger, *Model Country*, 133–35, 137, 153–57; Hanson, *Utopia*, 232–42; Barrán and Nahum, *Model Country*, IV, 47–51.

20. Wythe, *Industry*, 122–24; Finch, *Political Economy*, 153–58, 162–70; Albert, *World War I*, 228–32.

21. Hanson, *Utopia*, 56–62; Finch, *Political Economy*, 195–202. Vanger, *Model Country*, 138–39, 156–57; José P. Barrán and Benjamin Nahum, *Historia rural del Uruguay moderno*, 7 Vols., Montevideo: Ediciones de la Banda Oriental, 1967–1978, 663–65. Hanson, *Utopia*, 215–22, 86–93, 200–207, 240–41. Although Uruguayans complained endlessly about British corporate exploitation, the economist who studied this question most assiduously makes the case that British capitalists earned a reasonable 4 percent profit, see Hanson, *Utopia*, 207.

22. El Anglo, *Museo de la Revolución Industrial*, Fray Bentos, Uruguay.

23. Vanger, *Model Country*, 300, 341, 307; Vanger, *Visionary*, 55–57.

24. Alan Wells, *Latin America's Democratic Crusade: The Transnational Struggle against Dictatorship, 1920s–1960s*, New Haven: Yale University Press, 2023, 8–11, 45–56. Wells's excellent work only touches briefly on the Uruguayan experience, perhaps because it predated the period he studied, Vanger, *Visionary*, 47–49; Camilla Zeballos, "La extención del sufragio en el Uruguay de 1915: Una coyuntura pactada," *Revista Uruguaya de Ciencia Política*," Vol. 24, No. 1, 133–51.

25. Faraone, *Vivimos*, 50–52.

26. Vanger, *Model Country*, 122–29. Hanson, *Utopia*, 122–34, Barrán and Nahum, *Model Country*, IV, 147–49. Percy A. Martin and Earl M. Smith, "Labor Legislation in Uruguay," *Monthly Labor Review*, Vol. 25, No. 4 (October 1927) 10–17, especially 12–13; Peterson, "Workers, Officials, and the Creation of the Welfare State," 140–67. Peterson points out that a significant strike broke out in 1916 because workers' wages temporarily declined because

they worked fewer hours. Albert, *World War I*, 236–304, demonstrates that the war unleashed massive labor discontent and class conflict in Brazil, Peru, Argentina, and Chile. This was not the case in Uruguay!

27. Hanson, *Utopia*, 28–31, 147–50; Martin and Smith, "Labor Legislation," 10–12; Peterson, "Workers, Officials, and the Creation of the Welfare State," 14–16, 62–63.

28. Camilla Zeballos, "Extención del sufragio," 133–51; López-Alves, *State Formation*, 80; Real de Azúa, *Impulso*, 43–50.

29. Cynthia Jeffress Little, "Moral Reform and Feminism: A Case Study," *Journal of Interamerican Studies and World Affairs*, Vol. 17, No. 4 (November 1975), 386–97, especially 386–89.

30. Vanger, *Model Country*, 201–3; Fitzgibbon, *Portrait of a Democracy*, 128; Barrán and Nahum, *Model Country*, IV, 162–66. See also Real de Azúa, *El impuso y su freno*.

31. Ehrich, *Shield*, 71–81, 150–54.

32. Ehrich, *Shield*, 45, 105–7; Katherine M. Marino, *Feminism for the Americas: The Making of an International Human Rights Movement*, Chapel Hill: University of North Carolina Press, 2019, 13–19. Luisi's sister, Clotilde, also entered the university and became Uruguay's first practicing female attorney and later dean of the Women's University.

33. Ehrich, *Shield*, 82–84, 129–47; Little, "Moral Reform," 387. In addition to the liberal feminists, Catholics, Socialists, and Communists formed feminist organizations. Marino, *Feminism*, 23–39; 49–84. None of the essays in Stephanie Mitchell's edited *Women's Suffrage in the Americas*, Albuquerque: University of New Mexico Press, 2024, discusses the Uruguayan case.

34. James C. Knarr, *Uruguay and the United States, 1903-1929: Diplomacy in the Progressive Era*, Kent: Kent State University Press, 2012, 35–43, 53–54, 71–72.

35. Knarr, *Progressive Era*, 57–62, 106–9; Finch, *Political Economy*, 133–39; Faraone, *Vivimos*, 45–49; Koebel, *Uruguay*, 309.

36. Knarr, *Progressive Era*, 57–60. Albert, *World War I*, 40–41.

37. Knarr, *Progressive Era*, 77–106.

38. David S. Parker, *The Pen, the Sword, and the Law: Dueling and Democracy in Uruguay*, Montreal: McGill-Queens University Press, 2022, especially 116–22.

39. Barrán and Nahum, *Model Country*, IV, 168–85; Goran G. Lindahl, *Uruguay's New Path: A Study in Politics during the First Colegiado, 1919–1933*, Stockholm: Library and Institute of Ibero-American Studies, 1962, p. 189. Russell Fitzgibbon, "Adoption of a Collegiate Executive in Uruguay," *Journal of Politics*, Vol. 14, No. 4 (November 1952), 616–42. Fitzgibbon relates the anecdote at 617. I would contend that Model Country found the solution to a problem that no longer existed.

40. Vanger, *Model Country*, 244–61, 292–93, 331–39; Vanger, *Visionary*, 5–29, 47–52; Faraone, *Vivimos*, 41–42, 53–55, 60–64; Barrán and Nahum, *Model Country*, IV, 174–76; Oddone, "Uruguay, 1870–1930," 467–68.

41. Vanger, *Visionary*, 224–31; Peterson, "Workers, Officials, and the Creation of the Welfare State," 181–83. Ehrich, *Shield*, 83–87, 146–49.

42. Vanger, *Visionary*, 101–42, 255–65; Russell H. Fitzgibbon, *Uruguay: Portrait of a Democracy*, New Brunswick, NJ: Rutgers University Press, 1954, 230–44; Peterson, "Workers, Officials and the Creation of the Welfare State" 9; Lindahl, *Uruguay's New Path*, 34–42; Real de Azúa, *Impulso*, 33–34, also noted that references to God have been eliminated when taking an oath.

43. Martin and Smith, "Labor Legislation," 13.

44. Vanger, *Model Country*, 122–32, 350–51; Alan Knight, *Bandits and Liberals, Rebels and Saints*: Latin American since Independence, Lincoln: University of Nebraska Press, 2022, 21, 63–64; Alexander, *Organized Labor*, 21–27; Hanson, *Utopia*, 136–46.

45. Ehrich, *Shield*, 82–84, 129–47; Little, "Feminism," 387. Telephone operators at a switchboard responded to calls and placed them to the intended recipients. As the use of telephones increased, operators had to oversee an increasing number of lines (often over one hundred), which became unreasonable. Thus, the strikers demanded better wages and that the company hire more operators so that each only oversaw eighty phones.

46. Martin and Smith, "Labor Legislation," 15–16; Hanson; *Utopia*, 164–83; Faraone, *Vivimos*, 64–65; Phelps, *Migration of Industry*, 160, 212–13 states that companies paid 9 percent of payroll to the retirement system while employees contributed 5 percent of salary.

47. E. G. Collado and Simon G. Hanson, "Old Age Pensions in Uruguay," *Hispanic American Historical Review* (May 1936), 173–89. Hanson, *Utopia*, 150–64; Faraone, *Vivimos*, 64–65; Phelps, *Migration of Industry*, 211–13, complained about the negative effects of Uruguayan "socialism" on business.

48. Hanson, *Utopia*, 178–83.

49. Lindahl, *New Path*, 63–104; Farone, *Vivimos*, 54–57.

50. Lindahl, *New Path*, 105–46.

51. Mark J. Van Aken, "The Radicalization of the Uruguayan Student Movement," *The Americas*, Vol. 33, No. 1 (July 1976), 109–29.

52. Little, "Feminism," 394–95.

53. Finch, *Political Economy*, 79–90, 139–41; Knarr, *Progressive Era*, 131–35; Hanson, *Utopia*, 86–93.

54. Knarr, *Progressive Era*, 108–9; Phelps, *Migration of Industry*, 75–77.

55. Oddone, "Uruguay, 1870–1930," 472–75; Finch, *Political Economy*, 89.

Six

There Is Nowhere Like Uruguay, 1930–1955

This chapter focuses on the successes and occasional trials that Uruguay, often referred to as the Switzerland or Sweden of the Americas during these years, faced as it attempted to fulfill José Batlle's progressive legacy. Uruguayans' confident acceptance of their nation's exceptionalism, or as the Uruguayans called it, "*como el Uruguay no hay*"—there is nowhere like Uruguay, seemed merited as the country overcame the challenges of the Great Depression of 1930 and the tyranny of a short-lived dictatorship that threatened the country's democratic heritage. By the late-1930s, the economy had transformed itself from its reliance upon exported pastoral products to a more industrial one based on the principles of Import Substitution Industrialization (ISI). Although the two parties favored different parties in World War II, the majority of Uruguayans ultimately chose the Allies. Democracy resumed even before the war ended. As prosperity continued throughout the Korean conflict, policymakers found themselves in the fortunate position to be able to expand upon Batlle's progressive political, economic, and social programs. By 1955, many Uruguayans assumed that their exceptional nation would continue in its same path forever.[1]

THE GREAT DEPRESSION, 1929–1934

The Wall Street crash of October 24, 1929, known as Black Thursday, caused an economic tsunami that sent shock waves around the globe. As the global economy collapsed, Latin American states, including Uruguay, had to repay their debts to New York and London banks in gold even as tax receipts (mostly generated by export and import taxes) took a significant hit. To make matters worse, prices for most Latin American exports, already in decline by the late 1920s, weakened. As the unforeseen financial retraction caused by the banking crisis made securing new loans impossible, demand and prices for both agricultural products and industrial goods tumbled further. The collapse of international markets led to widespread unemployment, especially in sectors associated with the export trade. While the industrialized nations of Western Europe and the United States experienced the most severe consequences of the Great Depression, the collapse of world markets also affected Latin America.

In response to the Depression, Western Europe and the United States reacted with policies aimed at self-protection. According to classical liberal economic theory, a significant economic downturn required increasing tariffs to defend national industries from imports, coupled with reduced government spending to balance the budget. These measures, however, proved counterproductive in the globalized economies of the early 1930s. For Uruguay, Great Britain's decision to create an imperial preference tariff system that favored Commonwealth members (like Australia, Canada, and New Zealand) at the expense of nations like Argentina and Uruguay that supplied the identical products: wool, frozen and chilled beef, and mutton, proved nearly fatal.

Similarly, the United States' extraordinarily high Smoot-Hawley Tariff of 1930, increasing duties on imported agricultural products to 60 percent in an effort to protect U.S. farmers and ranchers had the same effect. By the end of 1932, the low point of the Depression in Uruguay, prices for its pastoral exports had dropped dramatically, down 58 percent from 1930. As a result, Uruguay's $25 million trade surplus in 1924 had reversed itself by 1931 and had become a trade deficit of almost $36 million. The nation's federal budget deficit for 1932 rose to 18 million pesos. The peso continued to lose value. By 1931, Uruguay owed its creditors almost $100 million. Further, creditors still expected to be paid in gold. As gold reserves dwindled, many nations abandoned the gold standard as did Uruguay.[2]

Despite Batlle's policy of economic nationalism designed to replace foreign-owned corporations and services with state-owned industries, British investors still possessed many of Uruguay's services: Montevideo's waterworks, its trolley system, and the railroads; while U.S. firms owned large *frigoríficos* (Swift and Armour), the cement factory (Portland), oil refineries, and auto assembly plants. British investments totaled $220 million; U.S. capitalists held assets valued at around $88 million, while French investors held property worth another $35 million. Whereas in the nineteenth century Uruguayans had owned the nation's assets (cattle, sheep, land, as well as the "industrial" saladeros), by the 1920s, foreigners owned a much larger share of Uruguay's wealth producing enterprises.[3]

To improve its balance of payments and further reduce its imports of U.S. manufactured goods, Uruguay raised taxes on the purchase of automobiles and other luxuries (sumptuary goods) beyond the reach of almost everybody, and increased tariffs on other imports. The tariff law excluded duties on machinery used in the country's own light industry facilities and on businesses that made products like cement and refined petroleum. Despite tariff reform, Uruguay partially defaulted on its debt in 1932, but by continuing to make interest payments, retained its decent credit rating.

To combat joblessness, the government restricted immigration, historically a source of productive labor and an engine of economic growth, to individuals who had sufficient funds to provide for themselves and their families for a year. Nevertheless, Black laborers who performed manual labor on the docks, in construction, factories, workshops, *frigoríficos*, and in low-level government jobs, found poverty at their doorstep. By lessening the number of foreigners, the government hoped that the thousands of former gaucho ranch hands and Blacks from Artigas and Rivera departments who had migrated to Montevideo and interior cities would find work. The 1932 act also prevented the entry of "undesirables," which included "the sick, vagrants, rogues, drug addicts, drunks, gypsies, Blacks, and Asians." (The president rescinded the law two years later.) The government attempted to balance the national budget by halting public works projects and slashing ordinary expenditures by 20 percent.[4]

Amid concerns about the declining economic situation, Uruguayans voted for change in the hotly contested election of 1930, the first following Batlle's death. Colorado candidate Gabriel Terra, Batlle's rival and businessman, won the 1931 to 1935 presidential term. Terra and Batlle had feuded over the years. Terra had voted against Batlle in 1910, and the rabidly anti-clerical Batlle (who could be petty) had criticized Terra for serving as a witness at his daughter's church wedding ceremony. As early as 1923, Terra broke with Batlle, publicly stating that he believed that colegiado system would not work; nevertheless, once he took office in 1931, he shared executive powers with the National Council of Administration as the Constitution of 1918 required. The following year the assembly passed the enabling legislation for women's suffrage. Their participation in a presidential election would be delayed until 1937 because of the events discussed in the next section.[5]

Terra's Colorado opponents joined a majority of Blancos in a legislative compromise soon nicknamed the Pork Barrel Pact (the Pact of Chinchulín). The batllista Colorados hoped that the creation of a new government enterprise would stimulate economic recovery and offer new jobs. By 1932, over thirty thousand Uruguayan workers found themselves unemployed. The Pact expanded Uruguay's experiment with ISI (import substitution industrialization) by creating a new state-owned corporation, ANCAP (The National Administration of Fuel, Alcohol, and Cement), a public–private joint enterprise. Giving the state-owned company monopoly status provided Uruguay with control over three essential industries (petroleum refining, cement manufacture for construction, and alcoholic beverage production) and created significant new employment. ANCAP proved profitable for the government.

Before ANCAP, Uruguay imported all of its refined gasoline from U.S. and British companies. Demand for gasoline, diesel, and kerosene had increased rapidly during the 1920s as the number of automobiles and trucks increased. Nationalists signed on to the Pork Barrel Pact because it offered Blancos proportional patronage opportunities and seats on the boards of all public corporations (a new form of coparticipation). Another significant state-run corporation, the *Administración Nacional de Usinas y Transmisiones Eléctricas* (UTE), expanded its domain by absorbing all of the privately owned telephone companies across the nation. Political bargaining

Figure 6.1 The ANCAP Petroleum Refinery at La Teja. Batlle's economic nationalism envisioned the creation of state-owned enterprises that would capture the domestic market from foreign-owned businesses. ANCAP, founded in 1931, required all petroleum that Uruguay purchased be refined by this state-owned corporation. The refinery at La Teja on the outskirts of Montevideo, pictured in this image, refined the vast majority of the petroleum. While foreign oil companies could market ANCAP-refined oil under their brand name, they could not undersell ANCAP. ANCAP also produced cement and certain alcoholic beverages. *Source*: Columbus Memorial Library.

like this caused a rift between the two factions of the Blancos over the spoils of patronage.[6]

The Depression encouraged some Uruguayans to turn to agriculture. New mechanization-enabled wheat farmers now met the needs of the domestic market, as did truck farmers who continued to produce vegetables and fruits grown on small farms near Montevideo. Farms dedicated to sunflowers and linseed produced vegetable oil for both domestic and export markets. Like the industrialization project, discussed later in this chapter, Uruguay became more self-sufficient by expanding agricultural production during the Depression. Crop diversification remained underdeveloped until the emergence of large-scale rice fields in the eastern part of the country and sugar cane in the northwest later in the century.[7]

In a persuasive essay, historian Alan Knight argued that the Great Depression had four effects on Latin America. First, in most countries it caused political instability. Second, it forced Latin America to reorient its export-driven economy toward a more balanced economy by experimenting with policies that encouraged the expansion of industry. Third, it forced the state to play a greater role regulating foreign-owned assets, expanding already popular economic nationalism. Finally, the Depression gave voice to working class people and forced Latin American governments to provide benefits to assist the urban unemployed. Fortuitously, Batlle's reforms provided Uruguay with an impressive head-start.[8]

THE COUP OF 1933: THE TERRA YEARS AND THE POLITICAL RESPONSE

Despite ANCAP, economic prospects showed no signs of improvement; in fact, by the end of 1932 the economy reached its nadir. The traditional solutions, reducing the budget by 20 percent and halting public works programs, only meant an unacceptable increase in unemployment. Deficits increased while the mortgage bank and pension system faced bankruptcy. The government could not afford to expand assistance programs for Uruguayans unable to provide for themselves. Exporters and ranchers, accustomed to high incomes, mourned the loss of the prosperity of the 1920s. Workers faced the rising cost of living even as their real wages fell. Almost everybody demanded change.[9]

Because traditional solutions had failed, both Luis Alberto de Herrera and President Terra blamed the *colegiado* system for the government's inertia. While Terra and his allies complained, Herrera threatened a march of his followers from eastern Uruguay to Montevideo modeled after Benito Mussolini's March on Rome that enabled him to seize power in 1923. Herrera hoped his march would gin up support for a new constitution.

President Terra had proposed a number of reforms to the colegiado but could not muster the required two-thirds majority in the legislature for any change. Fist fights broke out in the legislature. As one politician quipped, even securing the appointment of a new janitor resulted in a political battle in the National Council of Administration. The country's budget remained unbalanced, moving in the wrong direction. The loss of the British market for beef stung and that market would not be restored until 1935. As unemployment numbers increased to perhaps as many as forty thousand people, workers, notably from the frigoríficos in El Cerro, took to the streets. For the first time, significant numbers of Uruguayans lost faith in Batlle's system.[10]

Across the globe, the unprecedented trauma of the Great Depression caused people to question the efficacy of democratic governments. The Depression created political instability in almost all Latin American nations, as all but two (Colombia and Mexico) saw violent regime change in the early 1930s.

In January 1933, President Terra secretly met with Blanco leader Herrera to discuss the situation, and followed the meeting with a fiery speech in Rocha demanding a plebiscite on the constitution. Over the next two months he repositioned army commanders around the country to ensure their loyalty. On March 31, he executed an *auto-golpe* (a coup against his own government) calling for a new constitution that would abolish the *colegiado* and strengthen the hand of the chief executive. As Terra said to justify this measure, "It is the only road to assure the reform program of the revolution." Using the police, he dissolved the National Assembly and arrested the members of the National Council. A nine-person governing junta replaced the Assembly to provide him with legal advice and perform legislative functions. The coup formally realigned Terra's minority Colorado *lema* with Herrera's Nationalist faction against the remaining Colorados and Nationalists.[11]

Herrera, no stranger to political violence, had begun his career as a volunteer in both of Aparicio Saravia's revolts. Now a rancher with a prominent and wealthy wife, he remained the Nationalists' most influential politician and editor of the conservative newspaper *El Debate*. He ran unsuccessfully for president on numerous occasions but served in the legislature and on the National Council. Because of incidents like his surprising cross-party alliance with Terra, Herrera gained a reputation as a tactician rather than a man of principle. During the 1930s, both Terra and Herrera found much to admire in fascists' ideas. As the first Uruguayan politician to campaign from the rear of a railroad train and speak in front of mass gatherings, Herrera cultivated a populist image and dominated the Nationalists until his death in 1959.[12]

Terra appointed a constitutional assembly to rewrite the nation's foundational document. Bankers, foreign investors, and ranchers applauded the coup and the reforms of the Constitution of 1934 that restored the presidential system and reduced cabinet members to an advisory role. Under the terms of the constitution, Terra and Herrera's lemas each chose half of the senators and appointed 50 percent of the boards of directors of the Uruguayan state-owned corporations. The co-participation system of the Pork Barrel Pact that divided the spoils between the two parties now meant the division of patronage between Terra's Colorado lema and Herrera's Blanco lema to the exclusion of all others. As a favor to Herrera and the estancieros, the president reduced real estate and inheritance taxes. The new constitution also allowed a president to succeed himself in office, thereby permitting Terra's reelection in 1934.[13]

Terra's *auto-golpe* met with modest public opposition initially. Most dramatically, former president Baltasar Brum shot himself in front of a crowd of spectators after receiving the news about Terra's coup. University professors and students intermittently spoke out against the dictatorship as the government tamped down on the press. Short-lived coup attempts as well as an unsuccessful assassination attested to Terra's growing unpopularity by the following year. Parties on the left considered forming a "Popular Front" opposition (a coalition of Communists, Socialists, and more moderate reformers) as Chile had done. The next generation of the Batlle family and other politicians went into exile. Although by 1938 opposition had intensified, contemporaries still referred to Terra's administration as a "*dictablanda*" (a moderate regime) in comparison to other authoritarian governments of the 1930s. Political parties continued to operate, and growing numbers of citizens voiced their opposition to Terra and Herrera's admiration of the fascist regimes in Europe. (Terra had been Uruguay's minister to Rome and knew Mussolini.) *Estación Femenina* offered its usual menu of programs, including interviews with Paulina Luisi, a regime critic.[14]

Abandoning her stance as a pacifist favoring disarmament pacts in the 1920s, Luisi recognized Italy and Germany's authoritarianism and militarism as an

Figure 6.2 Torres-García's School with the Maestro. Torres-García was the founder of the School of the South. He argued that the art from the Southern Hemisphere deserved more attention. In addition, he became involved with the ideas of Universal Constructionism that were derived from the influence of Soviet art. *Source*: Museo-José Gurvich, Montevideo.

existential threat and helped to found the World Committee of Women against War and Fascism. She viewed Terra as a junior partner of his European colleagues, and after a brief trip to Europe, returned to participate in the struggle against his dictatorship. Italy's invasion of Ethiopia in 1935 aroused working class and university student protests in Montevideo, and women invaded the Assembly to read a petition denouncing the invasion. The Black-owned newspaper "*Nuestra Raza*" urged Black Uruguayans to take a stand against the Ethiopian invasion, while Federation of Uruguayan University Students (FEUU) compared Terra to Hitler. Despite the growing opposition, Terra retained sufficient influence to arrange for his brother-in law, General Alfredo Baldomir, an engineer and former police chief of Montevideo, to succeed him for the 1938–1942 presidential term.[15]

BOX 6.1: THE MODERNIST MOVEMENT

Artist Joaquín Torres-García, poet Juana de Ibarbourou, and architect Eladio Dieste each gained international reputations during the 1940s and 1950s as leaders of Latin America's modernist movement. Torres-García became one of the foremost Latin American participants in the Soviet-inspired Abstract

Constructivist school. He founded a studio, the Taller Torres-García, where he mentored a generation of artists in the "School of the South." He and his followers argued that artists in the Global South deserved recognition for their unique contributions to art, which he demonstrated in one of his best-known works that portrayed the Western Hemisphere upside down, minimizing the influence of the Global North. Poet Juana de Ibarbourou (1895–1979), first recognized for her work by Juan Zorrilla de San Martín, gained international recognition because of her sentimental lyrical feminist poems and stories filled with imagination and fantasy. Her favorite work, *Chico Carlo* (1944). consisted of seventeen short stories about her mother and her childhood in the city of Melo. An early feminist, she was nominated four times for the Nobel Prize in Literature. Eladio Dieste, trained as an engineer but best known as an architect influenced by Torres-García's ideas, designed and built structures like the Church of Christ the Worker (1957–1959) in Atlántida, recently named a UNESCO World Heritage site because of its unique construction. Its brick vaults support a thin roof made from tile, steel, and small amounts of cement that allows natural light to illuminate the sanctuary. With its sparsely furnished interior, the church bespeaks spirituality rather than grandeur.[16]

WORLD WAR II AND THE RETURN TO DEMOCRACY, 1938–1946

In 1938 Colorado General Alfredo Baldomir ascended to the presidency in the first national election in which women participated. Following his inaugural speech pledging a return to democracy, the moderate Baldomir publicly stated that he "favored a new Constitution and electoral laws," much to the dismay of Herrera and his Nationalists. In June, a crowd of two hundred thousand people gathered in front of Government House in the Plaza de Independencia and demanded just that. Three factors—the improving economy; the populace's overwhelming preference for the Allies; and the revulsion against the patently unfair provisions of the Constitution of 1934—began to open the political process. The provision that divided Senate seats equally between Colorados and Blancos especially rankled as the Colorados had earned twice as many votes as the Blancos in the election of 1937. But until Baldomir could reduce the Nationalist influence in the government, nothing would happen.[17]

As World War II approached, Herrera and his Nationalist followers openly espoused the cause of the fascist governments in Germany, Italy, and Spain. Herrera argued that the United States, because of past imperialistic behavior, presented a greater danger to Latin America than did Nazi Germany. Because of his influence, Uruguay remained officially neutral during the early years of World War II. Meanwhile, U.S. president Franklin D. Roosevelt unveiled his "Good Neighbor Policy," forgoing further interventions south of the Río Grande. Wooing the Latin American states took time and persistent efforts, beginning with FDR's initial good will tour in 1936, which included a stop in Uruguay.

But the United States' concrete proposals by the end of the decade, such as new lines of credit and opening commercial opportunities, caused sentiment in Latin America to shift toward the Allies, except in Argentina and Chile. When the United States approached Uruguay about building an airbase in 1940, despite Herrera's opposition, Baldomir, granted the United States the right to construct an "airport" at Laguna del Sauce. In addition, the government began jailing suspected German agents. The government revoked Radio Femenina's operating license briefly because one of its owners associated with a pro-Nazi organization. As the movement for a return to democracy strengthened, Baldomir dismissed three of Herrera's adherents from the cabinet in 1941, endng the Nationalists' influence. The following year Baldomir and the Colorados broke relations with the Axis powers and fully embraced the Allied cause. As a result, Uruguay's military would receive almost $8 million worth of equipment for the army, navy, and air force by war's end as part of a "Lend-Lease" program. Uruguay declared war on Germany and Japan in February 1945, although the Nationalists continued to oppose these steps.[18]

BOX 6.2: THE *GRAF SPEE* INCIDENT

The battle of the Río de la Plata in December,1939 caused many Uruguayans to reconsider their neutrality. A German pocket battleship, the *Graf Spee*, had sunk nine British merchantmen in the South Atlantic, but Captain Hans Langsdorff humanely rescued each sailor and returned him to shore. The British determined to stop this threat to trade. After a short battle, miles out in the Atlantic, in which three smaller British vessels damaged the *Graf Spee*, it took refuge in Montevideo's harbor. Captain Langsdorff asked local authorities if he could make repairs to his ship. After secretly consulting with the British Consul, the Baldomir government delayed action on Langsdorff's request and spread rumors of an approaching British fleet. Relying on international law that limited the time a vessel could remain in a neutral harbor, the Uruguayans refused to grant further refuge to the German vessel. Despite orders from Hitler to leave the harbor and fight to the last sailor, Langsdorff refused and helped his crew to take refuge in either Argentina or Uruguay. The ones who chose Uruguay were interred until the end of the war. He and a few sailors then scuttled the ship just outside the channel leading into the harbor. Langsdorff returned to the shore with these men, but shortly thereafter wrapped himself in the old imperial German flag (he was not a Nazi) and committed suicide in his hotel room.[19]

Despite the opposition of the Nationalists, Baldomir engineered what Uruguayans referred to as "the good *golpe*" of February 21, 1942, because it replaced the

Figure 6.3 The Scuttling of the *Graf Spee*. The Battle of the Atlantic eventually convinced Uruguay's Colorado leadership to join the Allied cause. Photographs of the scuttled *Graf Spee* demonstrate that Captain Ludendorff had no desire to harm Uruguayan shipping, as he carefully maneuvered the ship outside the harbor, planted charges, and blew up the ship. Captain Langsdorff and his crew who blew up the ship returned to Montevideo after which the Uruguayan government held the *Graf Spee* crew prisoners in the garrison of Sarandí de Yí for the duration of the war. The ship's sinking took considerable time. Citizens of Montevideo could watch the ship burn from their balconies in the Old City. *Source*: Museo Regional Mazzoni, Maldonado.

convoluted undemocratic form of government established by Terra's "bad *golpe*" of 1934. Baldomir's newly appointed Council of State made up of batllistas and members from minority parties drafted a new constitution that restored the system of proportional representation in the Senate; permitted the president to select his cabinet with the Assembly's confirmation; and allowed minority representation on the boards of state corporations. In November, Baldomir submitted the proposed Constitution of 1942 to a plebiscite that received approval by 77 percent of the electorate. In essence the reform displaced Herrera's influential ranchers and increased the political role of urban industrialists during Colorado president Juan José de Amézaga's term (1943–1947). Commentators compared Baldomir's actions to those of Máximo Tajes in 1887. Baldomir's good coup was part of the wave of democratization that swept Latin America as World War II swung in favor of the Allies.[20]

Amézaga, a politically progressive professor of constitutional law and a longtime battlista, presided over the final years of World War II. His administration dedicated itself to making restitution to those who suffered economic losses in the Terra years, the furtherance of wartime industrial and pastoral prosperity, and the expansion of labor's rights. As Uruguay's treasury became flush once again, Amézaga spent money to underwrite large public works projects, such as roads, Montevideo's airport, and the Rincón de Bonete dam at Paso de los Toros on the Río Negro to generate hydroelectric power. Wages and conditions improved for employees. Perhaps as a consequence of feminist influence at the San Francisco Convention that created the United Nations and declared the equality of men and women, the Assembly passed a statute providing women with the same legal rights as men.[21]

ECONOMIC RECOVERY AND INDUSTRIAL EXPANSION, 1935–1945

The circumstances surrounding the Great Depression and World War II allowed Uruguay to transition from a system based on the export of pastoral products to a more balanced economy with a significant manufacturing base. Nevertheless, exports of Uruguay's pastoral products remained vital. The nation desperately hoped to make an arrangement with Great Britain akin to Argentina's Roca-Runciman Treaty of 1933 that guaranteed Argentine agriculture and meat access to the British market at the same tariff rates granted to Commonwealth members. Uruguay finally secured an identical arrangement in 1935. During World War II, Uruguay extended credit to Great Britain for its purchases of beef, resulting in a huge cash surplus in Uruguay's favor by 1945. The United States reduced tariffs on Uruguayan products as part of FDR's goal of improving hemispheric relations, which opened U.S. markets to large quantities of Uruguayan wool.[22]

While the increasing British and U.S. demand for pastoral products allowed Uruguay's beef and wool industries to revive, the Depression and World War II created a shortage of imported goods to satisfy domestic consumers' needs. Argentine economist Raúl Prebisch theorized that these aforementioned external shocks offered Latin America the opportunity to develop state-directed, inward-looking industrial expansion, soon dubbed as import substitution industrialization, or ISI. In the case of Uruguay, Prebisch's argument proved accurate. By 1936, 4,310 more businesses operated than had been the case when the Depression began. The impetus toward further industrialization increased during the 1940s.

Uruguay had first encouraged industry with protective tariffs in 1875, 1886, and 1888. By the 1920s, tariffs protected numerous Uruguayan light industrial products destined for household use, mostly of which were manufactured in workshops and small factories. Terra and Baldomir offered tax credits and subsidies to further incentivize industrialists. Law 10,000 of 1941 created the Comptroller of Imports and Exports, a bureaucracy designed to prohibit the entry of competing foreign manufactured goods, furthering the artificial advantages of domestic industry and strengthening the state's control over the economy. Industrial products, such as woolen textiles, beverages, matches, paper products, soap, and furniture utilized raw materials found within Uruguay. Entrepreneurs imported tax-free the machinery necessary to produce these items. Already the third most industrialized nation in Latin America after Argentina and Mexico, the war years only strengthened that position.[23]

Economic self-sufficiency made additional strides forward because of Batlle's state-owned monopolies such as UTE, ANCAP, and the Institute of Industrial Chemistry. ANCAP operated differently from Uruguay's other state-owned corporations. It purchased crude oil from international petroleum companies like Shell, Exxon, and Atlantic and refined it at its La Teja refinery. But the foreign companies extracted an additional price for supplying the crude. They marketed some of the gasoline ANCAP refined under their own brands. ANCAP was prohibited from selling its gasoline at a lower price. Nevertheless, ANCAP's existence proved both vital and profitable because petroleum soon replaced coal as the nation's primary energy source.

During the war years, middle-class and elite Uruguayans regained confidence in the economy and deposited their capital in local banks or invested in new enterprises. As a result, foreign capital played little role in the new wave of industrialization. Three-quarters of the raw materials necessary for industry came from within the country. Further, the middle class and working class had sufficient income to purchase higher-end consumer goods. Its well-educated labor force proved eager to take these highly paid manufacturing jobs, and its transportation system of roads and railroads moved goods efficiently around the country. These factors allowed Uruguayan entrepreneurs in the late 1940s to advance to the next stage of industrialization, producing durable goods, such as refrigerators, mix-masters, vacuum cleaners, electrical appliances of all sorts, gas stoves, and radios. Those who owned ISI businesses grew wealthy.[24]

Lacking any petroleum or coal, Uruguay pioneered its alternative energy program after the war ended. In 1937 UTE had partnered with a German firm to design a dam on the Río Negro at Paso de los Toros. World War II forced the Germans to withdraw from the project, which the United States helped to complete. The resulting Rincón de Bonete dam supplied much of the domestic energy needs for decades. As energy consumption expanded, the government built additional hydroelectric plants at Rincón de Baygorria (also on the Río Negro) and at the Salto Grande's rapids (a joint project with Argentina). Uruguay did import necessary raw materials from its neighbors to manufacture new products. The Fábrica Uruguaya de Neumáticos, S.A. (Funsa) produced tires, inner tubes, and garden hoses from rubber imported from Brazil. Local entrepreneurs built two textile mills employing

Figure 6.4 Punta del Este, Uruguay's Premier Beach Resort. After ocean bathing became fashionable in the late nineteenth century, Argentine tourists and locals flocked to beaches in Montevideo's suburbs and, later, further east. After World War II, the United States helped to fund the construction of new hotels and casinos in the then remote town of Punta del Este. By the 1960s, jet-setters and celebrities from all over the world vacationed in exclusive apartments and, later, condominiums in the city as they still do today. Tourism remains an important revenue generator for the nation. Courtesy: Columbus Memorial Library.

roughly six thousand workers who fashioned Paraguayan cotton into inexpensive summer-weight clothing. The nation also imported tobacco, metal products, and some chemicals for industrial usage.[25]

Industry manufactured tools, radiators, pipes, and electric appliances out of scrap. Beverages, both soft drinks and wine, became important industries. The Paso de los Toros soft-drink company founded in 1929 produced a variety of fruit-flavored beverages. PepsiCo purchased the plant in 1951 and eliminated the local fruit flavors in favor of ones similar to U.S. products. (Grapefruit is still available.) Numerous small wineries dotted the countryside, some dating back to the nineteenth century. Uruguayans favored red wine made from Tannat grapes although most wineries produce both red and white varieties. Like Paso de los Toros beverages, these wines satisfied domestic demand.[26]

To sustain industry and the domestic market, entrepreneurs and policymakers argued that wages needed to be increased so that people could consume the products that Uruguayan factories manufactured. Thus, business prevailed upon the Baldomir and Amézaga governments to increase the size of the state's workforce. Industrial employees increased from roughly 54,000 in 1930 to 106,000 by the end of World

War II, and by another 60,000 by 1955. New legislation protected workers from wrongful termination; and even if management won the case, discharged employees received a pension. All public employees became eligible for retirement benefits. A Wage Coucil System, created in 1943, mediated the fairness of salaries. For the poorest urban dwellers who earned less than 200 pesos a month, the government enacted the Family Allowance Program, granting subsidies for children under the age of fourteen and up to eighteen if they continued their education. Rural workers shared the improvement in their standard of living. Both parties endorsed the relationship between business and labor that provided workers/consumers with good wages, hoping that high wages would compensate for the small size of Uruguay's domestic market. Future possibilities seemed endless for most Uruguayans as they possessed the most progressive welfare state in Latin America.[27]

After the racist fascist rhetoric of the 1930s and 1940s, post–World War II European and U.S. Blacks focused attention on the "New Negro," demanding greater opportunities. Although Uruguay's nineteenth-century censuses showed the Black population to be less than 1 percent, resulting in its reputation as South America's "white nation," equality for all citizens did not exist. The case of Adelia Silva de Sosa, a Black scholarship winner from Artigas temporarily denied her teaching position in Montevideo because of her skin color and accent, heightened public awareness of the disadvantages Black Uruguayans faced. Free public education seemingly offered opportunity to all, but families still had to purchase the obligatory school uniform as well as supplies, which poor families could not afford. As a result, of those Black students who attended school at all, many dropped out after the third grade to help with family finances, which deprived them of any future employment other than manual labor. Even Blacks who graduated from the university found few professional openings. For the remainder of the century, Black Uruguayans fought to change this situation.[28]

THE POSTWAR TRANSITION AND INTERNATIONAL RELATIONS

The successful conclusion of World War II offered its optimistic victors the opportunity to construct a new world order. In 1944 the Allies (the United States, Great Britain, the Soviet Union, and Nationalist China) drafted the Dumbarton Oaks proposal for an international organization designed to prevent future global bloodbaths and invited the world's nations to provide input. The Latin American states met in Mexico City to discuss possible modifications of the document. When the United Nations Conference on International Organization met in San Francisco in April 1945, Uruguay's delegates joined their colleagues and presented their ideas.

Given its troubled nineteenth-century history, Uruguay enthusiastically embraced the principal objective of the UN: to provide collective security to smaller nations against aggression by larger powers. Despite general agreement with the draft proposals, the smaller states hoped (unsuccessfully) that the final agreement would vest more authority in the General Assembly than in the Security Council where the four Allies and liberated France each held veto powers. The San Francisco Conference agreed that regional organizations like the Pan American Union would work in concert with the UN's mission, and that the UN would seek international solutions for worldwide economic, social, and human rights issues. Uruguay's legislature unanimously assented to the final document and thereby became an original member of the UN.[29]

After the war ended, the United States offered Uruguay a $20 million loan from the Import-Export Bank to pave the way for extensive public works at Punta del Este (Uruguay's premier beach resort that attracts thousands of Argentine tourists and celebrities from around the world) and at Piriápolis. Although the original loan certainly benefited the country over the years, it began a new cycle of debt that would have serious consequences in the 1950s. Some Uruguayans wondered whether their government had simply replaced British investors with Americans.[30]

Uruguay's pro-Allied stance during the war had caused friction with Argentina. Over the course of Baldomir's term, the tide had turned against conservative, fascist-leaning governments all around Latin America (except in Argentina). To show their pro-Allied sentiment, Uruguayan movie theaters screened Charlie Chaplin's film "The Great Dictator," a comedic parody of Hitler, banned in Argentina. Despite the Argentine government's threats, numerous Argentines crossed the La Plata to see it. Relations with President Juan Domingo Perón remained frosty until early 1948. Perón reduced wheat exports to Uruguay, forcing its government to subsidize farmers to make up the shortfall. In addition, he refused to allow Argentines to visit Uruguay's beaches, which damaged the tourist industry.

In 1947, however, Eva Perón stopped in Uruguay on her return from her "Rainbow Tour" in Europe. She had a cordial stay in Montevideo with newly inaugurated president Luis Batlle Berres and his Argentine wife. Shortly after, the two presidents met aboard ships in the Uruguay River and shook hands. Perón grudgingly agreed that the middle of the river was the border between the two countries and not the Uruguayan shore as Argentina had always claimed. Because of Perón's populist dictatorship and Batlle Berres's strong advocacy of democracy, the two leaders never became friendly, even though they shared certain policy objectives such as industrialization and better pay and benefits for workers.[31]

LUIS BATLLE BERRES AND THE WELFARE STATE, 1947–1955

Despite the Colorado party's division into two factions, List 14 (the more conservative lema led by César Batlle Pacheco and his brother Lorenzo, the sons of Batlle y Ordóñez) and List 15 (the more liberal faction led by their cousin, Luis Batlle Berres), the combined Colorado *lemas* easily won the 1996 election against the pro-Perón Nationalist candidate Luis Alberto de Herrera. The new president, who represented the rural wing of the Colorado party, pursued agricultural development as his primary goal. He formed the National Institute of Colonization and imported farm machinery so that Uruguay could raise more wheat and reduce its dependency on Argentine grain imports before 1948 when relations between the two countries improved.

More importantly, the president Tomás Berreta pressed Great Britain to pay off its 17 million pound sterling World War II debt, owed for the beef and wool the former had purchased on credit. Cash poor after the war, the British negotiated and signed the Anglo-Uruguayan Agreement of July 15, 1947, paying 10 percent of the sum owed in cash, and relinquishing their interest in the Aguas Corrientes Water Company and its purification plant (which became part of OSE), the trolleys (soon state-owned as the Municipal Transport Board or AMdeT), and the National Railroad (now the AFI, the State Railway Administration). The transfer of British concerns to Uruguayan state ownership pleased economic nationalists who had complained that British citizens monopolized the highest paying jobs in these industries. Both the water company and the railroad, however, needed additional investment to modernize their equipment, an expensive proposition. Shippers had already found that moving their goods by truck rather than rail was cheaper and more efficient, eventually dooming the rail system. Each acquisition of these previously foreign-owned private companies added hundreds of employees to the public payroll. Shortly after the debt settlement, the president died, making Vice President Luis Batlle Berres the new chief executive.[32]

Luis Batlle Berres had a close relationship with his uncle's family, as he and his six siblings lived next door to them as children. At the tender age of twenty-three, Batlle Berres won a seat in the Chamber of Deputies because of his uncle's influence, and shortly thereafter, engaged in the first of three duels he would fight with political opponents over the course of his career. He had been expelled from Uruguay during Terra's dictatorship but regained his seat in the Chamber during the Amézaga presidency. As a stanch supporter of the Allied cause, he looked favorably upon the post–World War II international arrangements for peace and security. At the same time, he boosted his personal profile by founding Radio Ariel where his dynamic speeches soon made him a popular favorite among progressive batllistas. Many writers would describe his presidency as the age of neo-batllismo.[33]

The successful ISI experiment caused both Colorados and Nationalists to envision Uruguay as an industrial nation able to advance its social welfare objectives. Based on the recent past, Batlle Berres and a majority of Colorados agreed that Uruguay's way forward lay in enhancing the power of the state by intervening in the economy, mediating social conflict, expanding public works, and redistributing wealth. The government furthered industrial development by increasing tariff protection and offering other incentives. Additional public employees joined the workforce, both in state-owned corporations and the bureaucracy. Workers consistently received healthy increases. As a result, industrial laborers became de facto partners of the state as most now voted Colorado or Blanco rather than Socialist or Communist. Public sector employees whose numbers rose to roughly 20 percent of the workforce also voted for one of the two traditional parties.

When World War II ended, advanced industrial economies in the United States and Europe resumed producing the capital equipment that Uruguay needed to expand its industrial production. Because of favorable conditions, especially the demand for Uruguayan wool during the Korean War, Uruguay's industrial production exploded, growing at the rate of 8.5 percent per annum in the decade between 1945 and 1955. Policymakers believed that between Uruguayan state-owned companies and privately owned factories and workshops, domestic consumers' demands for basic household commodities and electronics could be satisfied. Batlle Berres also believed that well-paying jobs would boost sales of domestically manufactured goods and improve most Uruguayans' standard of living. He even dreamed that Uruguay's industrial products could be marketed abroad.[34]

Batlle Berres's plans resembled those of post–World War II Western European Social Democrats in which favorable labor and welfare policies minimized class conflict and redistributed wealth. Uruguay's prosperity, he believed, would preserve democracy and fulfill his uncle's promise of providing order and social justice for all. To this end, Batlle Berres increased tariffs, provided subsidies for fledgling manufacturers, and increased workers' wages so that they could consume more Uruguayan made goods. These policies created a larger middle class and offered financial security to workers. Thus, Batlle Berres's program, which enjoyed considerable success from his inauguration until the end of the Korean War in 1953, resulted in the creation of a multi-class political alliance of industrialists, the middle class, and labor, all of whom foresaw a rosy future.[35]

The palpable optimism about Uruguay's future encouraged unusual social experiments. For example, a wealthy Uruguayan purchased thousands of acres in the Valle de Alegría (Valley of Happiness) in Lavalleja department and hired an engineer to divide it into sizable plots, each separated from its neighbor by a gully, a ridge or other natural phenomena. Architect Julio Vilamajó built over one hundred single-family houses made entirely from local materials. He introduced trees and populated the woods with birds and mammals. The resulting town of Villa Serrana became an idyllic rural retreat for retirees or vacationers who wished to take advantage of its calm, quiet natural surroundings. Its remote location, however, lacked electricity and the resort eventually lost favor. In recent years the addition of a dam, a swimming pool, and fine restaurants has revived the appeal of Villa Serrana.

Although most of Uruguay's industrial production utilized its own raw materials, it did need to import some items. For example, it purchased steel, chemicals, cotton, rubber for industrial use, and petroleum for ANCAP to process at its refinery at La Teja. ANCAP became the country's largest public corporation (Uruguayan crushed stone being an important component of cement), supplying the country's concrete needs during Montevideo's postwar construction boom. Machinery sporting the latest technology enabled the profitable expansion of the textile industry, especially in factories that wove Paraguayan cotton into thread and thereafter into inexpensive warm-weather clothing that Uruguayan consumers eagerly purchased. Uruguayan entrepreneurs also unveiled a profitable tire production industry, built several paper mills, and fashioned shoes and other leather products.

By 1955, manufacturing accounted for nearly 25 percent of Uruguay's gross domestic product, the second highest figure in Latin America after Argentina. Despite attempts to expand domestic industrial production further, by the mid-1950s competition from higher quality and less expensive U.S. imports, stalled Batlle Berres's dream of exporting Uruguayan manufactured goods. In 1955, President Eisenhower invited Batlle Berres to come to the United States to discuss trade. He made little headway, however, with his argument that if Uruguay continued to buy U.S. automobiles and factory machinery, it needed more favorable treatment for its beef and wool in U.S. markets. By 1957, both Swift and Armour pulled out of Uruguay, leaving thousands unemployed. While U.S. manufacturers refused to pay top dollar for Uruguay's wool tops (washed wool combed into parallel fibers in a bundle), they also showed little interest in importing Uruguayan knit woolen fabrics. Despite an impassioned speech, Batlle Berres unsuccessfully lobbied for greater access into the U.S. market in part because of a global shift in economic policy well outside of Uruguayan control.[36]

The Bretton Woods agreement of the 1940s that created the World Bank and the International Monetary Fund (IMF) encouraged governments to adopt free trade, eventually undercutting the protectionism necessary for industry to prosper in small nations like Uruguay. Uruguay's small population of about 2.5 million people limited its domestic market. Uruguayan industry relied on high tariffs to conceal its inefficiency and its lack of competitiveness in a free trade environment. As a result, by the mid-1950s some statesmen (but not Batlle Berres) urged Uruguay to rethink its economic strategy.[37]

During the prosperous years the middle class thrived. By 1952, Uruguayans enjoyed the highest per capita income of all Latin Americans. Except for the rural poor, fast abandoning impoverished towns and rural ranches for urban life, the nation's wealth was well distributed. Middle-class Uruguayans enjoyed an excellent standard of living, with urban households possessing all the amenities of modern life. The number of middle-class public employees continued to increase in the 1950s from 57,000 in 1935 to 168,500 in 1955. These numbers reflected the momentary prosperity but also created long-term obligations for the national treasury. Uruguay's economic growth between 1945 and 1955 warranted Batlle Berres and his advisers making the proud and justifiable claim that there was no place like Uruguay.[38]

Not only did the middle class prosper, but the shift from a pastoral to an industrial economy also benefited workers. By the 1950s, roughly one hundred thousand workers had become unionized in various labor federations, often ideologically affiliated in name with Socialists and Communists, but less concerned with controlling the means of production than in bread-and-butter issues like higher wages and improved working conditions. The Wage Councils successfully mediated disputes between workers, employers, and the state to reach satisfactory compromises on wage demands. Because of the success of the Wage Council agreement of 1943, Uruguayan legislators never created a national labor code, a typical occurrence elsewhere in Latin America. During good times like these, the lack of a code, which, for example, permitted employers to fire strikers and hire replacement workers did not matter. As a result, Uruguay's Luis Batlle Berres understandably rejected Argentina's

Juan Perón's populist and corporatist model of subsuming the labor movement (the famous *descamisados*) into the state. Instead, Uruguay's government and its unions had a tacit alliance. Socialist deputy Emilio Frugoni had floated this idea back in 1919 as a means of facilitating compromise between unions and management.[39] Workers' opinions about this arrangement changed after 1955 as economic conditions deteriorated.

During these prosperous years, Batlle Berres's government redistributed government funds to an ever-increasing number of citizens and broadened social benefits. Children could inherit their parent's pension benefits. Social welfare programs expanded in the early 1950s; for example, the government extended social security benefits to workers in all professions in 1954 (previously many agricultural workers, teachers, and police had been excluded). The Batlle Berres government provided women with extended maternity leave, and built new hospitals and schools, especially in rural areas. These new encumbrances, however, placed a heavy burden on the treasury, sustainable only if growth continued.[40]

Figure 6.5 The 1950 World Cup Presentation. This photo depicts FIFA President Jules Rimes giving the World Cup to the president of the Uruguayan Fútbol Association, Raúl Jude. Obdurio Varela, the captain of Uruguay's fútbol team in the 1950 World Cup final, facing a crowd of almost 200,000 frenzied Brazilian fans in the Maracanã Stadium who had just been guaranteed victory by Brazilian President Gertúlio Vargas, the captain told his teammates: "Forget those outside the pitch, each team has the same number of players." To the shock of all Brazil, Uruguay triumphed. Source: Museo del Fútbol, Montevideo.

BOX 6.3: HIGHLIGHT OF THE POSTWAR ERA: THE WORLD CUP VICTORY OF 1950

In 1950, Uruguayans waxed euphoric for several reasons. First, its economic prosperity and future prospects made people optimistic. Second, official ceremonies and parties celebrated the hundredth anniversary of Artigas's death. But nothing matched the national joy that erupted when Uruguay's *fútbol* (soccer) team won the World Cup for the second time. During the 1920s, Uruguay had proven its dominance at the sport by winning successive gold medals at the Olympic Games, and then the first FIFA (*Féderátion Internationale de Football*) World Cup competition in 1930. Uruguay next qualified for a World Cup bid in 1950, which Brazil hosted in its new Maracanã stadium in Río de Janeiro that held two hundred thousand fans. Uruguay's play during the season had been uneven. After demolishing Bolivia in the opening round and struggling through the next two matches, Uruguay's Celeste team faced a heavily favored Brazilian squad in the final match. Brazil's "beautiful game" featured a creative attacking style that gave it an early one-goal lead as the hometown crowd roared its approval, but in the second half, a defensive error allowed Uruguay to tie the score. With eleven minutes remaining, a second such error gave Uruguay the match and the World Cup, registering one of the most shocking upsets in the history of the game.[41]

THE SECOND *COLEGIADO:* JOSÉ BATLLE Y ORDÓÑEZ'S DREAM FULFILLED

In his inaugural speech in 1947, Batlle Berres had laid out his priorities: to work hard; to fight for his beliefs; and to dream about Uruguay's future, which depended upon a strong democracy and a government that would further socioeconomic equality. After implementing his social welfare policies, his poll numbers rose, causing rivals to fear his ambition. Some called him a populist. This new type of politician, personified by Juan Perón in Argentina and Getúlio Vargas in Brazil, had undermined democracy in Latin America by making exorbitant promises to win the votes of the masses, institute authoritarian regimes, and extend their terms in office. Batlle Berres promised not to follow this path, remaining true to Uruguay's democratic tradition.[42]

The election of 1950 resulted in the triumph of Batlle Berres's List 15 candidate Andrés Martínez Trueba. Shortly after his election, Martínez Trueba joined the leaders of List 14 (the Batlle Pacheco brothers) and proposed a referendum to resuscitate José Batlle y Ordóñez's colegiado in its original form. They recruited Nationalist leader Luis Alberto de Herrera, who had won the most presidential votes in 1950, to join them despite his bitter opposition to the original *colegiado*. A pragmatic politician, Herrera recognized the *colegiado* as an opportunity to gain co-participation in the government and to deny Batlle Berres a second presidential term. As a loyal batllista, Luis Batlle Berres felt he could not speak out against the idea. A commission recommended the necessary changes to the Constitution of 1942 and oversaw a plebiscite to approve the new charter. Uruguayans seemed utterly apathetic, as only 20 percent of voters approved it, 17 percent disapproved, and 63 percent failed to vote (the bare minimum to satisfy the requirement for approval).[43]

The Constitution of 1952 abolished the presidency and replaced it with a nine-person *colegiado* called the National Council of Government. Six seats would be proportionally divided between the sub-*lemas* of the majority party and three would belong to the highest vote-getting *lema* of the other party (Herrera's faction). Each year, a different majority member would take on the ceremonial title of president once Martínez Trueba's term ended in 1955. The parties agreed to divide patronage jobs on the boards of the public corporations, with the majority party receiving four seats and the minority three. This system restored the co-participation arrangement. The *colegiado*'s principles altered local government as well: a council in each department replaced the intendant.[44]

SIGNS OF TROUBLE: THE *COLEGIADO* BEGINS ITS TENURE

After the transition to the *colegiado*, Luis Batlle Berres's persuasive influence within the Colorado party assured the continuation of its plan of expanding the industrial sector. Although until 1956 growth rates and per capita incomes remained high, exports fell dramatically. The treasury surpluses accumulated during the Korean War evaporated as expenses for social programs, education, pensions, and unprofitable state-owned enterprises like the railroad mounted. Tariffs remained high in an attempt to exclude United States and European competition from the domestic market. By the mid-1950s, economists began to question the wisdom of the ISI industrial project as Uruguay's balance of payments turned negative when the price of wool fell after the Korean War ended. Meat exports stagnated as estancieros continued to graze cattle on grass instead of feeding them with silage which would have increased productivity. Uruguay learned that its small population of slightly over 2 million could not sustain the industrial base by itself.

In 1948, the United Nations Economic Commission for Latin America (CEPAL) under the leadership of Raúl Prebisch took on the mission of addressing long-term economic development for the region. In the 1950s, CEPAL argued for three solutions to the region's declining terms of trade (the price of exports falling relative to the rising cost of imports, resulting in a reduction of the population's standard of living). First, its experts theorized that Latin America needed to increase international trade rather than restrict it, which meant abandoning protectionism, one of the most sacred precepts of ISI. Second, it argued that the region needed more investment, but Uruguay's small domestic market deterred foreign investors. Finally, CEPAL suggested that a regional market would overcome some of the disadvantages that individual Latin American state economies faced when competing against U.S. and European goods. Unfortunately, none of these ideas came to fruition in the 1950s. By 1956 Uruguay's industrial production slowed as did the country's GDP, and inflation, the cruelest of all taxes because it strikes hardest at the poor, middle class, and pensioners, hovered between 10 percent and 20 percent annually.[45]

CONCLUSION

Difficult economic times bookended the twenty-five years discussed in this chapter. Uruguay weathered the Great Depression comparatively well despite the downturn in traditional exports and took advantage of changing circumstances to shift toward greater self-sufficiency by using protective tariffs, subsidies, and tax benefits to encourage manufacturing. Manufacturing increased after World War II as Uruguay began producing durable goods for household use. The prosperity from the early 1940s through the Korean War allowed the government to redistribute wealth and expand the progressive social welfare model that Batlle Berres's uncle had envisioned. Although a soft dictatorship emerged in the mid-1930s, Uruguay reasserted its democratic traditions during World War II. The diversified economy brought prosperity to industrialists, the middle class, government employees, and laborers. The optimism of the era encouraged both parties to reintroduce the *colegiado*, allegedly a more democratic political system, which restored co-participation in government and on the boards of the state-owned corporations. By 1955, Uruguayans enjoyed the highest per capita income in all of Latin America. But troubling economic signs had already emerged. Uruguay's response to this issue and other emerging problems will be the subject of chapter 7.

NOTES

1. The phrase is attributed to Efraín González Conzi, but the entire country quickly embraced it. It was the title for Hugo Ulive's 1957 film. It is also discussed in Fernando López-Alves, "Why Not Corporatism? Re-democratization and Regime Formation in Uruguay," in David Rock (ed.), *Latin America in the 1940s: War and Post-War Transitions*, Berkeley: University of California Press, 1994, 187–206; in Carlos Real de Azúa's essay, *Impulso*, 9–11, and in David Rock, *1940s*, 3–6.

2. Simon C. Hanson, *Utopia in Uruguay: Chapters in the Economic History of Uruguay*, New York: Oxford University Press, 1938, 248–51; Faraone, *Vivimos*, 73–76; M. H. J. Finch, *A Political Economy of Uruguay since 1870*, New York: St. Martin's Press, 1981, 141–43. Mariscal, *Debt Crises*, 203–9. For an excellent overview of the 1930s in the region, see Paulo Drinot and Alan Knight, *The Great Depression in Latin America*, Durham: Duke University Press, 2014.

3. Hanson, *Utopia*, 207–8, 248–50; Raúl Jacob, *El Uruguay de Terra, 1931–1938: Una crónica del terrismo*, Montevideo: Ediciones de Banda Oriental, 1983, 9–14, 20–21; Griffin, "Causal Factors," 25.

4. Hanson, *Utopia*, 251; Jacob, *Terra*, 13–16, 45. Marischal, *Debt Crises*, 210–13; Philip B. Taylor, "The Uruguayan Coup D'Etat of 1933," *Hispanic American Historical Review*, Vol. 32, No. 3 (August, 1952), 301–20, especially 302–3; Henry Finch, "Uruguay since 1930," in *Cambridge History of Latin America*, Vol. 8, New York: Cambridge University Press, 1991, 197; George Reid Andrews, *Blackness in the White Nation: A History of Afro-Uruguay*, Chapel Hill: University of North Carolina Press, 2010, 38–41, 93.

5. Jacob, *Terra*, 18–20.

6. Goran G. Lindahl, *Uruguay's New Path: A Study in Politics during the First Colegiado*, Stockholm: Library & Institute of Ibero-American Studies, 1962, 108–9, 163–72; Hanson, *Utopia*, 94–106; Jacob, *Terra*, 20–23, 46–51; Finch, "Uruguay since 1930," 198.

7. Finch, *Political Economy*, 64–65, 79–84; Pendle, *Uruguay*, 52.

8. Alan Knight, "The Great Depression in Latin America: An Overview," in Drinot and Knight, *Great Depression*, 276–312, especially, 298–305.

9. Jacob, *Terra*, 49–51; Pendle, *Uruguay*, 34.

10. Lindahl, *New Path*, 212–21; Hanson, *Utopia*, 250–53; Jacob, *Terra*, 29–34, 55–57; Russell H. Fitzgibbon, "Adoption of a Collegiate Executive in Uruguay," *Journal of Politics*, Vol. 14, No. 4 (November 1952), 616–42, at 620.

11. Jacob, *Terra*, 27–33, 55–56; Germán D'Elía, *El Uruguay Neo-Batllista, 1946–1958*, Montevideo: Ediciones de la Banda Oriental, 1982, 16–17; Taylor, "The Uruguayan Coup" 309–17; Faraone, *Vivimos*, 76–78; Philip Bates Taylor, Jr. *Government and Politics in Uruguay*, New Orleans: Tulane University, 1960, 24–26.

12. Eduardo Víctor Haedo, *Herrera: Caudillo Oriental*, Montevideo: Arca, 1969; Lindahl, *New Path*, 30–31.

13. Jacob, *Terra*, 55–64, Lindahl, *New Path*, 178–85; Faraone, *Vivimos*, 81–83. The text of the 1934 Constitution is in Russell Fitzgibbon, *The Constitutions of the Americas*, Chicago: University of Chicago Press, 1949, 715–61.

14. Juan Carlos Welker, *Baltasar Brum: Verbo y Acción*, Montevideo: Impresa Letras, SA., 1945; Jacob, *Terra*, 65–74, 117–18. Christine Ehrick, *Radio and the Gendered Soundscape: Women and Broadcasting in Argentina and Uruguay, 1930–1950*, New York: Cambridge University Press, 2015, 75–83.

15. See three essays in Pedro Cameselle-Pesce and Debbie Sharnak (eds.), *Uruguay in Transnational Perspective*, New York: Routledge, 2024; Katherine M. Marino, "For Peace and Freedom: Paulina Luisi and Global Anti-Fascism from Uruguay," 179–200; Vannina Sztainbol, "Black Anti-Fascism: The Transnational Politics of *Nuestra Raza*," 201–25; and Megan C. Strom, "Panorama Estudantil: Mapping the Transnational Solidarities and Ideologies of Uruguayan University Students (1908–1956)," 226–46.

16. Dawn Ades, *Art in Latin America: The Modern Era, 1820–1980*, New Haven: Yale University Press, 1989, 125, 143–44, 147, 241, 246, 285, 320–22, 358, 3, 137–39, 141–43,147, 344; Jorge Arbeleche, *Juana de Ibarbourou*, Montevideo: Arca Editorial, 1978.

17. Ana Frega, Mónica Maronna, and Yvette Trochon, *Baldomir y la Restauración Democratica (1938–1946)*, Montevideo: Ediciones de la Banda Oriental, 1987, 90–106; Faraone, *Vivimos*, 90–92; López-Alves, *Redemocratization*, 192–94.

18. Ana Frega, Mónica Maronna, and Yvette Trochan, *Baldomir y la restauración democrática (1938–1946)*, 25–44; Pendle, *Uruguay*, 83; Ehrick, *Radio*, 96–99.

19. Museum of the Battle of the Río de la Plata in Montevideo; Frega et al., *Baldomir*, 24–25. The movie, *The Battle of the River Plate*, was filmed in Montevideo in 1955.

20. Frega et al., *Baldomir*, 110–32, 48; Faraone, *Vivimos*, 90–92.

21. Frega et al., *Baldomir*, 132–47; Finch, "Uruguay since 1930," 202; Julio María Sanguinetti, *Luis Batlle Berres: El Uruguay del Optimismo*, Montevideo: Taurus, 2014, 26–27; Katherine M. Marino, *Feminism for the Americas: The Making of an International Human Rights Movement*, Chapel Hill: University of North Carolina Press, 2019, 191–221. UN delegate Isabel Pinto de Vidal, a longtime friend of Paulina Luisi, and one her colleagues became the two first females elected to the Senate in any Latin American nation.

22. Jacob, *Terra*, 111–14; Marschal, *Debt Crises*, 214.

23. Jacob, *Terra*, 83, 88–92; Finch, *Political Economy*, 8, 161–67; Faraone, *Vivimos*, 37–38; Carlos F. Díaz Alejandro, "Latin America in the 1930s," in Rosemary Thorp, *An Economic History of Twentieth Century Latin America: Latin America in the 1930s: The Role of the Periphery in World Crisis*, Palgrave Press, 2000, 37–38; Finch, "Uruguay since 1930," 203.

24. Jacob, *Terra*, 47–48, 94–100; Finch, *Political Economy*, 170–74; Frega, et.al., *Baldomir*, 25–26, 47, 64–65; Faraone, *Vivimos*, 92–93; Pendle, 57–61.

25. Wythe, *Industry*, 120; Russell H. Fitzgibbon, *Uruguay: Portrait of a Democracy*, New Brunswick, NJ: Rutgers University Press, 1954, 92–93.

26. Faraone, *Vivimos*, 93–98; Frega, *Baldomir*, 59.

27. Frega et al., *Baldomir*, 75–87, 99–118; Faraone, *Vivimos*, 101; Finch, *Political Economy*, 42–43, 59–62, and his "Uruguay since 1930," 203; Alexander, *Organized Labor*, 28–44.

28. Andrews, *Blackness*, 7–15, 40–49, 85–99. Mara Loveman, *National Colors: Racial Classification and the State in Latin America*, New York: Oxford University Press, 2014, agrees with these numbers and points out that the census was used primarily to measure a nation state's "progress" in the years up to the 1980s. Until World War II, race-based questions measured a nation's progress on the road to whiteness, see 9–10, 121–25. After the census question changed in 2009 to asking about having some Black ancestry, Uruguay's official Black population increased to about 5 percent.

29. Uruguayan Institute for International Law, *Uruguay and the United* Nations, New York: Manhattan Publishing Company, 1958.

30. Frega et al., *Baldomir*, 62–69; Finch, *Political Economy*, 171–73; Faraone, *Vivimos*, 95–96.

31. Frega et al. *Baldomir*, 25–26. 47, Farone, *Vivimos*, 92–93; Pendle, *Uruguay*, 57, 83; Sanguinetti, *Luis Batlle Berres*, 33–42.

32. Germán D'Elía, *El Uruguay neo-batllista, 1946–1958*, Montevideo: Ediciones de la Banda Oriental, 1982, 53–58; Real de Azúa, *Impulso*, 72–74; Finch, *Political Economy*, 218; Sanguinetti, *Luis Batlle Berres*, 45–47, 54.

33. Sanguinetti, *Luis Batlle Berres*, 15–37.

34. D'Elía, *Uruguay neo-batllista*, 27–51; López-Alves, "Re-democratization," in Rock, *1940s*, 196–200; Finch, "Uruguay since 1930," 204; Sanguinetti, *Luis Batlle Berres*, 49–52.

35. D'Elía, *Uruguay neo-batllista*, 50–51; Finch, "Uruguay since 1930," 204–5.

36. Sanguinetti, *Luis Batlle Berres*, 62–65, 118–20.

37. Rosemary Thorpe, "Latin American Economies in the 1940s," in Rock, *Latin America in the 1940s*, 46–50; D'Elía, *Uruguay neo-batllista*, 23–34, 75; Real de Azúa, *Impulso*, 58–64; Pendle, *Uruguay*, 78; Finch, *Political Economy*, 175–77, 181.

38. D'Elía, *Uruguay neo-batllista*, 33, 58–61; Griffin, "Causal Factors," 30–31; Faraone, *Vivimos*, 98–99.

39. D'Elía, *Uruguay neo-battlista*, 47–52; Pendle, *Uruguay*, 48–68; López-Alves, "Re-democratization" in Rock, *1940s*, 200–6.

40. Finch, *Political Economy*, 32–35. Pendle, *Uruguay*, 63; Sanguinetti, *Luis Batlle Berres*, 91–92.

41. Clemente A. Lisi, *A History of the World Cup, 1930–2018*, Lanham, MD: Rowman & Littlefield, 2019, 9–19, 44–60; Sanguinetti, *Luis Batlle Berres*, 83–85. In an interesting but unconvincing article, March Krotee notes that Uruguay's World Cup appearances slid downward along with its sociocultural standing, concluding with its failure to qualify in 1978, see Krotee, "The Rise and Demise of Sport: A Reflection of Uruguayan Society," *The Annals of the American Academy of Political and Social Science*," Vol. 445 (September 1979), 141–54.

42. Sanguinetti, *Luis Batlle Berres*, 49–50; Wells, *Democratic Crusade*, 11. For Wells, this distinction marks the key difference between the populists and democratic leaders of the era.

43. Fitzgibbon, "Collegiate Executive," *Journal of Politics*, 623–62; D'Elía, *Uruguay neo-batllista*, 61–65; Alexander T. Edelmann, "The Rise and Demise of Uruguay's Second Plural Executive," *The Journal of Politics*, Vol. 31, No. 1 (February 1969), 119–39, especially 125–26. The statistics come from Rosemary Thorpe, "The Latin American Economies in the 1940s," in Rock, *1940s*, 41–58, esp. p. 55; Finch, "Uruguay since 1930," 206–7. Also see Milton Vanger, "Uruguay Introduces Government by Committee," *American Political Science Review*, Vol. 48, No. 2 (June 1954), 500–513, esp. 504–9; and Sanguinetti, *Luis Batlle Berres*, 97–98. (The Chicago Cubs in these years also experimented with a similar idea and replaced the team's manager with nine coaches, each serving as manager for a game, but it did not improve their performance in the standings.)

44. D'Elía, *Uruguay neo-batllista*, 62–65, *La Constitución de 1952*, Montevideo: República Oriental del Uruguay, Poder Legislativo, 1953; Sanguinetti, *Luis Batlle Berres*, 99–105.

45. D'Elia, *Uruguay neo-batllista*, 36, 74–77; Finch, *Political Economy*, 221; Real de Azúa *Impulso*, 94–96, 103–7; Sanguinetti, *Luis Batlle Berres*, 133–34; Margarita Fajardo, "CEPAL, the International Monetary Fund of the Left? *American Historical Review* (June 2023), 588–615. Although the IMF and CEPAL agreed on many policies in the 1950s, they would eventually disagree strongly about the root causes and solutions for Latin America's lack of development.

Seven

Batllismo Challenged

Things Fall Apart, 1955–1985

Uruguay's post–World War II successes soured in the years after 1955. This decline undermined the case for Uruguayan exceptionalism as the most progressive republic in Latin America. Analysts have debated the cause of the malaise. Was it primarily due to an economic system that proved unworkable in a competitive free-market world where the premises of ISI batllismo no longer functioned, or did a moribund political system beholden to powerful constituencies inhibit a viable response? Neither of the two traditional parties had a constructive solution for the breakdown of what had been Latin America's most stable democracy and its most equitable socioeconomic system. Frustration led to calls for change from union members and young people belonging to the New Left, inspired by the revolutionary ideals of the Cuban Revolution of 1959. Inaction led to the perplexing collapse of Uruguayan society and economy resulting in a dark history that included a unique guerrilla conflict and a brutal military dictatorship that lasted until 1985. Unfortunately, this chapter weaves a very depressing tale about the events of these three decades.

THE POLITICAL AND ECONOMIC CRISIS OF THE 1950s

Uruguay's turn for the worse shocked its citizens, external observers, and adherents of the ISI structuralist economic theory of state-driven development that held the country up as South America's success story in 1955. Its well-educated, highly urbanized society had balanced the export of primary products with significant industry designed to satisfy the needs of the domestic market. ISI protectionist policies allowed factories to manufacture durable goods (appliances, furniture), to satisfy middle-class consumer demands. Uruguay enjoyed first-rate infrastructure: roads, telephones, and electrical services. It boasted the highest per capita income in all of Latin America.

All this evidence of material and social progress convinced the Colorado government to continue neo-batllista policies. This proved a misreading of the tarot cards.¹

After the adoption of the *colegiado*, Luis Batlle Berres and his liberal Colorado faction dominated the National Council of Government. His personal popularity with the voting public and his record as a successful chief executive made his voice, which argued for the expansion of ISI and the neo-batllista agenda, most persuasive. His program, however, depended upon the continued prosperity of the pastoral economy and an evolving industrial sector. Unfortunately, after the Korean War, global demand for agricultural and pastoral products weakened as European nations and the United States placed protective tariffs on South American beef. The invention of synthetic fibers reduced the demand for wool. Uruguay's income from exports shrank by 32 percent by the end of the decade. Despite these indicators of economic slowdown, Batlle Berres convinced the National Council to stay the course, importing costly industrial machinery and raw materials to expand the industrial base. Not only did the government spend the remainder of the treasury's reserves from the Korean War years, it borrowed money abroad.²

Over the decade, the budget fell deeper into arrears. Uruguay's population continued to eat well; estimates suggested that they consumed two-thirds of the meat butchered in the country, more meat per capita than any other nation. The Frigorífico Nacional, required to charge low prices, operated at a loss. Favored groups did well. For example, as a result of a 1940s labor agreement, every worker at the Frigorífico Nacional was entitled to take home four and a half pounds of beef after each shift! The bureaucracy continued to expand. A cycle of unemployment and inflation began because of the unbalanced budget resulting from a country living beyond its means. Consumer prices rose while the value of the peso slipped. Workers struggled to keep pace (the wage-price spiral), and labor became more militant. As the economy struggled, Wage Councils' decisions turned against labor. Trolley car workers and meat packers struck, enraged by rules that permitted employers to hire replacement workers for laborers on the picket line.³

Because of inflation and the decline in the peso's value, industrial production stagnated. The manufacturing sector had risen to 23 percent of GDP (gross domestic product) by 1955, but a decade later manufacturing grew a mere one additional percent. While ISI policies protected industry, Uruguay's small population of slightly over 2 million people could not sustain an industrial base by itself. But the very tariffs and subsidies that protected Uruguayan industry from foreign competition also promoted inefficiency and high labor costs, making Uruguayan products uncompetitive in global markets compared to comparable U.S. or European goods. Similar scenes were replicated across Latin America. While the batllista economic interventionist model worked well when external factors (the Great Depression and global wars) excluded competition, by the late 1950s circumstances had changed to the detriment of Uruguay and most of Latin America.⁴

Luis Batlle y Berres made one final attempt to salvage the situation for the Colorados as the election of 1958 approached. He offered bills in the Assembly that would have increased taxes and reduced some welfare benefits in an attempt to balance the budget. His cousins, heading the oppositional Colorado ticket, refused to support the legislation. This gridlock allowed the Nationalists to win the election and control six of the nine seats on the National Council, taking charge for the first time in almost one hundred years. As one writer commented, "Uruguay was a spectator stunned by its own crisis."[5]

THE NATIONALISTS TRY THEIR HAND, 1959–1967

During the 1950s, the Nationalist Party had reorganized and enlisted a new following. Their coalition included significant numbers of middle-class farmers and ranchers who joined Benito Nardone's *Liga Federal de Acción Ruralista* (Federal League of Rural Action). A vitriolic radio commentator with *caudillo*-like aspirations, Nardone revived the argument that urban parasites (the Colorados and the beneficiaries of their batllista policies) lived well because of the efforts of hard-working rural people who deserved a greater share of national wealth.

His message won political favor with Luis Alberto de Herrera and his long-standing *estanciero* following. To popularize their appeal, the Nationalists used the Bordaberry family's *Radio Rural* to spread their message. Nardone and Herrera shared strong pro-Catholic and anti-communist views, popular during the Cold War environment of the 1950s and 1960s, and blamed the corrupt *galedrudos* (Colorado middle-class politicians and their business and manufacturing backers) for Uruguay's disastrous economic condition. The election of 1958, then, would reorient the economy in favor of the ranching sector.[6]

The Blanco leadership recognized the changed dynamics of global economics. New policies stemming from the Bretton Woods Agreement that created the International Monetary Fund (IMF) and the World Bank profoundly influenced an increasingly intertwined free world with ideas of freer trade. While the generous U.S. Marshall Plan rebuilt Germany and a similar program restored Japan's economy, Latin America received no financial aid from the United States or the IMF in the 1950s. Instead, the IMF offered Latin America financial advisers and stable exchange rates based on the U.S. dollar, which also protected U.S. investments.[7]

Shortly after taking the reins of government, the Nationalist leadership invited the IMF to send economic specialists to make recommendations. Not surprisingly, the team suggested austerity measures: reducing the number of bureaucrats, tightening up welfare and pension benefits, and introducing a graduated income tax to raise revenue. These suggestions gored the sacred cow too deeply. Because many Nationalists held government positions or received pensions, Herrera and Nardone's coalition, already fractured by disputes over patronage, found these suggestions politically unpalatable. Patronage remained essential for both parties. By 1961, the public sector employed 21 percent of all workers. One administrator quipped that he "could get along better if I had a thousand employees instead of the seven-thousand they have given me." Thirty-two percent of the population received retirement or pension benefits. Past and future patronage recipients immobilized the political system.

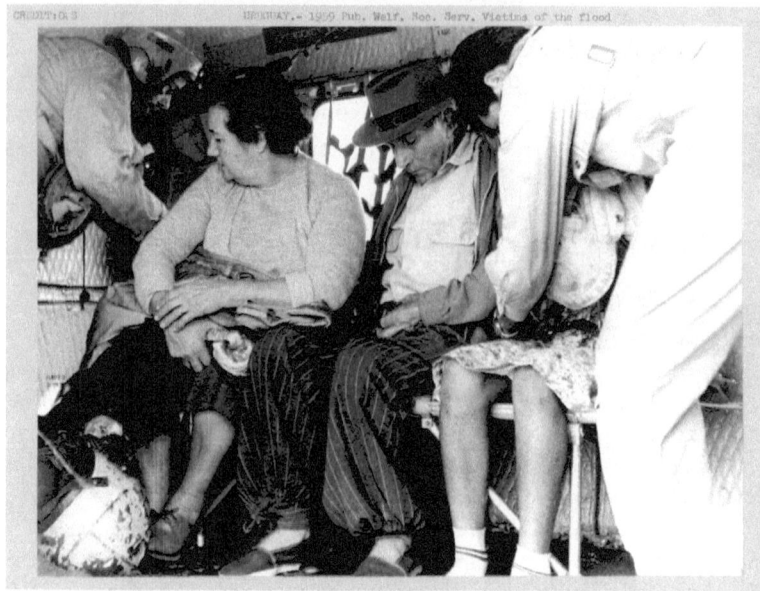

Figure 7.1 Evacuees from the Floods of 1959. The floods of 1959, the worst in more than a century, left thousands stranded without homes or possessions. As the Río Negro flooded its banks, military helicopters evacuated people fleeing the high waters and brought them to Montevideo where they received medical attention, food, clothing, and shelter. Volunteer groups and students brought supplies to shelters for distribution to the victims of this national disaster. The great flood of 1959 ruined crops and diminished the likelihood that the Nationalists would be able to solve the nation's economic woes. *Source*: Columbus Memorial Library.

Because neither traditional party introduced fiscal reforms, Uruguay experienced an extended period of stagflation (the combination of extremely low growth and high inflation) from 1960 to 1973.[8]

The Nationalists' limited reforms included the Monetary and Foreign Exchange Reform Law of 1959 that lowered certain tariffs, created a modest income tax and instituted some banking reforms. But for the political reasons cited above, the Nationalists refused most IMF suggestions. The state continued to play a major role in the economy. Critics of the IMF stabilization plan pointed out its unfair burden on workers, whose wages never kept pace with the rising cost of living during the 1960s. The Nationalists also experienced the misfortune of governing during the worst environmental disaster in the country's history, a pouring rain in 1959 that lasted a solid month. Towns and pastures flooded, and bodies floated out of graves. The Río Negro overflowed and drowned the hydroelectric dam at Rincón del Bonete, forcing engineers to dynamite it partially to avoid its complete destruction. The Uruguay River rose over fifty feet at Paysandú and Salto. The floods of

March and April 1959 reduced Uruguay's pastoral exports to their lowest point in generations.[9]

The Alliance for Progress, U.S. president John F. Kennedy's vision for improving relations with Latin America, announced in August 1961, offered a second opportunity for reform. The Alliance required each Latin American nation, after consultation with foreign experts, to create a ten-year development plan, something Uruguay had never done previously. U.S. economists hoped that plans would include dramatic reforms and dangled the carrot of development funding for approved plans. The Nationalist government formed the *Comisión de Inversiones y Desarrollo Económico* or CIDE, consisting of local and foreign experts, which collected statistical data and developed planning for seventeen sectors of the economy. Rising stars in the Nationalist government, such as Minister of Livestock Wilson Ferreira Aldunate, labored over the planning process.

Although both Herrera and Nardone had passed away by the time of the election of 1962, the willingness of the Blancos to entertain planning and reform propelled their new leaders to a slim victory. Because patronage and the welfare state provided social peace, the two parties secured 90 percent of the vote. As the planners worked, negative growth rates and a balance of payments deficit aggravated the cycle of inflation that continued throughout the 1960s. By 1965, consumer prices were rising about 40 percent annually and the peso (once three to the U.S. dollar) was now worth only a penny. Workers' real wages fell by 24 percent in the private sector and 40 percent in the public sector between 1957 and 1967. As a result, the middle-class empleados, especially bank employees, became the most militant union members. The deteriorating economic situation encouraged labor unions to coalesce into the National Workers Convention (CNT), which the Communist union dominated. As new elections approached in 1966, Uruguayans demanded that the planners unveil their ideas.[10]

The National Economic and Social Development Plan, introduced on the eve of elections, proposed reducing state programs while providing new services through increased efficiency. It offered structural agrarian reform, redistributing land to smaller producers and providing them with technology to boost livestock productivity and exports. Other proposals targeted export industrial development, income tax reform, the development of a Central Bank System, and much more. Although the National Council approved the report in February 1966, it never implemented any reforms. Three percent of the ranchers continued to own 44 percent of the land. When Uruguay defaulted on its debt in 1965, the CIDE experiment ended.[11]

By 1966, the flaws inherent in the batllista system had become readily apparent. Pensions, early retirements, and the bureaucracy's guaranteed lifetime employment placed a heavy burden on the treasury. The IMF loans burdened the country with an $800 million debt. (At the height of the Depression, Uruguay owed only $98 million.) Finally, benefits once conveyed were politically impossible to rescind. The decline in export sales made social programs unaffordable. As a result of the economic collapse, an estimated one hundred thousand Uruguayans abandoned their country in the 1960s seeking opportunity elsewhere. As in 1933, the National Council had displayed inertia in the face of crisis; hence, as the election approached, Colorado politicians made abolishing the *colegiado* system the focus of their campaign.[12]

THE CONSTITUTION OF 1967 AND THE RETURN OF PRESIDENTIAL GOVERNANCE

Colorado leaders urged voters to authorize a constitutional assembly to write a new document that would restore the presidential system. The Constitution of 1967, approved by plebiscite, provided for five-year presidential and congressional terms. It established the Central Bank to oversee monetary policy and a Social Security Bank to administer retirement funds. Because of ongoing protests, Article 168 of the Constitution granted the president authority to impose martial law under the *Medidas Prontas de Seguridad*, or Prompt Security Measures. These special powers far exceeded the chief executive's traditional police power granted in the event of invasion or rebellion. Article 168 allowed the president to limit free speech and freedom of the press, prevent strikes, break up protests, and respond to the emerging militant guerrilla threat. As in 1934, voters believed that changing the political system would remedy the country's economic woes. By ending the *colegiado*, the Constitution of 1967 closed the door on one of José Batlle y Ordóñez's bad ideas.[13]

Jorge Pacheco Arico (1968–1971), a former boxer and a conservative Colorado, ascended to the presidency following the sudden death of the elected chief executive late in 1967. Despite considerable opposition from Congress, Pacheco Arico took firm action in light of growing unrest. He censored the media, including internationally renowned leftist Eduardo Galeano's newspaper, outlawed the Socialist Party, and suspended the writ of habeas corpus. Despite the new political arrangement, the economic situation worsened. Inflation rose to 137 percent in 1967 and continued at that pace during the first half of 1968. Wages increased by only half that amount. To meet the crisis, Pacheco Arico reorganized his cabinet in May to include business leaders like César Charlone, Terra's finance minister during his dictatorship.

More importantly, he replaced the 1943 Wage Council System with a new entity, COPRIN (Council on Prices, Wages, and Productivity), designed to control runaway inflation and price increases. COPRIN's membership favored the government, which allowed it to freeze wages and prices to fix the economy. In June 1968, a wage freeze reduced the rate of inflation to 21 percent. Labor militants, students, and intellectuals, now even more disaffected with the traditional parties, led marches in the streets of Montevideo despite intense police crackdowns. Pacheco's economic measures did create some price stability and growth through 1970, laying the foundation for his future political ambitions.[14]

Pacheco Arico imposed full martial law for the first time in June 1968 and used the tool regularly thereafter. The combination of the wage-and-price freeze and the emergency security measures undermined the batllista policy of redistributing wealth. Strikes increased in frequency. Pacheco Arico would become increasingly authoritarian during the remainder of his term, which would intensify worker and student protests against the government. In 1971 he issued another decree that enabled him to utilize the army to assist the police as they cracked down on unrest. Despite COPRIN, the level of inflation had risen again by the end of 1971.[15]

POPULAR PROTEST AND THE TUPAMAROS, 1962–1973

As inflation continued to rise, students and workers voiced their concerns about the deteriorating social and economic situation. Uruguayans were not alone. Young people worldwide found themselves in the midst of a generational conflict with their parents over hairstyles, unisex clothing, rock music, and most importantly, political, economic, and social justice issues. The Cuban Revolution of 1959 inspired young people. When Fidel Castro visited Uruguay in June, enormous crowds applauded him. Another crowd cheered Castro's victory over the U.S.–inspired Bay of Pigs invasion. Young people, more willing to challenge the beliefs of their parents' generation, became activists. Polls taken in the mid-1960s suggested that 80 percent of students believed their government (the Chilean ambassador called it the "nine-headed monster") was corrupt and blamed it for the economic collapse.[16]

Workers agreed. A lawyer named Raúl Sendic, who had unionized sugar cane workers in Artigas department during the late 1950s, led them on several marches from Bella Unión to Montevideo, demanding a minimum wage and agrarian reform. When the Nationalist government ignored them, Sendic gathered middle-class union members, rural and urban workers like José (Pepe) Mujica, as well as intellectuals and university students belonging to the FEUU, into the MLN-T (*Movimiento de Liberación Nacional-Tupamaros*) or simply, the Tupamaros. He organized clandestine cells, one of which stole rifles from the shooting club in Colonia Suiza, the group's first military action, in July 1963. Other leftist groups and students who believed in using violence joined the Tupamaros. Four years later, the Tupamaros issued a proclamation that highlighted their slogan "There will be a Fatherland for all or there will be a Fatherland for none," indicating the birth of a violent revolution that would demand radical structural changes in Uruguayan society.[17]

In May 1968, students protested en masse against a proposed increase in bus fares in Montevideo. In response, police invaded the university campus, violating the principle of its autonomy. Other than snatching officers' caps as trophies and throwing rocks, initially the students protested peacefully. As the unrest continued, Pacheco used the Prompt Security Measures to break up demonstrations. Tensions escalated, especially after the police in August murdered a student named Líber Arce, which led to a massive protest in Montevideo. While the majority of students and intellectuals continued to believe in Uruguayan democracy, the police and political elites began to conflate student protesters with communists.[18]

Although student demonstrations lessened in October when classes reconvened, some student activists had become radicalized by the activities of Ernesto "Che" Guevara, one of the leaders of the Cuban Revolution of 1959 and the icon of the

Figure 7.2 Raúl Sendic Leading March of Sugar Cane Workers. The founder of the Tupamaros began his career as a lawyer defending the rights of sugar cane workers who, as agricultural laborers, traditionally earned the lowest wages in the republic. The sugar estates in Rivera department earned their owners' tremendous profits while the workers barely made ends meet. During the economic decline of the late 1950s and early 1960s, this situation only worsened. Sendic's role in leading marches elevated his stature and made him a logical leader of the Tupamaros. *Source*: Museo de la Memoria, Montevideo.

revolutionary left. He inspired a whole generation of young people. They endorsed the idea of armed conflict and initially formed much of the membership of the Tupamaros.[19]

The Tupamaros' military strategy differed from that of other Latin American guerrilla groups that generally followed Guevara's model. According to Che and French intellectual Regis Debray, successful guerrillas needed to create a secure *foco*, or base, in the remote countryside from which they could use propaganda to draw volunteers to their cause. The small guerrilla army could then safely enter into skirmishes with government forces until numerically large enough to defeat the national army. But as Fidel Castro told a Uruguayan journalist, "Your country lacks the geographic conditions for armed struggle: there are no mountains, no jungles." In addition, almost half the population, especially students and workers, lived in Montevideo, the most likely source of recruits.[20]

Abraham Guillen, a Spanish journalist living in Uruguay, devised the Tupamaros' strategy. He convinced Sendic and other leaders to organize multiple *focos* in Montevideo where members could hide in abandoned buildings, hold captives, and store food, supplies, money, arms, and explosives. Urban locations made spreading "armed propaganda" easy. The guerrillas hoped to gain the sympathies of the population through words as well as Robin Hood–like acts (redistributing stolen food and cash, for example). By the end of 1968, the guerrillas' tactics included robbing banks and kidnapping foreign diplomats, both viewed as agents of foreign exploitation. To preserve the anonymity of Tupamaro members, Sendic organized them into fifteen small cells of two to six individuals whose identity was known only to the Executive Committee.[21]

When the Tupamaros stepped up operations the following year, President Pacheco Arico expected that Montevideo's 3,500 member police force, many of whom had trained at a U.S. police academy in Georgetown, Maryland, could handle the challenge. They could not. Because the Tupamaros stole from the rich and left amusing messages behind after each escapade, their popularity soared. For example, the daring robbery of the most exclusive casino in Punta del Este, the San Rafael, in February 1969 ("the heist of the century"), provided them with a reputation as Robin Hood guerrillas. After receiving inside information about when to rob the casino, two Tupamaros, disguised as policemen, convinced the manager who was lunching nearby that he had to return to the casino because of a disturbance. Once inside, the "policemen" took his keys and emptied the safe of millions of dollars. After the robbery, Sendic learned that the haul included employee salaries and tips, which the Tupamaros returned to the workers. By mid-June, bank robberies and kidnappings of rich Uruguayans yielded sufficient money to purchase weapons and win new supporters.

The Tupamaros' Robin Hood–like image earned them international publicity. Radical leftists in the United States like the Black Panthers and the Black Power Movement spoke favorably of the Tupamaros as partners in the struggle against U.S. imperialism, but they were critical of their unwillingness to accept Marxist ideology. Instead, the Tupamaros made nationalistic references to José Artigas's ideas for social reform. International leftists also critiqued the Tupamaros' reluctance to embrace widespread violence.[22]

Over the next two years, the Tupamaros' tactics did become more violent as bombings and assassinations increased. Eventually, the police captured numerous Tupamaros and jailed them in Punta Carretas prison. To rescue their comrades, the Tupamaros turned to *Plan Satán*, which proposed kidnapping foreigners, including U.S. citizen Dan Mitrione, to exchange them for guerrilla leaders like Raúl Sendic and other Tupamaro commanders. Although the evidence is not clear, the Tupamaros certainly believed that Mitrione (officially an employee of the U.S. Agency for International Development [USAID]) was a CIA agent who trained police in torture techniques, intelligence gathering, and crowd control. The United States intensified pressure on Pacheco Areco's government to negotiate for Mitrione's release in exchange for all the imprisoned Tupamaros. When the deadline to release the prisoners passed, the hardline guerrilla leaders executed Mitrione. This bloody episode turned some Uruguayans against the Tupamaros.[23]

On January 8, 1971, the Tupamaros kidnapped another high-profile official, British ambassador Geoffrey Jackson. As his Daimler drove along the Rambla toward his office, a truck slammed into it. Two men overpowered his chauffeur, and hustled Jackson to captivity in a wet basement. During the first few weeks, his captors drugged him, tormented him with loud pop music, and endlessly interrogated him. His account of his captivity provides insights into the numerous women who participated in the Tupamaro movement. Although none held top leadership roles, participating in the guerrilla movement did liberate them from domesticity. He shared his captors' miserable living conditions with no toilet except a bucket and no shower. In September 1971, the Tupamaro captives concocted an escape plan that involved tunneling into the Montevideo sewer system, wading through waist-deep sewage and following the system's channels before exiting through manholes near selected safe houses. One hundred and eleven prisoners, including Sendic and Mujica, escaped. With no further need for Ambassador Jackson as a bargaining chip, the Tupamaros released him after two hundred and forty-four days in captivity. After this, President Pacheco turned the anti-guerrilla operation over to the military.[24]

THE ELECTION OF JUAN BORDABERRY AND THE DEFEAT OF THE TUPAMAROS, 1971–1972

As the Latin American nation with the longest standing democratic tradition, Uruguayans demanded that violence be tamped down to permit a peaceful election in 1971. With Pacheco removed from consideration (he tried to amend the Constitution to permit reelection, to no avail), the Colorados struggled to unify behind a single candidate. The Nationalists rallied behind their charismatic orator, Wilson Ferreira. The smaller leftist parties, the Socialists, Communists, and Christian Democrats along with disgruntled Colorados looking for a democratic, nonviolent path to change, formed a new party, the *Frente Amplio* (Broad Front).

To demonstrate that the Broad Front intended to work within the political system, they nominated General Líber Seregni as their presidential candidate. As the parties jostled at the polls, the Tupamaros, fearing they would lose all credibility if they disrupted the elections, agreed to an informal truce during the short campaign season. Like many on the left, they believed that the Frente Amplio might win. Further, both Wilson Ferreira Aldunate, conservative Colorado Zelmar Michelini, and Líber Seregni had multiple contacts within the Tupamaros, offering the guerrillas hope that they might achieve their agenda peacefully.[25]

But the Frente Amplio did not perform as well as expected, winning only 19 percent of the vote. Seregni and the Frente Amplio believed that the election had been rigged, and plausibly accused the CIA of contributing funds to the opposition. After Socialist Salvador Allende's surprise victory in Chile's election of 1970, certainly President Nixon and Secretary of State Henry Kissinger preferred that leftists lose the election in Uruguay. Because of the *lema* system, Colorado candidate, Juan María Bordaberry, who earned only 23 percent of the vote, won the presidency despite the fact that Blanco Wilson Ferreira had gained more votes. Ferreira refused to collaborate with Bordaberry, a relative unknown who seemed willing to grant the military complete control over the security situation.[26]

After the new government took office, violence resumed. The politically weakened Bordaberry allowed the military to manage the Tupamaro situation. The military itself was of two minds. Reform minded officers attempted to negotiate with Sendic and other leaders in July and August 1972. The Tupamaros agreed to surrender in exchange for the expropriation of Uruguay's five hundred largest estancias and their transformation into agricultural colonies, a demand which Bordaberry refused. The army now went on the offensive. When Tupamaro leader Hector Amadio Pérez and others who had been tortured provided information about the location of the guerrillas' hideouts, the military raided the buildings and captured some 2,500 Tupamaros, including Raúl Sendic, essentially eliminating the Tupamaros by the end of the year. Another five hundred Tupamaros fled to Argentina or Chile, both democratically ruled in 1973.[27]

BOX 7.1: THE MIRACLE IN THE ANDES, FLIGHT 571

On October 13, 1972, the Uruguayan rugby team along with family, friends, and a few other passengers, boarded a flight to Santiago, Chile, where they were scheduled to play a match. As they crossed the Andes, the copilot, confused by cloudy conditions, descended prematurely thirty-seven miles short of the airport and struck a mountain. The force of the crash sheared the tail and both wings off the plane, allowing the fuselage to slide down the glacier before crashing with great force into snow and ice, 11,700 feet above sea level. Huddling inside the plane and using torn padding from seats as extra clothing, the passengers discovered they had only a few chocolate bars, some dried plums, and almonds to eat. They found a transistor radio and listened for news about the search for the missing plane. After only eight days, the search ended. With their food gone, the survivors voted to eat the flesh of their deceased companions. On October 29, an avalanche buried the fuselage, killing eight more people and forcing the survivors to tunnel out. After ten weeks passed, the leaders decided that the strongest should hike out and find help. Without maps or instrumentation, Nando Parrado and Roberto Canessa crossed the border into Chile. After climbing a fifteen-thousand-foot mountain, the two trekked thirty-eight miles in ten days before seeing any humans. After the Chilean rescuers brought them to civilization, helicopters flew to the site crash and transported the remaining sixteen survivors to safety. Initially welcomed home as heroes after their seventy-two-day ordeal, Uruguayans became more ambivalent when news leaked that cannibalism had allowed them to survive. After Parrado and Canessa described the process of the vote, the survivors again became national heroes.[28]

THE NATIONAL SECURITY STATE: REPRESSION AND TORTURE, 1973–1985

The victory over the Tupamaros increased the military's influence and popularity, which allowed them to seize control gradually. In February 1973, Bordaberry attempted to remove the minister of defense and replace him with a general aligned with democratic ideals. Although the president attempted to rally the public to his side, he failed. Shortly thereafter, the military published "Document No. 4" that informed Uruguayans that the military would oversee all departments of government. COSENA (the National Security Council) comprised entirely of military officers, replaced Bordaberry's cabinet. This decision marked the beginning of Uruguay's bureaucratic military regime similar to the ones in Argentina and Brazil. The military announced that it its two most senior generals would retire each year, thereby preventing a one-man dictatorship such as General Augusto Pinochet's regime in Chile.

On June 27, 1973, the military initiated an *auto-golpe* (a coup against itself) and ordered Bordaberry to close the legislature and the judiciary, the last two democratically selected institutions in the country. Labor leaders in the CNT, which represented 90 percent of all workers, called for a general strike in response to the military takeover. The new government immediately outlawed the CNT, the union collapsed, and many union leaders, especially the communists, found themselves in prison. The military also prohibited the FEUU, whose membership had played such an important role in the Tupamaros, and purged the university faculty. The generals, as in the other Southern Cone nations and some Central American states, justified instituting the National Security State by arguing that the need to protect the collective well-being outweighed the luxury of protecting individual liberties. The Catholic Church alone protested these harsh tactics.[29]

The Cuban Revolution of 1959 that inspired the Left also provoked a response from conservative elements of Latin American society and the United States, each fearful about the spread of communism south of the Río Grande. As part of U.S. Cold War strategy, it trained officers, including those in the Uruguayan military, at the School of the Americas in Fort Gulick in the Panama Canal Zone. Other Uruguayans trained in France. In both locales, experts educated Latin Americans on defending their homeland against subversives by using counterinsurgency tactics. In addition, after 1960 the United States supplied Uruguay with $16 million of military equipment to suppress internal threats.

For the Uruguayan military, their mission would broaden to become a struggle not only against the Tupamaros and a holy war against communism, but also against the liberal, "corrupt" ideas of batllismo. By 1973 they viewed civilian politicians and the radical left equally as enemies of the state. The National Security State had two objectives. First, the military suspended civil liberties and imposed order to poison the roots of subversion, which meant the arrest, torture, and imprisonment of any remaining Tupamaros (or any "dangerous" individual). Second, the National Security State would reconstruct Uruguay by reforming the economy and curing the nation's social ills. To accomplish this, the military followed the ideas of French counterinsurgency theorist Roger Trinquier, who argued in his "Modern Warfare: A French View of Counterinsurgency" that the military's real work began after it defeated the rebels. In his opinion, the military should use propaganda and a firm hand to persuade citizens to accept the cleansing of society's problems before restoring democracy. Although only a figurehead, the military deposed Bordaberry in 1976 when he expressed greater ambitions. Other more compliant presidents would follow Bordaberry.[30]

The military interpreted existing Prompt Security Measures to permit the wholesale arrest, torture, and even murder of known dissidents. Those arrested included Jorge Batlle Ibáñez, a conservative Colorado follower of Pacheco and a future president. By 1975, Uruguay had the highest percentage per capita of political prisoners in the world, requiring the construction of new prisons. Uruguay's small geographical size and its relatively sparse population made controlling its population easy. As much as 10 percent of the population sought sanctuary elsewhere, especially in Argentina, a democracy until 1976. After the military coup there, Uruguay's military expanded its trajectory of transnational repression until it reached a crescendo shortly thereafter.

Uruguay joined Argentina, Chile, Paraguay, Bolivia, and later Brazil in Operation Condor. This secret illicit alliance allowed the military to target people in exile in other countries for their previous and current political activities, such as participating in the revolutionary Organization for Latin American Solidarity. Operation Condor required member states to exchange information about exiles, carry out joint operations, and repatriate exiles (unwillingly) to their home nations. It also carried out operations against exiles in the United States and Europe.[31]

The actions of the Uruguayan military seemed counterintuitive given the country's long tradition of military subordination to civilian government, but cold war logic had deeply divided Uruguayan society. Because of the argument demanding greater security, the military nearly doubled in size during the dictatorship, with an additional thirty thousand police supplementing the internal security mission. The regime redirected funding from education and social programs into the defense budget, which by 1983 ate up 49 percent of national revenues and blunted the government's economic reform efforts.

The appalling statistical evidence of kidnappings, executions, imprisonment, disappearances, torture, violence, and baby-stealing, though not as extreme as the numbers in Argentina or Chile, brought calls for justice for these human rights atrocities.

Newly elected U.S. president Jimmy Carter turned the spotlight on Uruguay's human rights violations. The United States suspended further military assistance to Uruguay after a hearing in the House of Representatives during which Wilson Ferreira described his near-death experience at the hands of assassins in Buenos Aires who succeeded in murdering two Uruguayan congressmen (Zelmar Michelini for one) who once had contacts with the Tupamaros. By the end of the dictatorship, the military had executed 90 individuals, disappeared another 167, and had arrested roughly sixty thousand people, many of whom were tortured and imprisoned (these numbers are disputed).[32]

To legitimize the regime, the military in 1976 passed a series of Institutional Acts (as had happened in Brazil) that suspended the constitution, redefined the government's powers, and limited individual liberties. The acts suspended the upcoming presidential election (Institutional Act 1) and allowed the generals to appoint the president (Institutional Act 2). Institutional Act 3 empowered the generals to appoint a new Army commander in chief annually, who, as the president of COSENA, had executive authority vested in him. Institutional Act 4 stripped fifteen thousand former politicians who had served in earlier governments of their political rights for fifteen years. Finally, Institutional Act 7 allowed the government to dismiss, without cause, any public employee; in part as a means of cleansing and reducing the size of the bureaucracy, a "cost-saving" measure of the National Security Doctrine's economic strategy. This act turned out to be a false economy given the number of additional armed service members and police on the public payroll.

In short, the military deepened its control of society *after* the internal guerrilla threat had been extinguished. Because the civilian populace held its democratic traditions dear, however, the military never gained political legitimacy. As a result, the military regime's ability to hold onto power rested upon its ability to fulfill the second objective of the National Security State: to remake Uruguayan society and the economy.[33]

BOX 7.2: CANDOMBÉ IN MONTEVIDEO

Reputedly Montevideo has the lengthiest Carnival season in the world, lasting sometimes as long as forty days. Because the military hoped to convince civilians that life was normal, the regime never canceled the *candombé* festivals that dated from the colonial period, preserved the traditions of the Afro-Uruguayan population, and acted as a social leveler. The festivities included two parades (*desfiles*) with *comparsas* (groups of performers) playing drums and other percussion. In the evenings, various groups of performers (musical, dance, or theatrical) traveled from *tablado* (stage) to *tablado* in each barrio. Performers with drums (the most important instrument in African culture) beat a rhythm while provocatively dressed women danced. During the 1970s, *candombé* organizers encouraged whites to participate in blackface, including the famous artist

Figure 7.3 Carnival Parade in Montevideo. In addition to the parades, each neighborhood formed a group of musicians and dancers to perform during the weeks of Carnival. These groups walk from neighborhood to neighborhood, putting on shows with drums, cymbals, and dance. Since the 1890s, barrios have decorated outdoor *tablados* (stages) for the roaming performers. At the end of the holiday, one group is selected as the winner. Shows also caricature important individuals like the president or perform plays with stock comedic figures. Whites as well as blacks participate in Carnival as an expression of the unity of Uruguayan culture. *Source*: Museo del Carnaval, Montevideo.

Carlos Páez Vileró, the father of one of the survivors of the famous plane crash. Because Páez Vileró had lived in the largely Afro-Uruguayan Barrio Sur for years, the people there encouraged him to join the festivities and paint numerous works highlighting the costumes and performances. The military encouraged the continuance of the candombé because it provided an outlet of fun for the populace although participants undoubtedly toned down skits that typically satirized political leaders.

THE NATIONAL SECURITY STATE: ECONOMIC REFORMS AND FAILURES

Having repressed the Tupamaros, the military realized (like the military in Brazil, Argentina, and Chile) that their credibility also depended upon their ability to reduce inflation and breathe new life into the economy. Theoretically, the military seemed uniquely positioned to make reforms for two reasons. First, it intended to institute a consistent, lengthy regime that would make implementing changes possible; and second, the absence of elections would insulate the military from popular opposition. Well aware of the failure of ISI, Bordaberry appointed a civilian, Harvard educated technocrat Alejandro Végh Villegas, as minister of the economy in 1974. Végh had gained practical experience working with both the Argentine and Brazilian military juntas. Like the Chicago boys (students of Nobel Prize–winning economist Milton Friedman) who advised Chilean dictator Augusto Pinochet, Végh believed that neoliberal, market-driven economics with a reduced state presence would improve the nation's finances.[34]

In line with free market beliefs, Bordaberry and his cabinet developed the *Plan Nacional de Desarrollo, 1973–1977*, which laid out the goals of dismantling protectionism, cutting social spending, reducing public sector employment, and privatizing some of the stated-owned corporations. Once aboard, Végh also hoped to diversify exports by adding select quality, higher-priced manufactured goods like fine leather jackets, tires, electrical appliances, and woolen sweaters for sale in global markets in the Middle East and Asia. Despite Végh's advocacy, the military rejected most of his ideas. Perhaps because he was the lone neoliberal voice in the administration, the regime agreed only to small tariff reductions and incentives to encourage foreign investment in an era where oil profiteers were seeking new locations for excess capital. By way of contrast, the "Chicago boys'" convinced Pinochet to implement full-throated orthodox neoliberalism with striking results in contrast to the effects of Uruguay's modest changes. Végh's plans to reduce the size of the bureaucracy and privatize some of the state-owned corporations met with no success, in part because many military officers and bureaucrats who oversaw public corporations and dispensed patronage received considerable rewards for doing so. Other Uruguayans viewed the welfare state as an entitlement and had no interest in neoliberal economics. Their combined resistance even to Végh's gradualist reform policies led him to resign in 1976.[35]

Although the regime theoretically promoted freer markets under the Law of Industrial Promotion of 1974, the military actually increased state interference in the economy by adding new preferential policies such as direct subsidies and tax rebates. These reduced the price of Uruguayan manufactured goods artificially and made them somewhat competitive in global markets. The military's policies enjoyed limited success between 1974 and 1978 as Uruguay's GDP grew by about 2.8 percent each year. Although this was the first sizable growth the country had experienced since 1955, because of inflation, the wealthy and middle class benefited most, while workers' income fell.

As a small nation, Uruguay's limited domestic market held little interest for foreign investors except for the banking and real estate sectors. The dictatorship eliminated barriers to foreign investments in real estate. Wealthy Argentines, who traditionally flocked to Uruguay's fine beaches like Punta del Este on the Eastern Shore, purchased second homes there. Argentine firms rebuilt and modernized portions of Montevideo, including the Old City. The military encouraged the construction of new hotels or the remodeling of older ones to cater to tourists. By the mid-1970s, the uptick in the economy and the easy accessibility of loans from international commercial banks allowed for significant infrastructure improvements. Tourism from Argentina and Europe brought in revenue beyond what the country had previously experienced.[36]

The military's freer market approach altered neo-batllista tenancy policies in Montevideo that had established rent control for the urban poor. Many residents of the Old City, the Barrio Sur and Barrio Palermo, lived in modest older apartments or in *conventillos* (tenements) that had often deteriorated over time because landlords had no financial incentive to make improvements. People often depended on neighborhood charitable services like soup kitchens to make ends meet.

As part of its urban renewal project, the military introduced the free-market Law of Rents in 1974 that maintained rent control for tenants who had leases predating the law but allowed landlords to raise rents on new lessees. Evicted tenants and their families moved into crowded boarding houses or squatted in abandoned buildings. The law permitted city government to condemn, demolish buildings, and clear the lots. The building boom put a modern face on the port district. Resettling the displaced tenants as the law required, but which the government viewed as a mere technicality, resulted in overcrowded makeshift government housing and a great deal of protest.[37]

The economic volatility experienced during the 1970s and 1980s resulted in large part from the two "oil shocks"—dramatic price increases for petroleum in 1973 and again in 1979. Petroleum producing nations had organized a cartel (OPEC) in the 1960s to control the market and increase crude oil prices. Because Uruguay produced no crude oil, the prices ANCAP paid for the petroleum it refined rose significantly, resulting in higher costs passed on to consumers. The 1979 shock brought on new rounds of inflation and ended GDP growth. As a result, the military abandoned the few free market policies that it had implemented. But those price increases also encouraged the military to begin the construction of two new hydroelectric power plants on the Río Negro to diversify Uruguay's energy supply.[38]

Although foreign entrepreneurs (other than Argentines) rarely invested in Uruguayan enterprises, the military government enjoyed success attracting loans from the IMF, the World Bank, and USAID in the 1970s. As Middle Eastern petroleum money parked in United States and European banks begged for investment opportunities, bankers offered loans at low but variable rates of interest. This privately held wealth attracted governments throughout Latin America. Easy money led to excessive spending, for which every Latin American country would pay a price during the "lost decade" of the 1980s. As a result of the "free" money, the military government increased Uruguay's foreign debt to about $2.25 billion, three times what the nation owed in the 1960s.[39]

The attempt to slash government spending largely failed because of opposition from the military who profited from dispensing patronage. They joined civilian-vested interests seeking to protect the neo-batllista economic system. The reallocation of a sizable portion of the budget to the military allowed it to increase officers' salaries despite Végh's hopes of reducing overall government expenditures. The system of rotating generals in charge of CONSENA operated like the *colegiado*, weakened central authority, and limited the possibility of reform. The number of state-owned businesses actually increased during the military period. Few state employees lost their jobs. Because of these factors, the military did little to resolve Uruguay's economic problems, which would worsen after the oil price shock of 1979.[40]

THE TRANSITION BACK TO DEMOCRACY

Because of growing publicity about the military's human rights violations, the Carter administration successfully pressured it to announce a timetable for Uruguay's return to democracy. The 1977 response stated that the military would draft a constitution by 1980 that would be subject to a plebiscite, followed by a presidential election in November 1981. Like Brazil, Uruguay transitioned slowly back to democracy as the military intended to delay exiting from power until it received assurances that it would not be held criminally liable for human rights transgressions.

When the draft Constitution of 1980 appeared, it retained the bureaucratic authoritarian regime and its prompt emergency measures (re-labeled as state of emergency powers) as well as the National Security Council. While many Colorado and Blanco politicians regained their political rights, Colorado Jorge Batlle and Nationalist Wilson Ferreira did not. The proposed Constitution banned the Frente Amplio from nominating a presidential candidate, and required the two major parties to agree upon a single candidate for each Assembly position. The document limited labor's right to strike. In the run-up to the plebiscite, the military throttled the press and launched a massive radio publicity campaign in favor of the "Yes" vote. Almost all observers, domestic and foreign, assumed that the military would easily win the plebiscite, just as General Pinochet had done in Chile earlier in the year.[41]

Eighty-five percent of the population turned out for the referendum. To everyone's surprise, the military suffered a humiliating defeat, with the "No" vote receiving 57 percent and the "Yes" vote only 43 percent. The vote reflected not only the unpopularity of the dictatorship but also the government's lack of legitimacy. No guerrilla threat existed anymore, and the military's economic development program had begun its death spiral. Most importantly, the plebiscite's failure demonstrated the persistence of the democratic tradition in Uruguay. Despite the setback, the military insisted that its departure would not be imminent. In 1981, the army appointed hard-liner General Gregorio Alvarez as president in the hopes that he could organize a popular pro-military party and win election democratically. Alvarez maintained the slow pace toward democracy by continuing the repression of regime opponents, limiting the free press, requiring the reorganization of the two traditional political parties, and denying political rights to banned party leaders.[42]

The second oil shock in 1979 had caused petroleum prices to double and by 1981 the country entered a deep recession. Real wages declined by 40 percent as the peso lost value. The arrival of the recession of 1981–1982 spelled the beginning of the end for the military. Like most Latin American nations, the military had taken advantage

Figure 7.4 Poster: José Batlle Would Vote No. When the military revealed the draft of the Constitution of 1980, silent civilian protest became widespread. One of the most effective forms of disapproval came from posters like this one, widely distributed throughout the country. Here, the artist evoked the name of José Batlle and his crusade for democracy to suggest why Uruguayans should reject the military's draft constitution.
Source: Museo de la Memoria, Montevideo.

of the easy credit available at *variable* interest rates in the 1970s. When the worldwide capital shortage caused interest rates to rise, Uruguay had difficulty paying its foreign debt, now over $4 billion. In the last years of the dictatorship, the economy actually contracted by nearly 10 percent. The military's hopes to attain legitimacy based upon economic prosperity evaporated.[43]

Other effects of the military's policies proved equally unpopular. In 1979 the military allowed unions to organize but banned many of labor's former leaders. On May 1, 1983 (Labor Day around the world), a hundred thousand workers rallied on behalf of a return to democracy. Within months, the unions joined together in a national labor confederation, the *Plenario Intersindical de Trabajadores* (PIT) that led massive protests against the dictatorship. Early the following year, PIT called for a general strike that provoked the military to outlaw the organization in a last-minute bid to hold onto power.[44]

For most Uruguayans the standard of living had declined during the dictatorship. The military sharply limited citizens' freedom of expression, cutting funds for research at universities and curtailing artistic performances and banning books deemed subversive. An estimated 380,000 Uruguayans, many of the country's middle class, artists, and intellectuals fled in the face of the repression. The military's multiple failures made returning the nation to civilian rule inevitable, but progress remained slow until the military received guarantees for amnesty.[45]

Following the rejection of the Constitution of 1980, young people joined the traditional parties. In 1982, the military scheduled primary elections to allow each Colorado and Blanco *sub-lema* to propose their presidential candidates. As the congressional election approached, the regime shuttered publications critical of this process. The elections of 1982, designed to select moderate, malleable party leaders with ties to the military, resulted in another popular rebuke, as the electorate voted for Nationalists and Colorados opposed to any further collaboration with the military. Despite this embarrassing loss, the military insisted on further delays.[46]

Uruguayans' patience wore thin with this news. Talks between party leaders and the military took place at the Parque Hotel, but produced no results. Large demonstrations, particularly by members of labor unions, began in the Uruguayan winter (July, August, and September) of 1983. Members of human rights groups, housing cooperatives, and women joined in the protests, banging pots to express their frustrations with the dire economic conditions. A massive rally by roughly four hundred thousand Uruguayans on November 27 at the Obelisk in Montevideo (the famous aerial photograph of the protest described the crowd as a "river of liberty,") demanded an end to the dictatorship and prompt elections. More protests followed after the press uncovered evidence of the torture and murder of Dr. Vladimir Roslik on April 15, 1984. An unauthorized general strike during which line commanders

Figure 7.5 The Statue of the Door, La Libertad. In the years since the restoration of civilian rule, Uruguayans have sought to memorialize the tragic circumstances of the military period and the freedom Uruguayans enjoyed in the years thereafter. This simple sculpture of a door opening symbolizes the freeing of some 2,800 political prisoners in 1984. Ironically, the prison was established just outside the town of La Libertad. *Source:* Author photo.

refused to arrest marching workers further convinced the generals to hasten the transition. In desperation, the government recalled Ambassador Végh from Washington DC to see whether he could rework his previous magic as minister of finance. He could not. The total collapse of the economy signaled the end of General Alvarez's hopes to cling to office.[47]

Because the military still enjoyed a monopoly of force, however, it insisted upon exacting conditions before it would turn the government over to civilians. The moderates within the military signaled a willingness to compromise by replacing General Alvarez with General Hugo Medina, a vocal supporter of negotiations. He agreed to rescind the demand for the continuation of the Council of National Security and approved the timetable for presidential elections in November 1984. He also released the Frente Amplio's Líber Seregni, from prison. The latter delivered a speech urging his party members to work for peace, adopt more moderate positions, and support the negotiations, as did former Tupamaro leader Raúl Sendic. Colorado Julio María Sanguinetti echoed these sentiments and signaled his willingness to work with the military and Seregni, declaring, "Revenge never! Justice always!" Nationalist leader Wilson Ferreira demurred. When he crossed the Uruguay River, hoping for a spontaneous popular uprising to end the dictatorship, his small crowd of followers dispersed and the military imprisoned him, negating any hopes that the Nationalists had of winning the election of 1984.[48]

In August both sides finalized the agreement known as the *Pacto de Club Naval* (the Naval Club Pact). The military dropped its restrictions on the press and repealed Institutional Acts 7 and 14 that authorized the government to fire civil servants at will and arrest citizens for political offenses. The military freed large numbers of political prisoners (but not Wilson Ferreira) and agreed to allow Frente Amplio members to vote in the election of 1984. The National Security Council remained as an advisory body only, restoring the primacy of the civilian branch of government. Institutional Act 18 restored the political rights of almost all political figures, even members of the Communist Party.

In return, the civilian negotiators from the Colorado and Broad Front parties orally agreed to ban Blanco Wilson Ferreira, the most ardent critic of the military and an advocate for agrarian reform, from the presidential election and to grant amnesty to military men for their actions during the dictatorship. Both Sanguinetti and Seregni signed off on the transition pact (Institutional Article 19) in August and scheduled elections for November. By outlawing the extreme sub-lema of the Nationalists, the moderates had achieved a consensus that would allow the restoration of democracy in Uruguay.[49]

THE PRESIDENTIAL ELECTION OF 1984

The Naval Club Pact required each *sub-lema* to nominate its candidate by August 25. Once again, the cumbersome double-simultaneous voting system gave the Colorados an advantage. The largest Colorado *sub-lema* chose Dr. Julio María

Sanguinetti as its presidential candidate while the more conservative Colorado *sub-lema* nominated Jorge Pacheco. Meanwhile, the Nationalists remained bitterly divided. Although Wilson Ferreira urged his followers to boycott the election, many refused. The internecine quarrel became so heated that Luis Lacalle (a future president) demanded that the campaign bus stop and let him off because he could not stand to ride any further with his colleagues. The Frente Amplio participated in the election with five separate sub-lemas uniting under the party's banner. These sub-lemas included the Communist and Socialist parties, both of which had had their political rights restored because they had opposed the Tupamaros. During the campaign the Broad Front developed an effective grass-roots organization that would bear fruit in the twenty-first century.[50]

For the first time, Uruguayan voters had the opportunity to view televised debates between the major party candidates, which benefited the Colorados, and the charismatic and distinguished Julio María Sanguinetti. The Colorados combined sub-lemas earned a plurality of 41 percent of the vote. The three Natonalist sub-lemas won 35 percent, and the Frente Amplio garnered roughly 20 percent, results resembling those of the 1971 election. The congressional elections produced equally mixed results as the Colorados secured a plurality in the Senate and Chamber of Deputies. Nearly every elected candidate came from the moderate or conservative wings of their parties. These results smoothed the democratic transition in the eyes of the military.[51]

Sanguinetti's campaign succeeded because of his pragmatic and moderate approach. He convinced voters that his Colorados would pursue fiscal conservativism, and when economic development resumed, the government would initiate new social programs. In other words, his government would balance Batlle-style redistribution policies with the resources provided by anticipated economic growth, marking a cautious return to Uruguay's traditional value-system. All parties and voters understood the need for a cautious approach toward retribution against the military as Sanguinetti donned the presidential sash in 1985.[52]

CONCLUSION

Uruguay's extreme traumas during the thirty years after 1955 are reminiscent of the social upheaval vividly described in African author Chinua Achebe's highly acclaimed novel *Things Fall Apart*. They also reminded Uruguayans that they were Latin Americans and not the Switzerland of the Americas. The destruction of the nation's traditional values resulted from the labyrinthine political system that lacked the dexterity to cope with the need for economic reform. Entrenched interests such as state employees, workers, retirees, and pension recipients constituted such a large percentage of the population that neither party had the political will to reform the bloated system. As export prices collapsed, the economic basis that funded the welfare state deteriorated. With no solution in sight, the Tupamaros on the far left and the military on the far right subverted the nation. Uruguay's home-grown guerrilla group brought terror to the streets of Montevideo and caused the military to respond with a brutal National Security State that in turn unleashed unthinkable violence and lawlessness without providing the promised economic reform. Popular condemnation of the regime's brutality forced a negotiated regime change in 1985. Known in the early 1950s as Latin America's most prosperous and socially advanced nation, could Uruguay's restore its identity as a successful socially progressive democracy? The final chapter of the book will try and answer this question.

NOTES

1. Charles Gillespie, *Negotiating Democracy: Politicians and Generals in Uruguay*, New York: Cambridge University Press, 1991, 1–3, 20–23.

2. Martin Weinstein, *Uruguay: Democracy at the Crossroads*, Boulder, CO.: Westview Press, 1988, 28–29; Germán D'Elia, *El Uruguay neo-batllista, 1946–1958*, Montevideo: Ediciones de la Banda Oriental, 1982, 74–77; Edelmann, "Rise and Demise," 130–33; M. H. J. Finch, "Three Perspectives on the Crisis in Uruguay," *Journal of Latin American Studies*, Vol. 3, No. 2 (November 1971), 173–90, at 176–77; Julio Maria Sanguinetti, *Luis Batlle Berres: El Uruguay del optimism*, Montevideo: Taurus, 2014, 124–25.

3. Alexander, *Organized Labor*, 20, 46–54; D'Elia, *Uruguay neo-batllista*, 79–82; Finch, "Three Perspectives," 173–74; Pendle, *Uruguay*, 49; Troy Andreas Araiza Kokinis, *Anarchist Popular Power: Dissident Labor and Armed Struggle in Uruguay, 1956–1976*, Chico, CA: AK Press, 2023, 124–33.

4. M. H. J. Finch, *A Political Economy of Uruguay since 1870*, New York: St. Martin's Press, 1981, 221, 233–35; Aldo Solari, *El Desarrollo Social del Uruguay en la post-guerra*, Montevideo: Editorial Alfa, 1967, 63–65.

5. Philip B. Taylor, "Interests and Institutional Dysfunction in Uruguay," in *American Political Science Review*, Vol. 57, No. 1 (March 1963), 62–74; Philip B. Taylor, *Government and Politics of Uruguay*, New Orleans: Tulane University Studies in Political Science, Vol. VII (1960), 63–65. The quotation is from Vania Markarian, *Uruguay, 1968: Student Activism from Global Counterculture to Molotov Cocktails*, Berkeley: University of California Press, 2017, 4.

6. Weinstein, *Crossroads*, 28–30. D'Elía, *Uruguay neo-batllista*, 78–84; Taylor, "Dysfunction," 65–66; Edelmann, "Rise and Demise," 131–33; Rosa Alonso Eloy and Carlos Demas, *Uruguay 1958–1968: Crisis y Estancamiento*, Montevideo: Ediciones de la Banda Oriental, 1986, 7, 21–23, 115–16; Finch, "Uruguay since 1930," 209–10; Sanguinetti, *Luis Batlle Berres*, 141–47.

7. Faraone, *Vivimos*, 116–18; D'Elia, *Uruguay neo-batllista*, 69–73, Thorpe, "Latin American Economies," 49–53.

8. Taylor, "Dysfunction," 66–67, 72; Gillespie, *Negotiating Democracy*, 30–32; Solari, *Desarrollo social*, 27, 51–52, 84, 139–54, 167–74; Weinstein, *Crossroads*, 81–85.

9. Finch, *Political Economy*, 237–39; Faraone, *Vivimos*, 121; Taylor, "Dysfunction," 67; Pendle, *Uruguay*, 70; Eloy and Demas, *Uruguay, 1958–1968*, 85–95; Tony Beckworth, *My Uruguay: Vignettes from a Way of Life*, Lexington, KY: private printing, 2017, 133–34.

10. Pendle, *Uruguay*, 104–5; Finch, *Political Economy*, 239–41; Alexander, *Organized Labor*, 67–71. Gillespie, *Negotiating Democracy*, 22–23. Edelmann, "Rise and Demise," 131–33. Herman Daly, "The Uruguayan Economy: Its Basic Structure and Current Problems,"

Journal of Latin American Studies, Vol. 7, No. 3 (July 1965), 316–30, esp. 320–29; Araiza Kokinis, *Anarchist*, 8–10.

11. Adolfo Garcé, "The Alliance for Progress in Uruguay: Political Dynamics, Legacy, and Lessons Learned," *Journal of Leadership Accountability and Ethics*, XVIII (4), 2021, 44–60, esp. 45–48; Finch, "Three Perspectives," 179, and Finch, *Political Economy*, 20–21. Simon Rottenberg (ed.), *Costa Rica and Uruguay: The Political Economy of Poverty, Equity and Growth*, New York: Oxford University Press, 1993, 247–48; Solari, *Desarrollo social*, 50, 133–46; Eloy and Demas, U*ruguay, 1958–1968*, 102–11, 121–33.

12. Taylor, "Dysfunction," 71–73; Finch, *Political Economy*, 241–42.

13. Faraone, *Vivimos*, 135–37. Edy Kaufman, *Uruguay in Transition: From Civilian to Military Rule*, New Brunswick, NJ: Transaction Books, 1979, 22–23; Alberto Pérez Pérez, *Constitución de la República Oriental del Uruguay*, 2 Vols., Montevideo: Universidad de la República, 1970. The constitution would be amended in 1997 so significantly that many refer to the current document as the Constitution of 1997.

14. Faraone, *Vivimos*, 139–40; Markarian, *Uruguay, 1968*, 10–14; Arturo C. Porzecanski, *Uruguay's Tupamaros: The Urban Guerrilla*, New York: Praeger Publishing, 1973, 57–60. Gillespie, *Negotiating Democracy*, 32–33; Debbie Sharnak, *Of Light and Shadow: Social Justice, Human Rights, and Accountability in Uruguay*, Philadelphia: University of Pennsylvania Press, 2023, 32–34; Finch, "Uruguay since 1930," 214–15; Howard Handelman, "Labor-Industrial Conflict and the Collapse of Uruguayan Democracy," *Journal of Interamerican Studies and World Affairs*, Vol. 23, No. 4 (November 1981), 371–94, esp. 374–76; Araiza Kokinis, *Anarchists*, 10–12.

15. Finch, *Political Economy*, 242; Finch, "Three Perspectives." 179–80; "Pacheco: A Man Who Became President by a Twist of Fate," *El Espectador*, July 30, 1998; Araiza Kokinis, *Anarchists*, 139, 168–69.

16. Markarian, *Uruguay, 1968*, 17–28; Van Aken, "Radicalization of Students." 126; Eloy and Demas, *Uruguay, 1958–1968*, 15–17, 23–31. Roberto García Ferreira, "Uruguay and the 'Cuban Issue,'" in Pedro Cameselle-Pesce and Debbie Sharnak, *Uruguay in Transnational Perspective*, New York: Routledge, 2024, 332–51. Tessa Bridal, *The Tree of Red Stars*, Minneapolis, MN: Milkweed Editions, 1997, is an excellent coming-of-age novel describing the experiences of a young upper-class woman and her friends who become caught up in the activities of the Tupamaros.

17. Weinstein, *Crossroads*, 39; Porzecanski, *Uruguay's Tupamaros*, 5–49; Van Aken, "Uruguayan Student Movement," 124–26; Sharnak, *Light and Shadow*, 28–30; Lindsey Churchill, *Becoming the Tupamaros: Solidarity and Transnational Revolutions in Uruguay and the United States*, Nashville: Vanderbilt University Press, 2014, 12–19; Pablo Blum, *The Robin Hood Guerrillas: The Epic Journey of Uruguay's Tupamaros*, Orlando, FL: Creative Space, 2014, 30–34.

18. Markarian, *Uruguay, 1968*, 29–61; Solari, *Desarrollo social*, 122–30; Sharnak, *Of Light and Shadow*, 34–36.

19. Markarian, *Uruguay, 1968*, 29–61; Solari, *Desarrollo social*, 122–30; Sharnak, *Of Light and Shadow*, 34–36.

20. Abraham Guillen, Donald C. Hodges (eds.), *Philosophy of the Urban Guerrilla: The Writings of Abraham Guillen*. New York: Harper Collins, 1973; Pablo Brum, *The Robin Hood Guerrillas: The Epic Journey of Uruguay's Tupamaros*, Orlando: Creative Space, 2014, 36, 43. Castro's quotation is on page 70.

21. Porzecanski, *Uruguay's Tupamaros*, xi–xii, 4, 27–49; Stephan G. Rabe, *Kissinger and Latin America: International Human Rights and Diplomacy*, Ithaca, Cornell University Press, 2020, 26, 103–4.

22. Brum, *Robin Hood Guerrillas*, 81–137; Churchill, *Transnational Revolutionaries*, 56–66, 69–91. Ironically, the Tupamaros never addressed the issue of the problems facing Blacks in Uruguay.

23. Porzecanski, *Uruguay's Tupamaros*, 55–56; Kaufman. *Uruguay in Transition:* 34–35. Gillespie, *Negotiating Democracy*, 40–43; David Kohut and Olga Vilella, *Historical Dictionary of the Dirty Wars*, third ed., Lanham, MD: Rowman & Littlefield, 2017, 356–57; Sharnak, *Of Light and Shadow*, 30–31.; Rabe, *Kissinger*, 106; Brum, *Robin Hood Guerrillas*, 139–71 Brum reviewed all the relevant documents and is skeptical about the claims about Mitrione.

24. Geoffrey Jackson, *Peoples' Prison*, London: Faber & Faber, 1973. Churchill, *Transnational Revolutionaries*, 120–49. Only the FAU (the anarchists) and the Maoists refused to join the Frente Amplio; Araiza Kokinis, *Anarchists*, 150–51. Brum, *Robin Hood Guerrillas*, 206–23.

25. Brum, *Robin Hood Guerrillas*, 223–24, 248; Jimena Alonso, "Christian Democratic Parties of Uruguay and Chile in the Discussion of Unity of the Left (1964–1971)," in Cameselle-Pesce and Sharnak, *Transnational*, 287–306, esp. 297–301.

26. Kaufman, *Uruguay in Transition*, 16–18; Finch, *Political Economy*, 62, 247–48; Francesca Lessa, *The Condor Trials: Transnational Repression and Human Rights in South America*, New Haven: Yale University Press, 2022, 15–17; Eloy and Demas, *Uruguay, 1958–1968*, 23–30. Kaufman, *Uruguay in Transition*, 43–45. Gillespie, *Negotiating Democracy*, 46–49; Sharnak, *Of Light and Shadow*, 37–44.

27. Weinstein, *Crossroads*, 40–41; Porzecanski, *Uruguay's Tupamaros*, 59–70. Gillespie, *Negotiating Democracy*, 43–45; Finch, "Uruguay since 1930," 218–20; Brum, *Robin Hood Guerrillas*, 287–309.

28. Andes Museum, 1972, Montevideo, Uruguay; Nando Parrado, *Miracle in the Andes: Seventy-Two Days on the Mountain and My Long Trek Home*, New York: Crown Publishers, 2006; Roberto Canessa, *I Had to Survive: How a Plane Crash in the Andes Inspired My Calling to Save Lives*, New York: Atria Books, 2016. See also the film, "Alive" and the documentary "Snowbound."

29. Weinstein, *Crossroads*, 44–48; Alexander, *Organized Labor*, 71–75; Finch, *Political Economy*, 247–50; Kaufman, *Uruguay in Transition*, 26–30, 38–42, 45–46, 81–82; Brum, *Robin Hood Guerrillas*, 312–27.

30. Kaufman, *Uruguay in Transition*, 55–68; Weinstein, *Crossroad*, 48–52; Finch, "Uruguay since 1930," 223; Brum, *Robin Hood Guerrillas*, 233–35.

31. Finch, *Political Economy*, 248–50; Porzecanski, *Uruguay's Tupamaros*, 74–76; Kaufman, *Uruguay in Transition*, 11, 14–15, 28. Gillespie, *Negotiating Democracy*, 44–45; John Dinger, *The Condor Years: The Secret History of South America's Assassination Alliance*, New York: The New Press, 2005. Lessa, *Condor Trials*, 17–20, 30–31, 85–109, is a remarkably detailed work of scholarship.

32. Weinstein, *Crossroads*, 48–54; Sharnak, *Of Light and Shadow*, 83–97; Rabe, *Kissinger*, 112–16.

33. Weinstein, *Crossroads*, 53–55; Kaufman, *Uruguay in Transition*, 73–78; Gillespie, *Negotiating Democracy*, 50–52.

34. Weinstein, *Crossroads*, 56; Gillespie, *Negotiating Democracy*, 53–56; Glen Biglaiser, *Guardians of the Nation? Economists, Generals, and Economic Reform in Latin America*, Notre Dame, IN: Notre Dame University Press, 2002, 2–9, 111–13.

35. Finch, *Political Economy*, 252–53; Gillespie, *Negotiating Democracy*, 57–59, 65–67; Biglaiser, *Guardians*, 40, 41–50.
36. Finch, *Political Economy*, 260–64; Weinstein, *Crossroads*, 56–59; Rottenberg, *Costa Rica and Uruguay*, 268–70; Marichal, *Debt Crises*, 233.
37. Lauren A. Benton, "Reshaping the Urban Core: The Politics of Housing in Authoritarian Uruguay," *Latin American Research Review*, Vol. 21, No. 2 (1986), 33–52.
38. Rottenberg, *Costa Rica and Uruguay*, 277–92, 303–4, 389.
39. Weinstein, *Crossroads*, 59–61, 63. Finch, *Political Economy*, 267–69; Kaufman, *Uruguay in Transition*, 83–86.
40. Weinstein, *Crossroads*, 56–57. Finch, *Political Economy*, 268; Biglaiser, *Guardians*, 117–37.
41. Sharnak, *Of Light and Shadow*, 108–22.
42. Weinstein, *Crossroads*, 58–65.
43. Weinstein, *Crossroads*, 81–82; Gillespie, *Negotiating Democracy*, 80–103; Alexander, *Organized Labor*, 76–77; Sharnak, *Of Light and Shadow*, 132–33, 156; Luis Roniger and Mario Sznajder, *The Legacy of Human Rights Violations in the Southern Cone: Argentina, Chile, and Uruguay*, New York: Oxford University Press 1999, 78–80.
44. Weinstein, *Crossroads*, 67–73; Finch, *Political Economy*, 261–66, 278.
45. Finch, *Political Economy*, 269–71; Kaufman, *Uruguay in Transition*, 82–83, 95, Salgado, *Teatro Solis*, 199–200.
46. Luis E. González, "Uruguay, 1980–1981: An Unexpected Opening," *Latin American Studies Association*, Vol. 18, No. 3 (1983), 63–76, at 63–65, 68–69. Kaufmann, *Uruguay in Transition*, 83–86; Sharnak, *Of Light and Shadow*, 154–57.
47. Weinstein, *Crossroads*, 77–80; Juan J. Linz and Alfred Stepan, *Problems of Democratic Transition and Consolidation: Southern Europe, South America, and Post-Communist Europe*, Baltimore: Johns Hopkins University Press, 1996, 152–53. Gillespie, *Negotiating Democracy*, 60–75; Sharnak, *Of Light and Shadow*, 136–67; Luis Roniger and Mario Sznajder, *The Legacy of Human Rights Violations in the Southern Cone: Argentina, Chile, and Uruguay*, New York: Oxford University Press, 1999, 78–80, 229–42.
48. Weinstein *Crossroads*, 83; Gillespie, *Negotiating Democracy*, 104–27.
49. Weinstein, *Crossroads*, 84–85; Gillespie, *Negotiating Democracy*, 130–59.
50. Weinstein, *Crossroads*, 86–87; Gillespie, *Negotiating Democracy*, 160–91.
51. Weinstein, *Crossroads*, 86–90; Finch, "Uruguay since 1930," 226–27.
52. Gillespie, *Negotiating* Democracy, 195–218; Sharnak, *Of Light and Shadow*, 172–78.

Eight

The Renaissance

Uruguay, 1985–2024

Like the other Southern Cone nations, Uruguay faced seemingly insurmountable problems on the eve of its return to democracy. After undergoing a twenty-five-year economic debacle resulting in lower living standards, Tupamaro violence that undermined security, and a brutal, repressive dictatorship that saw more people imprisoned per capita than anywhere in the world, Uruguayans rightfully felt uncertain about their future in 1985. To provide hope, the leaders of the three parties met and agreed upon broad goals consistent with the nation's traditions. First, Uruguay would return to an electoral democracy in which parties would compromise. Second, the government would entertain new strategies for reviving the economy without jettisoning the premises of the neo-batllista state; and third, when finances improved, government would spend some resources advancing progressive socioeconomic reforms. This broad agreement served Uruguay well. While other Southern Cone nations vacillated from one political extreme to the other, Uruguay maintained a steady course. This chapter will assess Uruguay's progress after 1985 and suggest reasons why it moved forward while Argentina, Brazil, and Chile have struggled.

THE RESTORATION OF DEMOCRACY AND NEOLIBERALISM, 1985–2005

The year 1984 completed the formal transition to democracy and initiated four consecutive presidential elections in which moderates from the two traditional parties were victorious. Julio María Sanguinetti had garnered only 39 percent of the popular vote, and therefore needed to collaborate with other parties that held the majority in the legislature. Like other South American nations, they agreed to pay off the burdensome foreign debt in order to regain a good credit rating, rebuild the economy, and address labor and pensioners' need to recoup their lost standard of living. The moderate leadership of the Colorado and Nationalist parties also accepted the military's demand for amnesty despite its human rights violations.[1]

Most importantly, Sanguinetti and his centrist allies in the other parties agreed that Uruguay must be governed constitutionally and democratically. In accordance with the Constitution of 1967, regular elections would be held under the "byzantine electoral system" with its *lemas* and *sub-lemas*. Each of the five parties within the Frente Amplio coalition followed the lead of presidential candidate General Líber Seregni and renounced violence in favor of electoral democracy as did recently released members of the Tupamaros such as Raúl Sendic and José Mujica. After Wilson Ferreira's death in March 1984, his faction abandoned their extreme oppositional positions and joined forces with the conservative Nationalists. Colorados reaffirmed their democratic beliefs. Uruguay's high level of political participation and the parties' ability to negotiate to solve problems reinforced Uruguay's reputation as Latin America's most democratic nation. At the conclusion of Sanguinetti's term, an informal poll indicated that 87 percent of the population believed that reformist (neo-battlista) democracy would provide the best future for the country.[2]

With the collapse of the Soviet Union in 1989, the United States became the world's only super-power. Economists encouraged Latin American nations to adopt the principles of the so-called Washington Consensus, broadly supported by the International Monetary Fund (IMF) and World Bank, in order to recover from the debt crisis of the 1980s. That project encouraged Latin American nations to replace the state-dominated economy with a free-market system and impose fiscal discipline by raising taxes or cutting domestic spending to pay off debt. Sanguinetti's administration agreed to pay off its nearly $5 billion debt, mostly incurred by the military. Leaders of all three parties concurred in order to restore relations with the many governments that had shunned the military.

Because the debt was manageable in comparison to the enormous sums that Mexico and Brazil owed, Uruguay located private banks willing to restructure its loans after the World Bank and the IMF guaranteed them. Despite this solution to the debt crisis, the foundations of Uruguay's economy remained shaky, resting upon the traditional exports of pastoral products and some light industrial goods. The gross domestic product (GDP) stagnated, initially preventing Sanguinetti from doing much to alleviate the poverty of unionized workers, public employees, or retirees. As a result, numerous strikes occurred in 1985 and 1986, coupled with women banging pots as they marched through the streets, the universal urban Latin American message of displeasure with government policies. By the end of Sanguinetti's term, finances improved and the restored Wage Councils mediated modest increases for workers. The inclusion of Frente Amplio leaders in the governing coalition allowed them to convince workers to accept these settlements. Although for most Latin American workers, the 1980s constituted the "lost decade" with triple-digit inflation, for Uruguayans, the Sanguinetti administration's economic policies and declining inflation allowed for some improvement.[3]

Most controversially, Sanguinetti and the legislature implemented the oral understanding made at the Naval Club meeting prohibiting trials of either military officers (discussed later in the chapter) or Tupamaros. Sanguinetti, seeking national reconciliation, commuted the sentences of convicted guerrillas and freed all remaining political prisoners, including Raúl Sendic and José Mujica. The former spent time in Europe and Cuba before returning to Uruguay and perishing from Charcot's disease in 1989, while Mujica became involved in politics in the Frente Amplio coalition, winning a seat in the Chamber of Deputies and later becoming president. Sanguinetti restored the political rights of exiles, allowing many to regain their jobs in the government bureaucracy.[4]

The question of justice for the families of murdered and disappeared victims of the dictatorship posed thorny problems. Although the Frente Amplio and many Nationalists wanted to put military leaders on trial, President Sanguinetti shared the sentiments of democratic leaders in Chile and Argentina that seeking prosecutions of those alleged to have violated human rights would jeopardize the transition to democracy and provoke the military to reassert power. Using its investigatory powers, Congress compiled a list of forty-six cases of human rights violations. In August, 1986, Sanguinetti convinced the Colorado majority (willingly) and the Nationalist minority (grudgingly) to pass the Law of General Expiation (the Expiry Law, Law 15.848) granting the military immunity for their deeds. Frente Amplio legislators opposed the bill.

The statute sparked an uproar. Under the Constitution of 1967, if opponents of a bill gathered the signatures of 25 percent of the electorate, the government was required to hold a referendum on the legislation. Labor leaders, students and leftist politicians gathered over six hundred thousand signatures favoring a referendum, well in excess of the required number. President Sanguinetti and the Colorados campaigned in favor of the Expiry Law against opponents of the bill, making the case that a vote in favor of the law would preserve democracy against a fresh military takeover and would further national reconciliation. Wilson Ferreira agreed with Sanguinetti, while General Líber Seregni did not, arguing that the country could not ignore the military's crimes. Eighty-five percent of eligible voters participated and upheld the Expiry Law by a margin of 56 percent of the votes against 43 percent opposed. Sanguineti opined that there were neither winners nor losers in the referendum (echoing the familiar language of compromise) because the outcome had been decided by a fair political process following open debate. Most Uruguayans considered the question closed. As in Chile in 1990 where Pinochet remained a threat, moderate civilian politicians and the public at large prevailed because they feared that putting the military on trial would result in a return to dictatorship.[5]

The centrist coalition triumphed again in 1989. To the surprise of observers, Nationalist candidate Luis Alberto Lacalle, the grandson of Luis Alberto de Herrera, won the election with a plurality of 37 percent and then entered into a coalition with Jorge Batlle's Colorado faction. Lacalle's victory represented the continuation of Uruguay's political class wherein certain families (in this case the Herrera descendants leading the Nationalists, and the Batlle descendants, the Colorados) produced another generation of leaders (the line would continue further when Lacalle's son Luis Lacalle Pou became president in 2020). Given the insistence of the IMF on reforms, Lacalle pressed for neoliberal economic reforms. In theory, neoliberals sought to impose austerity (reduce government spending) by selling off state-owned businesses (privatization) and by reducing social spending (pensions and wages—politically impossible in Uruguay). Neo-liberals also sought to free business from government regulations, allowing them to operate more efficiently. Because import substitution industrialization (ISI) had failed to generate new development, Lacalle's new administration favored more foreign investment.

Lacalle's proposals seemed reasonable to outsiders. He introduced the Public Enterprises Law of 1990 that would have privatized ANTEL, the national telephone company, the state insurance monopoly, the national airline, and ANCAP's hard liquor monopoly. By selling these businesses, the government theorized, Uruguay would save money by laying off public employees. Debate swirled. Although both chambers approved the reform legislation, Frente Amplio and the labor unions objected, and gathered enough signatures to force a referendum in December 1992. The idea of reforming state-owned corporations proved such anathema that 72 percent of the population rejected the measure. Lacalle next tried to reform Social Security by raising the age of eligibility, but voters rejected that notion by an even wider margin. Working within a coalition that did not believe in neoliberalism, Lacalle's reforms had no chance.[6]

When the third post-dictatorship presidential election turned out to be a virtual three-way tie (Sanguinetti received 34 percent, the Nationalist got 33 percent, and the Frente Amplio candidate, Tabaré Vázquez, slightly less), Sanguinetti urged his colleagues to unify behind him because his political skills would make progress possible. Because of the awkward results in the past two elections, at long last the parties agreed to simplify presidential elections by abolishing the lema system and requiring each party to nominate a single candidate. If no candidate achieved a majority in the election, the two highest vote getters would compete in a run-off. Because this statute fundamentally changed the electoral system, many Uruguayans refer to the legislation as the Constitution of 1997. Polls showed that the Uruguayan people overwhelmingly approved of the reform and that the electorate seemed comfortable with the increasingly influential Frente Amplio because of its consistently moderate tone. Most importantly, with the conclusion of each successful election, the likelihood of a military coup diminished.[7]

Sanguinetti and his allies managed to reform the pension system. By the end of the twentieth century, Uruguay contributed a far greater share of its GDP (12 percent) to its pension fund than any other country in the Americas. Actuaries predicted that by 2020 that percentage would rise to 20 percent, a completely unmanageable amount. Pension reform had been on the agenda for years, but had always faced stiff opposition from recipients. The government finally agreed upon a mixed public/private pension system (like Chile's) that succeeded politically. Those who earned a lower income would have their money placed in a defined benefit pension fund managed by the state pension bank, as had always been the case. Middle-income workers had the ability to put some money into an account managed by a private fund. The greater one's income, the more discretion the individual had to invest in private funds. Other statutes that the coalition passed, the Law Promoting Foreign and National Investment in Industry and Mining, demonstrated Uruguay's new-found interest in promoting a more neoliberal economic policy. Another statute funded free preschool for four- and five-year-old children and helped Sanguinetti fulfill his promise as a reformer. While popular opinion accepted moderate reforms, it acted as a brake on more extreme neoliberal economic measures.[8]

Nevertheless, in 1999 the economy fell into recession, caused principally by Argentina's debt crisis. ("When Argentina catches a cold, Uruguay gets pneumonia.") Uruguayans received a second shock when they turned on their televisions the day following the first round of the presidential elections and learned that Frente Amplio candidate, Socialist physician Tabaré Vázquez, had received 40 percent of the vote and led after the first round. For the traditional parties, this result could not stand. As a result, the Nationalist candidate, who had received the smallest percentage of votes, agreed to support Colorado Jorge Batlle, the grandnephew of José Batlle and the son of former president Luis Batlle Berres, in the second round. Batlle, now seventy-two years old, promised to continue to advocate for moderate free-market policies and to create a Peace Commission to investigate the fate of the disappeared. These proposals carried Batlle to the presidential office.[9]

The tenuous coalition splintered in 2002 as the recession deepened. Argentine tourists could no longer afford vacations on Uruguayan beaches, and many Argentine entrepreneurs withdrew their capital from Uruguayan banks. Batlle let the peso float in 2002, which created a bank run, as Uruguayans and Argentines scrambled to withdraw their savings and reinvest it in safer currencies such as the U.S. dollar or the Euro. To prevent a financial collapse, Batlle called for a bank holiday, precipitating riots in the street. Unemployment reached 20 percent, real wages fell, over 40 percent of the population dropped below the poverty line, and inflation increased. With the assistance of an emergency loan from the United States, the first direct loan President George W. Bush had approved for any Latin American nation, Batlle stabilized the situation. Shortly thereafter, the IMF lent money to Uruguay payable over a lengthier period of time, which allowed the government to satisfy its debt to the United States. In the meantime, over a hundred thousand Uruguayans emigrated.[10]

Under IMF pressure, Batlle's government proposed a modest change for the inefficient state-owned ANCAP. As part of a new austerity program, the administration planned to permit private entrepreneurs to invest in the division that produced alcoholic spirits. Although the legislature approved these changes, the Frente Amplio turned out enough voters (over 60 percent) who disapproved of this tinkering with ANCAP and nullified the measure. Other austerity measures proved acceptable to Frente Amplio. Batlle's promise to balance the budget by 2004 and his progress in reducing inflation pleased the IMF. By the end of his administration, the growth rate had increased to an impressive 13 percent and inflation decreased, partly due to other factors discussed later. Nevertheless, the public remained unhappy with the moderate parties' response to the economic crisis.[11]

ECONOMIC REVIVAL: MERCOSUR AND EXPANDED MARKETS

A partial solution to Uruguay's stagnant economy materialized in the 1990s: a means of expanding its markets. ISI had failed because the nation's small population provided insufficient domestic consumers to sustain large-scale industry. In addition, its high labor costs and outdated manufacturing equipment rendered it uncompetitive internationally. Therefore, the possibility of entry into a broader transnational market organized like the European Union that also offered some protection against global competition excited both politicians and business leaders.

The idea of a Latin American common market dated back to 1960, but it took the debt crisis and the widespread adoption of "sober" economic policies (neoliberalism) to convince Brazil and Argentina to propose a customs union that would include Uruguay and Paraguay. The proposed treaty created a common external tariff against nonmembers, eliminated custom duties within the common market, deregulated agriculture, and potentially allowed for the privatization of some state industries and banking. The partners dubbed the new free trade zone the *Mercado Común del Sur*, or Mercosur for short. To prevent disputes, Mercosur's administrators created a body of agreed-upon civil law policies concerning issues such as the environment, public health, and standards for products.[12]

When President Lacalle signed the Treaty of Asunción in March 1991, he voiced some misgivings, namely that Brazil and Argentina, who combined generated over 90 percent of Mercosur's GDP, would dominate the customs union. The Mercosur agreement bound the four parties into a common goal of promoting democracy and a more open, liberal economy that encouraged freer trade and capital flow between nations. The treaty opened Brazilian and Argentine markets to Uruguayan goods, garnering an enormous financial advantage for the country. These policies benefited Uruguay and strengthened its role within Mercosur as a service economy because of its well-educated populace's foreign language abilities and IT skills.[13]

During Mercosur's first decade, Uruguay's trade with Brazil and Argentina increased fivefold, such that exports and imports from the two constituted almost 50 percent of Uruguay's GDP. Uruguay's service economy grew significantly during the 1990s as tourism and banking accounted for about 35 percent of its GDP. The dairy industry expanded enormously as a consequence of Mercosur membership. Its regulations required that cheeses, wherever manufactured, have a standard texture, flavor, and color. Uruguayan dairy farmers sold their milk, cheese, and other dairy products to a cooperative, Conaprole, which in turn exported them to Brazil. Today, Brazil remains the largest purchaser of Uruguayan dairy items.[14]

The issue of new members raised political controversies. The treaty required that the admission of a new permanent member required a unanimous vote. In 2004, Venezuela's Hugo Chávez had sufficient clout to bypass the formal steps (with which Chile and Bolivia had complied) required for associate membership. Chávez promised to use oil revenues to aid his friends in the Southern Cone as part of his ambition to play a larger role on the world stage, and as a counterpoise to U.S. influence. In 2013 Venezuela requested full membership status at a propitious moment. Mercosur had just suspended Paraguay's membership because of a lapse in its democratic practices. The remaining three presidents (Brazil's Luiz Inácio Lula de Silva, Argentina's Cristina Fernández de Kirchner, and Uruguay's José Mujica), all members of the leftist Pink Tide, voted to admit Venezuela. Three years later, the members suspended Venezuela indefinitely until President Nicolás Maduro agreed to hold free elections and desist from human rights abuses, which he has yet to do. In the meantime, Colombia, Peru, Ecuador, Suriname, and Guyana have become associate members.[15]

By 2019, Mercosur had become the fifth-largest trade bloc in the world. From the outset it hoped to expand its advantages as a large Regional Trade Association to gain a special status with the EU. Negotiators authored a draft agreement in 2019, but EU leaders had reservations about Brazil's logging operations in the Amazon. In addition, French farmers objected to the wholesale importation of Argentine beef, which threatened their own production. Any arrangement with the EU seems unlikely as of 2025. As a result, Mercosur nations have pursued bilateral agreements with other trading partners, such as China.[16]

THE PROGRESSIVE PRESIDENTS TAKE OFFICE: THE FRENTE AMPLIO, 2005–2015

Although Uruguay's economy began to recover during the final year of Jorge Batlle's presidency, the electorate was ready for change. In much of Latin America, voters rejected the neoliberal economic measures that had wreaked hardship on the poor, leading to the resurgence of the far left in Venezuela, Bolivia, and Ecuador, earning them the nickname of the "Pink Tide." They swept to power with widespread popular support based on the premise that they would undo neoliberal legislation. Between 1999 and 2016 (the dates vary from country to country), Hugo Chávez's Venezuela, Evo Morales's Bolivia, and Rafael Correa's Ecuador adopted policies that redistributed national wealth to the poorest members of society and abandoned the path of the Washington Consensus, the IMF, and the World Bank. Pink Tide leaders in Brazil (Lula) and Argentina (Néstor Kirchner) also spent vast sums on social welfare projects.[17]

In 2004, Uruguayans rejected both of the traditional parties. The election of Frente Amplio's Tabaré Vázquez as president, as well as the party's sweep of the congressional elections, suggested that Uruguay would be joining Latin America's Pink

Tide. This did not happen. President Vázquez campaigned on his promise to abide by Uruguay's democratic tradition and moderate left reformism rather than seeking radical structural changes as proposed by Chávez, Morales, and Correa. Tabaré Vázquez's biography as a respected oncologist convinced voters that, while moving leftward, he would continue Uruguay's political, economic, and social trajectory. To the surprise of observers, Vázquez won an outright majority in the first round (the first time this had happened since the Colorados' victory in 1950), thereby avoiding a repetition of the 2000 election where the two traditional parties joined forces in the run-off to deprive him of the presidency. The victory of the Frente Amplio marked the beginning of fifteen years of progressive reforms.[18]

As a first step, President Vázquez and the Frente Amplio fulfilled their promise to deepen democracy by creating broadly based advisory councils in marginalized communities that drafted legislation for congressional consideration. This more participatory form of democracy encouraged new ideas for change. For example, one advisory council drew up recommendations to reform the education statute. They compiled ideas drawn from regional assemblies that included roughly twenty thousand participants, mostly students and teachers. Legislators then drafted a bill that adopted most of the council's recommendations. The statute reaffirmed the nation's long-standing commitment to universal public education, but also adopted the committee's recommendation requiring that education receive a fixed percentage of GDP as its allocation. Law 18,437 of 2008 committed the government to provide free early childhood education, adult continuing education, and funded laptops for all primary school students although rural schools still had some disadvantages like transportation.[19]

The Frente Amplio also utilized participatory democracy to reform the Wage Councils, the social security system, and health care. The Wage Councils, reinstated after the era of the dictatorship, were disbanded in 1992 during Lacalle's neoliberal reforms. The Frente Amplio reinstated the councils and allowed additional workers' organizations to bring wage disputes forward. As a result, new legislation allowed rural workers, public administrators, and domestic servants to engage in collective bargaining. In the spirit of moderation, the government set minimum and maximum levels of wage increases. In part because of this process, real wages for employees rose more than 50 percent between 2005 and 2014.[20]

The government successfully reformed social security. As part of the neoliberal reforms of the 1990s, the government had allowed high-income employees to invest a portion of their contributions in a private pension system. Although the private system offered greater returns in prosperous times, it also put pensioners at greater risk. Citizen groups successfully advocated for a change that simplified the application for social security and unemployment benefits. A second provision allowed people invested in the private system to return their funds to the public system.

During the neoliberal years, the health care system also included a private option, similar to the one in Pinochet's Chile. After much discussion within citizens' councils, the Frente Amplio's legislation increased participation and funding for the public health care system. In short, the Frente Amplio's methodology of creating greater consensus using participatory democracy redistributed wealth more broadly. These reforms, however, did not undertake deep structural changes in the system (no discussions occurred about tax reform, for example), but merely tinkered with it. The combination of the Frente Amplio's restraint in limiting new public spending, coupled with greater income resulting from the commodity boom, led to a decade of positive economic growth and reform while maintaining the Frente's popularity.[21]

President Vázquez's thorniest problem arose when a Finnish corporation, UPM, sought to establish the Botnia wood pulp plant near Fray Bentos in 2003. No longer did Uruguay's landscape look as it had in the days of the gaucho, with rolling grasslands and the occasional lonely ombú tree providing shade. Now forests of eucalyptus trees, fated to be ground into pulpwood, grew everywhere. The thin, absolutely straight trees, clustered closely together, matured in about ten years at which time workers logged them, removed the bark, let them dry in the sun, and trimmed them to a uniform size for trucking to the mill. UPM owned 370,000 acres planted in trees. Ranchers quickly learned that they could plant eucalyptus on the prairie, and that once the seedlings had sprouted to a sufficient height, they could graze cattle beneath them, realizing a second source of income from the same acreage.

Despite the theoretical unity that Mercosur had established between partners, Uruguay's licensing of UMP's plant at Fray Bentos raised concerns about pollution in the town of Gualaguaychú, Argentina, just across the river. In April, 2005 its citizens and environmental allies led a demonstration that prevented traffic from crossing the San Martín bridge into Uruguay. The blockades continued sporadically as environmental groups and Argentina's government filed a complaint with the International Court of Justice. Argentina's President Néstor Kirchner proved unwilling to curb the protesters, which damaged Uruguayan commerce and threatened the summer (January through March) tourist season. The International Court eventually found in favor of Uruguay in 2010. The ruling did not deter sporadic protests. Vázquez's successor established a cordial relationship with Argentine President Cristina Fernández de Kirchner who convinced the Gualaguaychú protesters to refrain from blocking the bridge. In exchange, the new Uruguayan president agreed to monitor jointly the environmental condition of the river with Argentina.[22]

Tabaré Vázquez's 60 percent approval rating, despite vetoing a bill to legalize abortion, convinced voters to deliver a plurality of votes to former Tupamaro guerrilla José "Pepe" Mujica in the 2009 presidential election. During the dictatorship, Mujica had been shot, tortured, and imprisoned for fourteen years, resulting in ongoing physical issues. Known for his modest lifestyle, Mujica drove an old Volkswagen Beetle and refused to live in the presidential palace, preferring to reside in his modest farmhouse just outside Montevideo. He donated 90 percent of his salary to charity, and refused to wear a necktie on formal occasions, even when he met with President Barack Obama during a state visit. More importantly, like Vázquez, Mujica promised to follow his predecessor's moderate economic policies.[23]

BOX 8.1: ENERGY

In 2007, Uruguay's growth slowed because oil prices had reached the astronomical sum of $145 a barrel. Tired of fluctuating petroleum prices, Tabaré Vázquez and his cabinet set a goal of energy independence. After rejecting nuclear power, the government accepted the proposal of physicist Ramón Méndez Galain who suggested that a combination of wind and solar power could solve Uruguay's energy needs. Galain served as national director of energy under both progressive presidents. His $6 billion plan, roughly the equivalent of 12 percent of Uruguay's GDP, proposed installing wind turbines throughout the east and north of the country. Twenty private turbine manufacturers bid on the project. When each company agreed to match the lowest bidders' contract, Uruguay accepted every proposal and aggressively adopted wind power. The companies installed turbines at their own expense, and the state-owned electric company (UTE) sold the electricity to consumers at a guaranteed profitable price for twenty years. By 2023, wind generated 40 percent of the country's electricity. Four dams produced enough hydroelectric power to contribute an additional 40 percent for the energy grid, while solar and biomass chips provided lesser amounts. In total, 98 percent of Uruguay's energy needs today come from renewable sources. Cities replaced diesel-powered buses with electric ones and joined the International Alliance for the Decarbonization of Transport with hopes of encouraging truckers to convert to green hydrogen. The use of clean energy usage makes Montevideo one of Latin America's most livable cities. Today, Uruguay, Denmark, and Iceland are the three nations leaving the smallest carbon footprint on the planet.[24]

Mujica dedicated much of his term to expanding the personal liberties of Uruguay's underrepresented citizens and seeking justice for the victims of the military dictatorship (discussed in a later sections) while leaving the details of economic policy in the hands of his capable vice president. Over the course of the decade, Frente Amplio reduced poverty levels from 40 percent in 2004 to 9 percent in 2014, the lowest in Latin America. During the same years, real wages rose 52 percent and indigency declined to about 2 percent while expenditures for social programs rose from 60 percent of the budget to 75 percent. According to the GINI index, the progressive governments had successfully reduced income inequality. How had the Frente Amplio secured the resources to achieve these social gains?[25]

CHINA AND THE COMMODITY BOOM, 2004–2014

At the beginning of the twenty-first century, China gained membership into the World Trade Association and initiated its "going out" policy: engaging in global trade in a major way. Remarkably bereft of raw materials given its geographical enormity, China had to seek essential commodities in the international marketplace and turned to Latin America and Africa to supply its need for petroleum, iron ore, and copper. China's thirst for these products increased their prices resulting in significant boosts to Latin American economies. As a result, the region's annual growth rate between 2004 and 2011 increased by roughly 3.6 percent, even taking into account the Great Recession of 2008. After 2014, Chinese purchases of commodities receded somewhat as it became more consumer oriented. Nevertheless, the China boom allowed Latin American nations to invest in their own people and redistribute profits to the poorest sectors of society. While some Latin American nations (Argentina, Brazil, Ecuador, and Venezuela) emphasized redistribution to the near exclusion of development, others like Uruguay followed a more balanced approach and did both. In fact, domestic investment in Uruguay grew steadily over the boom years as did the use of technology.[26]

Until 2006, Uruguay had imported more goods than it exported to China, resulting in an unfavorable trade balance. The uptick in Chinese demand reversed this trend. Although Uruguay offered no mineral commodities for sale, the Chinese textile industry placed a premium on fine Uruguayan wool tops and even on uncarded wool, sales of which brought the nation prosperity unknown since the mid-1950s. To a lesser degree, the cattle industry made inroads into Chinese markets, both for quality beef, and after 2019, for powdered milk. The resulting wave of prosperity allowed the Frente Amplio government to meet existing loan repayment obligations and provide for the expansion of social benefits during the presidencies of the progressive presidents. Since 2016, when China and Uruguay signed a trade agreement following President Mujica's state visit to Beijing, the former has become Uruguay's most important trading partner. It did *not*, however, commit the error of entirely relying upon the commodity boom to improve its economy.[27]

In addition to purchasing Uruguayan commodities, Chinese businesses invested in Uruguay. Between 2006 and 2015, Chery Mobile assembled automobiles in Uruguay as part of a joint venture with Uruguay's Oferal and Argentina's Socma, producing over thirty cars per day. These inexpensive cars temporarily displaced the *cachilas* (vintage cars) and the omnipresent Brazilian-made Volkswagens that once dominated Montevideo's streets. China chose Uruguayan firms as reliable partners because they could market these jointly produced items to other Mercosur nations, especially Brazil and Argentina. Uruguay's skilled and well-educated workforce, as well as its stable political system, also encouraged Chinese corporate investors. In addition to automobiles, Chinese firms became involved in textile, telecommunication, and chemical companies in Uruguay. Sometimes Chinese imports competed successfully with Uruguayan manufacturers, no longer protected by the ISI tariff regimen. Those manufacturers that operated in specialized niche markets more easily survived Chinese competition.[28]

After 2014 China's interest in Latin America diversified under President Xi Jinping's "Belt and Road Initiative" (OBOR), a global infrastructure construction plan funded by loans through the China Development Bank. Xi's vision challenged

U.S. and Western Europe's domination of financing large development projects in the Global South. Although the most grandiose of these projects, President Xi's hope to construct an inter-oceanic canal through Nicaragua, failed to materialize, other infrastructure projects have moved forward. Uruguay signed a memorandum of understanding that outlined a series of projects for Uruguay. It became the first Mercosur nation to sign such an agreement with China.[29]

Transportation links and electrification ranked high on the types of projects the Chinese favored. In August, 2018, after Tabaré Vázquez's visit, China promised it would build a new Central Railroad, which was expected to transport pulpwood from the recently constructed UPM plant at Paso de los Toros to the port of Montevideo. The new mill will outproduce the other two pulp mills combined. Unfortunately, when China's economy shut down during the COVID crisis, work on the railroad ceased. Chinese companies participated in UTE's wind power project and brought electrification to the sparsely settled north by constructing more wind farms. China also promised to develop a new fishing port on the Atlantic. China's development program appealed to Latin Americans because Xi seemed more forgiving and generous about alternative modes of payments when some countries had difficulties meeting their obligations.[30]

Has China's involvement with Uruguay as a new trading partner benefited the country and allowed it to avoid the "resource curse": economists' notion that commodity exporters often fritter away for political purposes the profits earned from an export boom? As previously noted, the progressive Frente Amplio governments did redistribute wealth significantly between 2005 and 2015. As a result, Uruguay enjoyed the highest income equality ranking under the GINI index in all of Latin America at the end of the progressive period. But the country also achieved a balance between economic growth and the progressive redistribution of resources. These results paid political dividends as the Frente Amplio won the presidency for the third successive time in 2015.[31]

THE QUESTION OF AMNESTY FOR THE MILITARY AND POLICE AFTER 1989

Undaunted by the Expiry Law and the referenda of 1989 and 2009, opponents of amnesty sought to find loopholes to prosecute the military on behalf of victims. For example, the statute did allow presidents to initiate investigations of claims of human rights abuses. President Jorge Batlle took advantage of this clause to create the Peace Commission to find children of twenty-six imprisoned Tupamaro women, later tortured and disappeared, whose babies had been adopted by military families. The preliminary findings of the commission suggested that twenty-nine dissidents had been killed in Uruguayan prisons while an additional 150 individuals who had fled to Argentina met their demise there. Because former president Juan María Bordaberry was not a member of the military, the commission found that he did not enjoy the benefit of the Expiry Law. Found guilty but in ill-health, ex-President

Bordaberry remained under house arrest until his death in 2011. General Gregorio Alvarez, a civilian at the time of his presidency, also fell outside the Expiry Law. Convicted of ordering the kidnapping and torture of Uruguayan exiles in Argentina as part of Operation Condor, he too remained in prison until his death.[32]

For President José Mujica, the issue of securing justice for victims of the dictatorship was personal. In the 1990s, Senator Zelmar Michelini's son created and led an annual "March for Truth, Memory, and Never Again" as survivors sought justice. The government's new paper currency after 1993 did not honor military heroes, but rather gave homage to poets, artists, academics, and musicians. Human rights activists had long criticized Uruguay for its inaction, and opened a case before the International Human Rights Court to force change. Amnesty International estimated that Uruguay's military had disappeared 197 citizens and executed another 202. In 2011, the verdict in the case of *Gelman v. Uruguay* in the Inter-American Court of Human Rights required Uruguay to rethink its amnesty policy. Because of the ongoing outcry against the military's abuses, the Frente Amplio majority in the Assembly overturned the Expiry Law and replaced it with Act 18.831, which reclassified the military's human rights abuses as "crimes against humanity." Under international law, human rights' violations are not subject to statutes of limitations. In a very controversial decision, the Supreme Court struck down two key articles of the statute, holding that Uruguay's statute of limitations meant that Act 18.831 could not be applied retroactively to the injustices of the dictatorship. Women who had been abused by the military had been building their cases by collecting many testimonials. Although many provided depositions by 2021, the government has apparently decided not to move forward with charges. While the quest for justice remains unlikely to be satisfied, these women's collective memories have impacted society. As of 2023, only twenty-three policemen or military had been sentenced.[33]

THE FRENTE AMPLIO AND PROGRESSIVE PERSONAL LIBERTIES, 2005–2015

The Frente Amplio had promised not only to distribute wealth more equitably, but also to improve its citizens' health and well-being. As a practicing oncologist, Dr. Vázquez understood the dangers of tobacco and lent his prestige to the anti-tobacco campaign. He pointed out that more people worldwide died from smoking every year than the total number of casualties in the two world wars combined. In 2006, the Assembly passed legislation that banned smoking in bars, restaurants, offices, and other enclosed public places, the first Latin American nation to do so. Public opinion polls showed that 80 percent of the population agreed. When Philip Morris sued Uruguay for requiring graphic warnings on cigarette packs, Uruguay won the litigation in an international court, setting an example for other countries seeking to limit Big Tobacco's products. In 2018, during his second term, Dr. Vázquez convinced the Assembly to pass legislation requiring manufacturers of comestibles to place labels on their products if they contained excessive salt, fat, or sugar (most soft drinks). Ironically, after the success of the anti-smoking campaign, President Vázquez would die of lung cancer shortly after his second term as president ended.[34]

The Frente Amplio, like many of the Pink Tide governments, also fought for an expanded interpretation of human rights, which included more personal liberties for disadvantaged groups. Uruguay had always been among the most progressive Latin American states regarding women's rights. Beginning with the democratic and progressive José Batlle years, Uruguayan women gained equal access to primary and secondary education and secured the right to vote. They gained property rights such as the ability to open bank accounts in their own names. In the post–World War II era, the state recognized their equal status in law regarding the raising of children and in the workplace although courts often ignored the latter law.[35]

The second wave of feminism beginning in the 1970s attempted to reform civil and criminal legal codes to expand women's reproductive freedom; specifically, access to contraception and abortion. Both of these issues posed moral questions that raised vigorous opposition. Women and their advocates, which included many male public figures, also wanted a statute protecting victims of domestic violence, long unpunished. In 2017, legislation ended the defense of a "crime of passion" in the event of a murder of an adulterous wife. The Frente Amplio advanced abortion rights. While ethically controversial, these progressive reforms placed no additional financial burdens on the treasury. Uruguayan feminists hoped to advance the careers of female politicians, but while women have won seats in the legislature, no woman has been elected president.[36]

The issue of legalizing abortion polarized society. Advocates for change saw the matter as a question of liberty, privacy, and public health, while opponents wanted to uphold the right to life and family values. Under the 1938 constitution, compassionate (victims of rape) and therapeutic (to save the life of the mother) abortion became legal. Following the landmark decision of *Roe v. Wade* in the United States, women in Uruguay pressured political leaders to grant them a similar freedom of choice. In September of 2012, the legislature passed a bill legalizing elective abortion (for any reason) during the first trimester and thereafter for victims of rape or incest. Although social conservatives and the Catholic Church attempted to annul the reform through a referendum, they could not muster sufficient signatures to bring the issue forward.[37]

In 2007 the Frente Amplio voted to make Uruguay the first Latin American nation to legalize same-sex civil unions. After five years of cohabitation, same-sex couples could formally prove a union and obtain social security benefits, inheritance rights, and joint property rights. They could also adopt children. The following year a senator, working with a pro-LGBT lawyer and the "Black Sheep" organization, drafted a bill permitting same-sex marriage. The bill caused controversy, with former president Sanguinetti favoring it and former president Lacalle opposing it. Similar bills had been enacted into law in Argentina and Brazil. After much debate, the legislation passed in 2013 with support from all three parties. Although a bare majority of voters approved of the measure in 2012, by 2017 three-quarters of all Uruguayans favored it.[38]

In 2018 the Frente Amplio moved forward with the "Freedom of Identity" bill that guaranteed personal freedoms for transgendered people. The law stated that anybody could create their own personality based upon their chosen gender identity. This allowed individuals to change their names, even children under the age of thirteen after a professional consultation and with their parents' consent. Further, the law obligated the National Health Care system to pay for hormone therapy and sex reassignment surgery. More conservative citizens attempted to undo this socially progressive legislation but could not garner enough signatures for a referendum.[39]

President Mujica also pressed forward with a campaign to legalize marijuana, another reform that may have generated revenue. For over forty years, Latin American nations had argued that the explosion of drug use, illegal trafficking, and resulting violence was the fault of consuming nations like the United States, where the demand for drugs escalated rapidly. In 2013, the Organization of American States (OAS) suggested that its members ought to rethink their laws about drug use. Uruguay's recreational use statute permitted people over the age of eighteen to join a social club, limited in size, where they could purchase an ounce and a half of pot from a pharmacy every month for personal consumption. The statute also allowed people to cultivate modest amounts for personal use. The Frente Amplio government argued that the legislation would minimize pot smoking and not lead to the consumption of other drugs.[40]

TABARÉ VÁZQUEZ'S SECOND TERM, 2015–2020

Former president Tabaré Vázquez had retained the popularity he rightly earned during his first administration. But by 2015, the China boom had slowed and dampened progressives' prospects for additional reforms, especially after they lost their majority in the Assembly. The economic slowdown inhibited the ability of the government to redistribute more resources and eventually dragged President Tabaré Vázquez's popularity below the 30 percent level. Conservatives believed that Mujica's reforms had gone too far and that the new administration needed to put a brake on further innovations. The Assembly refused to fund some of Mujica's proposed infrastructure expenditures because of tighter finances and China's delays on implementing the Belt and Road Initiative.[41]

The question whether the government could make additional progressive social reforms awakened fears that Uruguay would be unable to escape the "middle income trap (MIT)," the status of a country remaining ensnared at a mid-level of development below the wealthy United States, Western Europe, Japan, China, and Southeast Asia, but above the impoverished nations of the Global South. Countries fall into the MIT because they cannot compete globally in labor intensive industries (like textiles) because their workers earn high wages. They also cannot compete in the manufacture of high-value products or services (high-tech goods, for example) because their productivity is too low. Even though Uruguay (and Chile) had briefly reached the high-development group during the boom years, the slowing economy after 2016 moved them downward to where the middle-income trap awaited them.[42]

Economists suggest several steps a nation should take to attain permanently a high level of development. Local businessmen and the state must invest significant resources into building sustainable infrastructure, employing innovative technology to become more competitive, and developing a human capital by promoting education and health care access. Remaining in the high-income range requires a nation to invest at least 25 percent of its GDP in education, infrastructure, and technology. During their periods of rapid development, China, Japan, and the "Little Tigers" of East Asia (Hong Kong, Singapore, South Korea, and Taiwan) spent more than 40 percent of their revenue in these three categories. Although Uruguay outspends all other Latin American nation, its total is only 20 percent.[43]

Uruguay needs to do more. In terms of human resources, its population is well educated and healthy. Although education is free through the university level, too few students complete secondary school. The government has wholeheartedly embraced technology. Even without China's promised infrastructure improvements, Uruguay continued to build roads that facilitated the rapid transportation of goods. With their Chinese partner, Huawei, Uruguay developed a fiber optic network service that reaches most of the country. As noted earlier, the country embraced green energy, generating electricity almost exclusively from wind farms, hydroelectric power, solar, and burned pulpwood residue. To gain more investment revenue, Uruguay needs to revise its tax structure and form more public–private partnerships. No longer does the livestock industry dominate the export economy. By 2023, fully 25 percent of exports came from pulpwood; grains, especially rice, provided another 25 percent; textiles and other products, including beef, supplied a lesser amount.

BOX 8.2: PHILANTHROPY AND THE MEVIR PROGRAM

Local landowner and award-winning stockbreeder Alberto Gallinal Heber, the owner of San Pedro de Timote, originated a philanthropic endeavor called the Movement to End Unhealthy Rural Housing (*Movimiento para la Erradicación de la Viviendo Rural Insalubre*) in 1967 to build homes for the rural poor. The influential Dr. Gallinal Heber convinced the government to pass Law 13.640 to initiate the program, intended in part to slow migration from rural areas to Montevideo. Post-dictatorship governments have endorsed the program. MEVIR's supervising board oversees townspeople engaged in sweat equity programs (ninety-six hours a month) to construct tiny houses, a school, and a police station. Upon completion, the beneficiaries participate in a lottery to choose the house that they will occupy. The National Housing Fund pays for 70 percent of the construction, and the new owners repay the remaining 30 percent under the terms of a low-rate mortgage. The process has resulted in the formation of communities instead of rural slums. The government connects the new homes with electricity, water, and sanitation. MEVIR has significantly improved the quality of life in rural areas during the twenty-first century.[44]

In response to popular claims in 2016 that the Frente Amplio no longer had a reform agenda, President Vázquez advanced several ideas. The government provided laptops to all students in secondary schools, and accelerated the expansion of the fiberoptic network. It pushed for an agreement with UPM to build a third pulp mill at Paso de los Toros (near Durazno) on the Río Negro. Completed in 2023, the mill has brought employment to thousands of Uruguayans and has bipartisan support from the political parties. Uruguay is now the third-largest bleached pulpwood producer in Latin America. President Vázquez also signed the Ibirapitá Plan that distributed four hundred thousand computer tablets to low-income retirees over the age of sixty-five. These machines allowed the elderly to access information about social programs and benefits for which they were eligible and gave them access to the internet to communicate with friends and relatives to lessen their isolation.[45]

Although corruption is rare in Uruguay, scandal reached near the top of Vázquez's second administration. The indictment of Vice President Raúl Sendic, the son of the former Tupamaro guerrilla and a youthful Frente Amplio politician, soured many on the party. Auditors uncovered financial irregularities in ANCAP's books during the time Sendic was its manager. Sendic further lost public credibility when he could not produce documentation proving he had received a medical degree from the University of Havana as he claimed. Finally, prosecutors proved that Sendic used ANCAP accounts to purchase clothes, jewelry, and electronic equipment for himself, behavior that stood in marked contrast to former president Mujica's penurious lifestyle. As a result, Sendic resigned in 2017.[46]

By the time of the presidential election of 2019, Tabaré Vázquez's popularity had waned despite the fact that over the last fifteen years Frente Amplio's policies had resulted in dramatically reduced poverty rates and greater income equality. While progressive elements called for more radical systemic change in the tax structure to make the rich pay more, an opposition group called *Un Solo Uruguay* took the opposite point of view. The members of this organization proposed that the nation's spending priorities ought to be altered. Calling for a reduction of excessive social spending and lowering taxes on the upper middle classes, Un Solo Uruguay proposed that government should invest more in agriculture and manufacturing. This group and other disenchanted members of the electorate would change the direction of the country in the presidential election of 2019.[47]

RETURN OF THE NATIONALISTS, 2020–2025

By 2019, other Latin American nations had also turned away from the Pink Tide. As Frente Amplio's popularity declined, National Party leader Luis Lacalle Pou, a law graduate from the Catholic University and son of former Nationalist president Luis Alberto Lacalle, won the election by promising an expansion of free-market opportunities and a more conservative outlook on social issues. Earlier in his career he had opposed the abortion law and gay marriage. In the first round, he garnered the largest percentage of the vote (about 28 percent) and narrowly won in the second round by creating a coalition of center-right to extreme right parties that combined earned slightly more than half the vote. President Lacalle Pou was determined to take Uruguay in a new direction.[48]

During the campaign, he promised major reforms, bundled together in the "Law of Urgent Consideration," which the president signed in July, 2020. It contained 857 separate articles that modified some of the measures of the progressive years. Immediately, the labor unions and Frente Amplio began collecting signatures to repeal 135 of the measures that affected ANCAP, labor unions, social security, and public housing. After all the procedural requirement had been met, the vote occurred late in 2022. The referendum to repeal the legislation failed, even though it won a majority in Montevideo, Paysandú, and urbanized Canelones department. Lacalle's reforms, however, did not undermine his basic support for the country's social democratic reformist tradition.[49]

Lacalle Pou won widespread acclaim for his reasonable and prompt response to the COVID-19 crisis. When hospitals reported the first COVID cases on March 13, 2020, the government went into immediate lockdown and closed the Argentine border (the Brazil border remained more fluid). After short lockdowns, Lacalle Pou focused on voluntary guidelines, testing, and vaccines. All students had laptops; thus, instruction continued uninterrupted. He urged Uruguayans to reduce social gatherings outside the family and practice social distancing, suggesting Montevideans could walk individually on the Rambla. The government initiated widespread testing and successfully traced and isolated infected persons. Like other nations in the Global South, Uruguay initially had difficulty procuring vaccines, but eventually China offered the Sino-Vac and Uruguay received shipments of the Pfizer vaccine in 2021. Within a relatively short amount of time, about 86 percent of the population had received at least one dose. Although about 1 million Uruguayans contracted COVID, the country recorded only 7,617 deaths. As a result of Lacalle Pou's policies and Uruguay's generally healthy and well-off population, face-to-face instruction resumed in May 2021 and borders reopened by the end of the year. To counter the economic effects of the pandemic and reduce exposure, the government expanded unemployment benefits to some, and increased subsidies to the poor and eased credit restrictions.[50]

BOX 8.3: COVID-19 AND YERBA MATE

Some readers familiar with Uruguay may find it odd that this book has only made occasional reference to yerba mate, the quintessential national drink. Its relevance here is because COVID-19 completely disrupted the social conventions associated with the beverage. Since colonial times, drinking yerba mate has been a ritual shared between family members, friends, business associates, and workers on the job. Sharing mate is a sign of friendship and respect. The familiar sight of a man carrying a thermos of hot water under his arm is part of the urban landscape. To make the tea, the server pours boiling water into a mate (bowl) containing yerba (tea leaves). The recipient then sips the caffeinated beverage through a *bombilla* (metal straw) with a strainer at the base and passes it to others. COVID-19 changed that timeless tradition. As COVID spread, health authorities advised that social contacts spread the disease and warned about the dangers of sharing a bombilla with non-family members. As a result, the practice of communal mate drinking stopped and now (at least to this observer) is still limited to couples and families.[51]

The ill effects of COVID reduced Uruguay's gross national product (GNP) by nearly 6 percent in 2020. Because Mercosur's attempts to ink a pact with the EU stalled in 2019, President Lacalle Pou sought an alternative, a bilateral agreement with China or a tie to other free trade zones such as the Trans-Pacific Partnership. He hoped to obtain a tariff reduction for Uruguayan beef in the China market similar to the advantages that Australia and New Zealand enjoyed. (China's tariff is already lower than that of the United States and the EU.) Further, Chinese firms buy the entire cow and not just choice cuts like western consumers. In return, Uruguay offered to open its doors to more Chinese products at advantageous tariff rates. But as Uruguay attempted to move further away from Mercosur, its partner, Brazil, vetoed these plans.[52]

Early in 2022, *The Economist* published a very favorable analysis of Uruguay's status in line with this author's thesis. The article highlighted the fact that Uruguay has the largest middle class in Latin America, close to the lowest levels of inequality, and has essentially eliminated extreme poverty. Its economy is balanced and sound. In addition, its faith in democracy remains unshakable. Unfortunately, in February 2023, scandal tarnished the nation's image when a court convicted the nation's security chief and a close friend of the president of influence peddling, associating with criminals and selling fake Uruguayan birth certificates so that Russians could obtain genuine Uruguayan passports. Because of a de-emphasis on border security after the signing of Mercosur, gangs began using Montevideo to ship guns and drugs from Argentina to Brazil. Drug lords ferried cocaine from Peru and Colombia through Uruguay to EU nations. As a result of gangs and drugs, criminal activity has increased such that security is now a concern of citizens.

Despite these problems, the president remained popular. The country experienced a severe water shortage in July 2023 after a third straight year of drought. Both reservoirs on the Santa Lucia River that provided water for Montevideo drained down to 1 percent of capacity. Lacalle Pou avoided absolute prohibitions and instead urged voluntary usage restrictions such as not watering lawns. Because Montevideo's piped water became unsafe, the government recommended bottled water and supplied it free to poorer communities. It desalinated water from the Río de la Plata, and excluded from the ban workers in poorer communities who made their living by washing cars, suggesting instead ways in which they could reuse water. Finally, that November, the skies opened and delivered plentiful rain.[53]

CONCLUSION

The Uruguayan renaissance required the full-throated commitment of all three political parties to democracy in 1985. This agreement created an atmosphere of compromise that tempered discussions about economics and social policy. The elimination of the lema system in favor of a second-round run-off increased the likelihood that the most popular presidential candidate would win. Although the Frente Amplio initially resisted reforms to the neo-battlista state, the three parties supported Mercosur and encouraged foreign investment, the development of new exports, the use of high-end technology, and freer trade. These policies allowed Uruguay to resume economic growth, particularly (but not exclusively) during the years of the commodity boom from 2005 to 2014. The parties' agreement to compromise also extended to supporting moderate, socially progressive legislation without resorting to exorbitant financial handouts that bankrupted its "Pink Tide" neighbors. All parties accepted Frente Amplio legislation expanding the rights of women, gays, and transgendered

Figure 8.1 A Group of Gauchos Drinking Yerba Mate. Uruguayans enjoy their favorite drink of mate at virtually any time of day. As a highly caffeinated beverage, yerba mate is particularly enjoyable in the afternoon. Although this image portrays a country scene, urban Uruguayan men commonly carry a thermos of hot water under one arm so that they can refill the bowl as the day goes on. *Source*: Columbus Memorial Library.

people. By 2024, Uruguay had the largest middle class in all of Latin America, had almost eliminated extreme poverty, and enjoyed the least income inequality on the continent. As this book went to press, Uruguayans elected Frente Amplio's Yamandú Orsi as president for the 2025–2030 term. He ran on a platform of "safe change that will not be radical," maintaining the principles that have governed the nation since the end of the dictatorship and made it once again South America's success story.[54]

NOTES

1. Weinstein, *Crossroads*, 86–90; Charles Gillespie, *Negotiating Democracy: Politicians and Generals in Uruguay*, Cambridge: Cambridge University Press, 1991, 218–19.

2. Gillespie, *Negotiating Democracy*, 228–38. The quoted phrase is Weinstein's, "*Crossroads*," 126; Finch, "Uruguay since 1930," 231.

3. Alexander, *Organized Labor*, 77–79; Weinstein, *Crossroad*, 95–99; Gillespie, *Negotiating Democracy*, 220–27; M. H. J. Finch, "Uruguay since 1930," 228–29.

4. Gillespie, *Negotiating Democracy*, 218–21; Weinstein, *Crossroads*, 101–9, Gerardo Caetano, *Historia minima de Uruguay*, Mexico: El Colegio de Mexico, 2020, 234–35. For a vivid novel about Mujica's life, see Carolina de Robertis, *The President and the Frog*, New York: Alfred A. Knopf, 2021. Luis Roniger and Mario Sznajder, *The Legacy of Human Rights Violations in the Southern Cone: Argentina, Chile, and Uruguay*, New York: Oxford University Press, 1999, 80–81.

5. Debbie Sharnak, *Of Light and Shadow: Social Justice, Human Rights, and Accountability in Uruguay*, Philadelphia: University of Pennsylvania Press, 2023, 191–219, 229–231. Sharnak argues that Sanguinetti's decision promoted peace and democracy, while the trials in Argentina prompted three military revolts and the Rettig Commission Report in Chile caused great anxiety. Francesca Lessa, *The Condor Trials: Transnational Repression and Human Rights in South America*, New Haven: Yale University Press, 2022, 176; Roniger and Sznajder, *Human Rights Violations*, 79–89, 165; Finch, "Uruguay since 1930," 229–230.

6. Gerardo Caetano, *Historia minima de Uruguay*, Mexico: El Colegio de Mexico, 2020, 237–38, 241–42; Glen Biglaiser, *Guardians of the Nation? Economists, Generals and Economic Reform in Latin America*, Notre Dame: Naotre Dame University Press, 2002, 166–67. William Beezley (ed.), *The World Today Series: Latin America, 2020–2022*, fifty-fourth edition, Lanham, MD: Rowman & Littlefield, 399.

7. Juan J. Linz and Alfred Stepan, *Problems of Democratic Transition and Consolidation: Southern Europe,* South America, and Post-Communist Europe, Baltimore: Johns Hopkins University Press, 1996, 155–64.

8. Caetano, *Historia mínima*, 242–46.

9. Beezley, *Latin America*, 399; Caetano, *Historia mínima*, 249–51.

10. Caetano, *Historia mínima*, 251–54.

11. Beezley, *Latin America*, 399–400; Caetano, *Historia mínima*, 255–57.

12. Peter Coffey, "The Historical Background to Integration in Latin America," in Peter Coffey (ed.), *Latin America—MERCOSUR*, Boston: Kluwer Academic Publishers, 1998, 2–18. See also Francesco Duina, *The Social Construction of Free Trade: The European Union, Nafta, and Mercosur*, Princeton: Princeton University Press, 2006, 19–21, 74–75, 101; Gillespie, *Negotiating Democracy*, 232.

13. Carlos Eduardo López Rodriguez, *Uruguay*, in Coffee (ed.), *MERCOSUR*, 155–77. Paul Cammack, "MERCOSUR: From Domestic Concerns to Regional Influence," in Glenn

Hook and Ian Kearns, *Sub-regionalism and World Order*, New York: St. Martin's Press, 1999, 95–97, 112–14. Caetano, *Historia mínima*, 239–40.

14. Coffee, *MERCOSUR*, 10–12; Duina, *Social Construction*, 32–42, 101–6, 127–29, 164.

15. "Mercosur Suspends Venezuela for Failure to Follow Rules," Associated Press, December 2, 2016.

16. Council on Foreign Relations, Mercosur report, December 18, 2023.

17. Steve Ellner (ed.), *Latin America's Pink Tide: Breakthrough and Shortcomings*, Lanham, MD: Rowman & Littlefield, 2020, 22–79.

18. Caetano, *Historia Minima*, 258–62; Nicolás Betancourt and José Miguel Busquets, "The Frente Amplio's Government in Uruguay: Policy Strategies and Results," in Ellner (ed.), *Pink Tide*, 113–36, and their edited volume, *El Decenio progresista: Las políticas públicas de Vázquez a Mugica*, Montevideo: Instituto de Ciencia Política, 2016.

19. Betancur and Busquets, "Frente Amplio," 115–17.

20. Betancur and Busquets, "Frente Amplio," 117–18.

21. Betancur and Busquets, "Frente Amplio," 118–25.

22. "Uruguayan Mill Can Operate Despite Breach of Treaty, UN Court Rules," UN News Service, April 20, 2010.

23. Marc Becker, *Twentieth Century Latin American Revolutions*, Lanham, MD: Rowman & Littlefield, 2017, 226–28; Beezley, *Latin America*, 400–401; Pablo Brum, *The Robin Hood Guerrillas: The Epic Journey of Uruguay's Tupamaros*, Orlando: Creative Space, 2014, 350–51.

24. Noah Gallagher Shannon, "What Does Sustainable Living Look Like? Maybe Like Uruguay," *New York Times*, October 5, 2022, Magazine section; Erika Beras, interviewing Ramón Méndez Galain, NPR, "All Things Considered," October 6, 2023; *Merco Press*, May 22, 2021.

25. Caetano, *Historia mínima*, 267–69; Betancourt and Busquets, "Frente Amplio," 128–29.

26. David B. H. Denoon (ed.), *China, the United States, and the Future of Latin America*, New York: New York University Press, 2017, 5–7. Caetano, *Historia mínima*, 265–66. For a study focusing on the larger South American nations, see Carol Wise, *Dragonomics: How Latin America Is Maximizing (or Missing Out On) China's International Development Strategy*, New Haven: Yale University Press, 2020.

27. Kevin P. Gallagher, *The China Triangle: Latin America's China Boom and the Fate of the Washington Consensus*, New York: Oxford University Press, 2016, 42–47. In 2017, for example, Uruguay exported $2.5 billion worth of primarily agricultural products while importing only $1.7 billion of manufactured items.

28. Gallagher, *China Triangle*, 55–58.

29. Gallagher, *China Triangle*, 190; The Global American, "Uruguay and China Sign an MOA" (September 2022).

30. Gallagher, *China Triangle*, 112–13, 146–53.

31. Betancourt and Busquets, "Frente Amplio," 127–30. Caetano, *Historia mínima*, 269–70; Gallagher, *China Triangle*, 93–101. Wise, *Dragonomics*, 156–57, 228–35.

32. David Kohut and Olga Vilella, *Historical Dictionary of the Dirty Wars*, third ed. Lanham, MD: Rowman & Littlefield, 2017, 360–61. See also Francesca Lessa, *Memory and Transitional Justice in Argentina and Uruguay: Against Impunity*, New York: Palgrave Macmillan, 2013; and Lessa, *The Condor Trials-Transnational Repression and Human Rights in South America*, New Haven: Yale University Press, 2022, 179, 183–96.

33. Kohut and Vilella, *Dirty Wars*, 361–62; Lessa, *Condor Trials*, 204–6, 226–27; Roniger and Sznajder, *Human Rights Violations*, 119–21, 212–13. Poet Juan Zorrilla de San Martín

graces the 20-peso note, José Pedro Varela, the educator the 50-peso note, composer Eduardo Fabini the 100-peso note, painter Pedro Figari the 200-peso note, Alfredo Vásquez Acevedo, an educator on the 500-peso note, poet Juana de Ibarbarou on the 1,000-peso note, and priest Dámaso Antonio Larrañaga on the 2,000-peso note. Mariana Achugar and Gabriela Fried Amilivia, "Wounds That Won't Heal: *Mujeres* Case Challenges to Uruguay's Post-Transitional Culture of Impunity," in Pedro Cameselle-Pesce and Debbie Sharnak, *Uruguay in Transnational Perspective*, New York: Routledge, 2024, 352–81.

34. Pan-American Health Organization Bulletin, 2018.

35. Asunción Lavrin, *Women, Feminism, and Social Change in Argentina, Chile, and Uruguay*, Lincoln: University of Nebraska Press, 1995.

36. Karen Kampworth (ed.), *Gender and Populism in Latin America: Passionate Politics*, University Park, PA: Pennsylvania State University Press, 2010, 5–6, 223–26; Mala Htun, *Sex and the State: Abortion, Divorce, and the Family under Latin American Dictatorships and Democracies*, New York: Cambridge University Press, 2003, 115, 59–67, 117–19.

37. Beezley, *Latin America*, 402; Htun, *Sex and the State*, 142–54, 173–76.

38. "Same-Sex Marriage Bill Comes into Force in Uruguay," BBC News, August 5, 2013; Omar G. Encarnación, *Out in the Periphery: Latin America's Gay Rights Revolution*, New York: Oxford University Press, 2016, 51, 69–70.

39. Caetano, *Historia mínima*, 271–72.

40. Beezley, *Latin America*, 402; "Uruguay Cannabis Growers' Clubs, Registration Begins," BBC News, October 31, 2014.

41. Caetano, *Historia mínima*, 270–73.

42. Eva Plaus, Paper 685, *Asian Development Bank Institute*, March, 2017, 1–19; Patrice Franko, *The Puzzle of Latin American Economic Development*, fourth ed., Lanham, MD: Rowman & Littlefield, 2019, 242–96.

43. Plaus, "Paper 685," p. 11. She argued that Latin American nations need to use performance requirements when they fund or partially fund a project; Franko, *Puzzle*, 247–68.

44. "MEVIR: Uruguay's Little House on the Prairie," *Serial Localism: WordPress.com*, March 8, 2016. "*Edición Homenaje al Centenario del. Dr. Alberto Gallinal Heber*," Ministerio de Turismo y Deporte, Uruguay, 2024, 47.

45. Caetano, *Historia mínima*, 273–75. Apparently, students who graduate from private secondary schools are not always included in official statistics.

46. Bentancourt and Busquets, "Frente Amplio," 131.

47. Betancourt and Busquets, "Frente Amplio," 127–31.

48. "Lacalle Wins Presidency as Rival Concedes," BBC News, November 28, 2019.

49. "Uruguay Referendum Votes to Keep Law of Urgent Consideration Referendum," in *Latin American News Digest*, January 23–30, 2024.

50. Johns Hopkins University of Median Coronavirus Resource System, March 10, 2023; Elizabeth Bukacos, Patricia Carbolla, and Miguel Mello, *Latin American Journal of Central Banking*, June 2023; Luis Alberto Moreno, "Latin America's Lost Decades: The Toll of Inequality in the Age of COVID-19, *Foreign Affairs*, January–February, 2021, 138–49.

51. Pite, *Yerba Maté*, 3, 201–3.

52. *The Economist*, "China's Post-Covid Rebound Will Create Winners and Losers in Latin America," January 21, 2023, 25–26; *New York Times*, July 20, 2023.

53. *The Economist*, "Why Uruguay? What Latin America's Success Story Can Teach Its Neighbors," February 26, 2022, 33–34; *The Economist*, "Is Uruguay Losing its Sheen," April 15, 2023, 30.

54. *The Economist*, "Is Uruguay too Stable for its own Good," November 30, 2024, 27.

Select Bibliography

The following bibliography contains books that I found especially useful in creating this synthesis of Uruguay's history. While the majority are in English, I have included a number of critical works by Uruguayan scholars. Because this textbook did not require primary documentation, I did not venture into its principal archive, the *Archivo General de la Nación*. Unlike many Latin American nations whose archives are scattered in several locations, Uruguay's governmental archives are all conveniently housed together. Many of the scholars named in this bibliography made excellent use of these resources.

Acevedo Vásquez, Eduardo. *Anales Históricos del Uruguay*, 6 Vols. Montevideo: Casa Barreiro y Ramos, 1933–1934.
Acree, William. *Everyday Reading: Print Culture and Collective Identity in the Río de la Plata, 1780–1910*. Nashville: Vanderbilt University Press, 2009.
Albert, Bill. *South America and the First World War: The Impact of the War on Brazil, Argentina, Peru and Chile*. Cambridge: Cambridge University Press, 2002.
Alexander, Robert J. *A History of Organized Labor in Uruguay and Paraguay*. Westport, CT: Praeger Publishers, 2005.
Andrews, George Reid. *Blackness in the White Nation: A History of Afro-Uruguay*. Chapel Hill: University of North Carolina Press, 2010.
Araiza Kokinis, Troy Andreas. *Anarchist Popular Power: Dissident Labor and Armed Struggle in Uruguay, 1956–76*. Chico, CA: AK Press, 2023.
Barrán, José P., and Benjamín Nahum. *Historia rural del Uruguay moderno*, 7 Vols. Montevideo: Ediciones de la Banda Oriental, 1967–1978.
Becker, Marc. *Twentieth Century Latin American Revolutions*. Lanham, MD: Rowman & Littlefield, 2017.
Beezley, William H. *The World Today Series: Latin America, 2020–2022*. Lanham, MD: Rowman & Littlefield, 2021.

Biglaiser, Glen. *Guardians of the Nation? Economists, Generals and Economic Reform in Latin America*. Notre Dame: Notre Dame University Press, 2002.

Blanchard, Peter. *Fearful Vassals: Urban Elite Loyalty in the Viceroyalty of La Plata, 1776–1810*. Pittsburgh: University of Pittsburgh Press, 2020.

Blanchard, Peter. *Under the Flags of Freedom: Slave Soldiers and the Wars of Independence in Spanish South America*. Pittsburgh: University of Pittsburgh Press, 2008.

Brum, Pablo. *The Robin Hood Guerrillas: The Epic Journey of Uruguay's Tupamaros*. Orlando: Creative Space, 2014.

Borucki, Alex. *From Shipmates to Soldiers: Emerging Black Identities in the Río de la Plata*. Albuquerque: University of New Mexico Press, 2015.

Brown, Jonathan C. *A Brief History of Argentina*, second ed. New York: Checkmark Books, 2011.

Caetano, Gerardo. *Historia minima de Uruguay*. Mexico: El Colegio de México, 2020.

Cameselle-Pesce, Pedro, and Debbie Sharnak, eds. *Uruguay in Transnational Perspective*. New York: Routledge, 2024.

Chasteen, John. *Heroes on Horseback: A Life and Times of the Last Gaucho Caudillo*. Albuquerque: University of New Mexico Press, 1995.

Churchill, Leslie. *Becoming the Tupamaros: Solidarity and Transnational Revolution in Uruguay and the United States*. Nashville: Vanderbilt University Press, 2014.

Darwin, Charles. abridged. *The Voyage of the Beagle*. London: Penguin Books, 1989.

D'Elia, Germán. *El Uruguay neo-batllista, 1946–1958*. Montevideo: Ediciones de la Banda Oriental, 1982.

Demaria, Isidoro. *Montevideo Antiguo: Tradiciones y Recuerdos*, 2 Vols., II, 342–45. Montevideo: El Siglo Ilustrado, 1888.

Demaria, Isidoro. *Rasgos biográficos de Don Joaquín Suárez*. Montevideo: Imprenta a vapor de El Ferrocarríl, 1881.

Drinot, Paul, and Alan Knight. *The Great Depression in Latin America*. Durham: Duke University Press, 2014.

Ehrick, Christine. *The Shield of the Weak: Feminism and the State in Uruguay, 1903–1933*. Albuquerque: University of New Mexico Press, 2005.

Erbig, Jr., Jeffrey Alan. *Where Caciques and Mapmakers Met: Border-Making in Eighteenth Century South America*. Chapel Hill: University of North Carolina Press, 2020.

Eloy, Rosa Alonso, and Carlos Demas. *Uruguay 1958–1968: Crises y estancamiento*. Montevideo: Ediciones de la Banda Oriental, 1986.

Encarnación, Omar G. *Out in the Periphery: Latin America's Gay Rights Revolution*. New York: Oxford University Press, 2016.

Faraone, Roque. *El Uruguay en que vivimos, 1900–1968*. Montevideo: Arca Editorial, 1968.

Fernández Saldaña, José M. *Diccionario Uruguayo de biografías, 1810–1940*. Montevideo: Editorial Amerindia, 1945.

Ferns, Henry Stanley, *Great Britain and Argentina in the Nineteenth Century*. Oxford: The Clarendon Press, 1960.

Finch, M. H. J. *A Political Economy of Uruguay since 1870*. New York: St. Martin's Press, 1981.

Fitzgibbon, Russell H. *Uruguay: Portrait of a Democracy*. New Brunswick, NJ: Rutgers University Press, 1954.

Frega, Ana, Mónica Maronna, and Yvette Trochan. *Baldomir y la restauración democrática (1938–1946)*. Montevideo: Ediciones de la Banda Oriental, 1987.

Gandia, Enríque. *Los treinte y tres orientales y la independencia del Uruguay*. Buenos Aires: Espasa-Calpe Argentina, S.A., 1939.

Ganson, Barbara. *The Guaranis under Spanish Rule in the Río de la Plata*. Palo Alto: Stanford University Press, 2014.

Gillespie, Charles. *Negotiating Democracy: Politicians and Generals in Uruguay*. Cambridge: Cambridge University Press, 1991.

González Laurino, Carolina. *La construcción de la identidad uruguaya*. Montevideo: Universidad Católica, 2001.

Halperín-Donghi, Tulio. *Politics, Economics and Society in Argentina in the Revolutionary Period*. Cambridge: Cambridge University Press, 1975.

Hanson, Simon C. *Utopia in Uruguay: Chapters in the Economic History of Uruguay*. New York: Oxford University Press, 1938.

Hudson, William Henry. *The Purple Land: Being the Narrative of One Richard Lamb's Adventures in the Banda Oriental*. New York: Grossett & Dunlap, 1904.

Jacob, Raúl. *El Uruguay de Terra, 1931–1938: Una crónica del terrismo*. Montevideo: Ediciones de la Banda Oriental, 1983.

Jackson, Geoffrey. *Peoples' Prison*. London: Faber & Faber, 1973.

Kampwirth, Karen. *Gender and Populism in Latin America: Passionate Politics*. University Park: Pennsylvania State University Press, 2010.

Katra, William H. *José Artigas and the Federal League in Uruguay's War of Independence, 1810–1820*. Madison: Farleigh Dickenson University Press, 2017.

Kaufman, Edy. *Uruguay in Transition: From Civilian to Military Rule*. New Brunswick, NJ: Transaction Books, 1979.

Knarr, James C. *Uruguay and the United States, 1903–1929: Diplomacy in the Progressive Era*. Kent: Kent State University Press, 2012.

Knight, Alan. *Bandits and Liberals, Rebels and Saints: Latin American since Independence*. Lincoln: University of Nebraska Press, 2022.

Koebel, William Henry. *Uruguay*. London: T.F. Unwin, 1911.

Lessa, Francisca. *The Condor Trials: Transnational Repression and Human Rights in South America*. New Haven: Yale University Press, 2022.

Lessa, Francisca. *Memory and Transnational Justice in Argentina and Uruguay: Against Impunity*. New York: Palgrave and MacMillan, 2013.

Lessa, Francisca. *The Condor Trials-Transnational Repression and Human Rights in South America*. New Haven: Yale University Press, 2022.

Lindahl, Goran G. *Uruguay's New Path: A Study in Politics during the First Colegiado*. Stockholm: Library & Institute of Ibero-American Studies, 1962.

López-Alves, Fernando. *State Formation and Democracy in Latin America*. Durham: Duke University Press, 2000.

Lynch, John. *The Spanish American Revolutions, 1808–1826*. New York: Oxford University Press, 1986.

Marino, Katherine M. *Feminism for the Americas: The Making of an International Human Rights Movement*. Chapel Hill: University of North Carolina Press, 2019.

Markarian, Vania. *Uruguay, 1968: Student Activism from Global Counterculture to Molotov Cocktails*. Oakland: University of California Press, 2017.

Martínez Lamas, Julio. *Requeza y pobreza del Uruguay: Estudios de las causes que retardant el progreso nacional*. Montevideo: Palacio del Libro, 1930.

Mariscal, Carlos. *A Century of Debt Crises in Latin America: From Independence to the Great Depression, 1820–1930.* Princeton: Princeton University Press, 1989.

McLean, David. *War, Diplomacy, and Informal Empire: Britain and the Republics of La Plata.* London: British Academic Pres, 1995.

Méndez Vives, Enrique. *El Uruguay de la modernación.* Montevideo: Ediciones de la Banda Oriental, 1977.

Pedemonte, Juan Carlos. *Hombres con Dueño: crónica de la esclavitud en el Uruguay.* Montevideo: Editorial Independencia, n.d.

Pendle, George. Uruguay. 3rd ed. London: Oxford University Press, 1965.

Pi Hugarte, Renzo. *Los Indios del Uruguay.* Quito: Abya-Yala, 1995.

Pite, Rebeka. *Sharing Yerba Maté: How South America's Most Popular Drink Defined a Nation.* Chapel Hill: University of North Carolina Press, 2023.

Pivel Devoto, Juan A. *Historia de los partidos y las ideas políticas en el Uruguay: La definición de los bandos, 1829–1838,* 2 Vols. Montevideo: Editorial Medina, 1956.

Pivel Devoto, Juan A., and Ranieri de Pivel Devoto. *La Guerra Grande, 1839–1851.* Montevideo: Editorial Medina, 1971.

Prado, Fabrício. *Edge of Empire: Atlantic Network and Revolution in Bourbon Río de la Plata.* Oakland: University of California Press, 2015.

Real de Azúa, Carlos. *El impulso y su freno: Tres decades de batllismo y los raises de la crises Uruguayo.* Montevideo: Ediciones de la Banda Oriental, 1964.

Rock, David (ed.). *Latin America in the 1940s: War and Post-War Transitions.* Berkeley: University of California Press, 1994.

Roniger, Luis and Maria Sznajder, *The Legacy of Human Rights Violations in the Southern Cone, Argentina, Chile and Uruguay.* New York: Oxford University Press, 1999.

Salgado, Susanna. *The Teatro Solís: 150 Years of Opera, Concert, and Ballet in Montevideo.* Middletown, CT: Wesleyan University Press, 2003.

Sanguinetti, Julio Maria. *Luis Batlle Berres: El Uruguay del optimismo.* Montevideo: Taurus, 2014.

Sharnak, Debbie. *Of Light and Shadow: Social Justice, Human Rights, and Accountability in Uruguay.* Philadelphia: University of Pennsylvania Press, 2023.

Solari, Aldo. *El Desarrollo Social del Uruguay en la postguerra.* Montevideo: Editorial Alfa, 1967.

Street, John. *Artigas and the Emancipation of Uruguay.* Cambridge: Cambridge University Press, 1959.

Vanger, Milton. *José Batlle y Ordóñez: The Creator of his Times, 1902–1907.* Cambridge: Harvard University Press, 1963.

Vanger, Milton. *The Model Country: José Batlle y Ordóñez of Uruguay, 1907–1915.* Hanover, NH: University Press of New England, 1980.

Verdesio, Gustavo. *Forgotten Conquests: Re-Reading New World History from the Margins.* Philadelphia: Temple University Press, 2001.

Weinstein, Marvin. *Uruguay: Democracy at the Crossroads.* Boulder: CO: Westview Press, 1988

Whigham, Thomas C. *The Paraguayan War,* 2 Vols. Lincoln: University of Nebraska Press, 2002.

Wise, Carol. *How Latin America Is Maximizing (or Missing Out on) China's International Development Strategy.* New Haven: Yale University Press, 2020.

Index

Page references for images are italicized.

abortion, 202
abrazo de Monzón, 42–44
Acevedo Díaz, Eduardo (historical novelist), 84
advisory councils, 196
AFE. *See* State Railway Administration of Uruguay
Afro-Uruguayans, 14, 16, 19, 54, 55, 59, 61, 64, 80, 114, 176–77, *177*. *See also* Blacks; enslaved people
age of leather, 9, 19
agriculture, 3, 10, 20, 95, 140, 143, 151–52; cheese, 194; colonies, 114; rice, 204; technology, 140, 151–52
Alliance for Progress, 167
"Alto," (Halt!), 122, 126
Alvarez, Gregorio, 180–81, 183, 201
Alvear, Carlos Antonio de, 34
Amadio Pérez, Hector, 173
AMdeT (Municipal Transport Board), 152
Amézaga, Juan José de, 147, 149, 152
amnesty, 181, 190, 193, 200–201
anarchism, 97
ANCAP (National Administration of Fuel, Alcohol, and Cement): attempts to reform, 193, 204, 205; established, 139, *140*, 141, 148, 153

Anglo-Uruguayan Agreement of 1947, 147–52
anti-tobacco legislation, 201
Aparicio, Timoteo, 71, 80–81, 82
Argentina, 1, 10, 31–32, 40, 42, 51, 53, 54, 55, 68, 71, 79, 82, 86, 101, 102, 151, 174, 175, 177, 189, 193, 194, 197
Ariel Student Center, 129
armed propaganda, 171
Arroyo de Vacas, 9
Arroyo Grande, 59
article 168 of 1966 Constitution. *See* Prompt Security Measures
Artigas, José Gervasio: Blandengue officer, 26–27, 30–31; democracy, 37–38, *37*; Federal League Protector, 34–41; gaucho lifestyle, 27–28; in exile, 41, 52, 55; military leader, 32–36, *33*, *36*; and national identity, 27, 85, 99, 171; social reforms, 31
artisans, 14, 96
Atlantic world, 1, 12
austerity. *See* neo-liberalism
Azara, Félix (Blandengue captain), 30–31, 38

217

Banco de la República Oriental del Uruguay, 87, 117
Banda Oriental, 1, 16, 17, 19, 20, 26, 27, 30–45, 51
bandeirantes, 10
banks: crisis, 137, 141; mortgage bank, 117; National Insurance bank, 117
Baldomir, Alfredo, 143, 144–48
barbed wire, 89, *90*, 96
Baring Brothers Bank, 87
Batlle, Lorenzo (President), 61, 70–73, 109
Batlle Berres, Luis, 151–58, 164, 193
Batlle Ibáñez, Jorge, 175, 180, 191, 193–94, 195
Batlle y Ordóñez, José, *113*, 115, 120, 122–23, 124, 126–27, 129, 130, 137, 139, 141, 156, 158, 168, *181*, 193, 202; Democratic reforms, 109–10, 116, 126, 131; editor of *El Día*, 109; journalist, 82, 101; labor reforms, 115, 121, 122; politician, 110, 112; president, 114–15, 116, 120–22; social welfare, 109, 127–29; shield of the weak, 122–23
Batlle Pacheco, César, 151, 156
Batlle Pacheco, Lorenzo, 151, 156
Batoví, 14, 31
beef products, 138, 141, 147; canned cornned beef, 92, 94, 116; hides, 20, 41, 66; jerky (*tasajo*) 14, 66; meat extract, 92, *93*; refrigerated or frozen, 94, 114; tallow (grease), 14, 19, 66. See also *saladero*
Belgium, 94
Belt and Road Initiative, 199–200
Beresford, William, 26
Berro, Bernardo, 65, 68, 70
Black Panthers, 171
Blacks, 12, 14–16, 33, 38, 41, 42, 64, 81, *83*, 139, 143, 150, 160n28, *177*, 187n22. See also Afro-Uruguayans; enslaved people
Blanco party, 56, 57, 68, 70, 71, 101–2, 110, 112, 129, 144. See also Nationalist party
Blandengues, 17, 30, 33, 39
Blanes, Juan Manuel, *29*, *30*, *33*, 39–40, *43*, *58*, *70*, *72*, 84
bola, 5, 6, 32

Bolívar, Simón, 27–28
Bonaparte, Napoleon, 26, 28
Bordaberry, Juan, 173, 174, 175, 178, 200–201
Botnia (pulp plant), 197
branding, 14, 89
Brazil, 1, 10; colonial border disputes 11–14, 17; dictatorships, 174, 175, 177; invasions, 31, 41–45, 51, 53, 55; Mercosur, 189–94; uneasy allies, 56, 64, 68–70, 79, 82, 102
Bretton Woods Agreement, 154, 165
British Intervention, 25–27, 57–64
Brown, Admiral William (Guillermo), 34, 59, 60
Brum, Baltasar, 115, 125, *125*, 127, 142
Buceo, 34, 59
budget deficits, 138
budget reductions, 139
Buenos Aires, 8, 13, 16, 17, 57, 60; junta and autonomy, 31–32; rivalry with Montevideo and Banda Oriental, 25–26, 27, 31, 34–35, 40
bureaucracy and state building, 81, 82, 97, 128, 152, 154
bureaucratic military regime, 176
Bush, George W., 193

cabildo, 17, 19, 26, 31, 38
Cabot, Sebastian, 8
cachilas, 199
Cagancha, 57
Calera de las Huérfanes, 11
calidad, 16
candombé, 16, 176–77
cannibalism, 8
capital equipment, 153, 164
Caruso, Enrique, 96
Castro, Fidel, 169–71
catalanense, 4
Catholic Church, 52, 73, 98, 100, 127
Catholic Ladies League, 123
cattle, 199; Durham, 114, 194; creole cattle, 9, 60, 89, 92, 114; feed, 86; Herefords, 60, 94, 114; pedigreed, 89
Carter, Jimmie, 176
Caruso, Enrique, 96

caudillos, 28, 51, 110; Guerra Grande, 57–61; as presidents 54–57
Cedula of 1754, 17–18
Central Bank, Social Security Bank, 168
centralism, 52, 81. *See also* stability
Central Uruguay Railroad Co., 91, 200
CEPAL (United Nations Economic Commission for Latin America), 157–58
Cerritos, 59, 61
cerritos de indios, 5
Cerro, 17, 96, 112, 114, 124
Cevallos, Pedro de, 13, 17
Chair Law of 1918, 128. *See also* women
Chaná, 3, 5, 10
Charles III, 16–17
Charles IV, 31
Charrúa: colonial era, 8, 9–10, 13, 22nn10–12; during independence, 28, 31, 33; extermination of, 55, 84; lifeways, 6; pre-Hispanic, 1, 3, 5–6
Chávez, Hugo, 195, 196
Chery Mobile automobiles, 199
Chicago boys, 178. *See also* neo-liberalism
Chile, 79, 82, 175, 177, 189, 191, 192, 195
China, 195, 198–200; exports and imports, 198–200. *See also* Belt and Road Initiative
Church of Christ the Worker, 144
CIDE (Investment and Economic Development Commission), 167
Cisplatine Province, 41–42
Cisplatine War, 44
civil marriage, 100
CNT (National Workers' Convention), 167; labor union, 167, 174
codification of legal codes, 81
Cold War, 174
colegiado (plural executive) 126–27, 139, 141, 156–58, 168
collective security, 150–51. *See also* transnational
College of Engineering, 99
Colonia, 5, 13, 20, 32, 34, 44, 60
Colônia do Sacramento, 12–13
Colorado party: battlismo, 112, 116, 124; caudillo origins, 56, 57, 60, 68, 82, 101–2, 110; moderate reformers, 168, 172, 182, 190, 191, 196; neo-batllismo 142, 144–45, 152, 165
comercio libre (imperial free trade), 17
commodity boom, 198–200, 208
common market, 194–95. *See also* Mercosur (Mercado Común del Sur)
"*como el Uruguay no hay*," 137
Compte, Auguste, 79
Constitution Day, 85
constitutions: Constitution of 1830, 51–54, 53; Constitution of 1918, 127–28, 139; Constitution of 1934, 142; Constitution of 1942, 147, 157; Constitution of 1952, 157; Constitution of 1967, 168, 190; Constitution of 1997, 192
consulado (Chamber of Commerce), 17, 26
co-participation in government, 71, 73, 101, 110, 127, 131, 142, 157
COPRIN (Commission on Prices, Wages, and Productivity), 168–69
Correa, Rafael, 195
corruption, 82, 205
COSENA (National Security Council), 174
cost of living, 166
cotton textiles, 149, 153
coup of 1933, 141–42
COVID-19, 206–7; economic effects, 207
crisis of 1950s, 157–58, 164–68
cuareimense, 4
Cuareim River, 4, 61
Cuban Revolution, 163, 169–70
cuchillas, 2
Cuestas, Juan Lindolfo, 86, 91, 102
curriculum, primary school, 99

dairy products, 194
Darwin, Charles, 3–4, 19, 28–29, 79
death penalty, 115
Debray, Regis, 170
defense budget, 175
del Puerto, Francisco, 8
democracy: batllista universal suffrage, 121, 125–26, 144, 145, 172, 180; elite dominated 37–38, 88, 112; post-dictatorship revival, 190, 191, 194, 196, 197, 207, 208
departments (provinces), 52
Depression of 1930, 137–41, 158

Depressions of 1868 and 1873, 71, 73
developmental liberalism. *See* positivism
El Día, 109–10
Díaz de Solís, Juan, 6–8, 96
dictablanda, 142
dictatorship, 163, 164, 189, 201
Dieste, Eladio, 143–44
disease, 10, 20, 71, *72*
diversification of exports, 147, 178
divisa, 56, *56*, 74n6
divorce law, 110, 115, 122–23
domestic capital, 87, 97, 117–19, 148, 199
domestic market, 178
domestic servants, 14, 128
domestic violence, 202
Dorrego, Manuel, 34, 85
double-simultaneous voting, 115–16
drought, 207–8
drug smuggling, 207
duels, 126, 152
durable goods, 148, 163. *See also* manufacturing
Durazno, 54, 66, 91

economic decline, 164–65, 179–80
economic nationalism, 114–15, 116, 130, 138, 151
La Educación del Pueblo, 98
education and literacy, 97, 98–99, 101, 120–21, 131, 150; Law of Public Education, 98; Public Education Reform of 2008, 196
eight-hour day movement, 97, 121–22, 124
election of 1903, 110
election of 1984, 183–84
Elío, Francisco Javier de, 27, 31–33
elite women, 62–63. *See also* Fragosa de Rivera, Bernadina
emphyteusis (tenancy), 54
empleados, 97, 167
enclosure movement, 89–90, 95
enslaved people, 10, 14–16, 20, 33, 34, 59, 64. *See also* Blacks
entes autónomos (state-owned corporation), 116–31, 138, 139, 153, 179. *See also* ANCAP; OSE; UTE
entrepreneurs, 80, 117–18, 153

Estación Femenina (Women's Radio Station), 142
estancia, 17–18, 66, 114, 115
estanciero, 18–19, 30, 31–32, 42, 54, 56, 64, 81, 142, 157
Ethiopia, invasion of, 143
eucalyptus, 197
European Union, 194, 195
exceptionalism, xii, 114, 115, 137, 163, 207
Exodus of 1811, Great, 33–34, *36*, 38
exports, 19, 66, 67, 71, 73, 92–94, 102, 137–38, 141, 147, 157; Diversification, 178, 194, 200, 204

Fábrica Nacional de Papel (National Paper Factory Inc.), 119
Fábrica Uruguaya de Neumáticos (National Tire Company), 148
Family Allowance Program, 150
fascists, 142–43
"The Fatherland Legend," 84
federalism, 52
Federal League, 35–40, 41
feminism: first wave, 123–24, 128, 144; second wave, 202
Ferdinand VII, King, 31
Fernández de Kirchner, Cristina, 195, 197
Ferreira, Wilson, 172–73, 176, 180, 183, 190, 191
FEUU (Federation of Uruguayan University Students), 143, 169, 174
fiberoptic technology, 204, 205
financial crisis of 1890, 87
financial crisis of 2002, 193
Flight 571, 173–74
flood of 1959, *166*, 166–67
Flores, Venancio, 61, 65, 80; assassination of 70, *70*; fusionist, 65; in Guerra Grande, 61; presidency, 68–69; rebellion of 1864, 68–69; War of Triple Alliance, 68–70
Florida (city), 84
foco, 170–71
foreign debt, 130, 137, 138, 167, 189, 190, 199
foreign investment, 82, 85, 86–87, 91–92, 102, 138, 154, 178, 179, 192; Law

Promoting Foreign and National Investment, 193
foreign legions in Guerra Grande, 59–60
FORU (Regional Federation of Uruguayan Workers), 97, 121. *See also* labor movement
Fragosa de Rivera, Bernadina, 61, 62–63, *63*
France, 57–64, 73, 75n16, 75n20, 94
Franciscans, 11
Fray Bentos, 92
freer trade, 163, 165, 178, 190, 192, 193. *See also* neo-liberalism
Frente Amplio, 172–73, 180, 184, 190, 191, 192, 193, 195–203
frigorífico, 94, 114, 119, 130, 139, 154; Armour and Company, 114, 124; Fray Bentos (El Anglo), 114; Frigorífico Nacional, 130, 164; Frigorífico Uruguaya, 112; Swift and Company, 114, *119*, 124
frigorifico workers, 164
Frugoni, Emilio, 155
fusionist movement, 65, 68, 71

Galeano, Eduardo, 168
Gallinal Heber, Alberto, 204
Garibaldi, Guisseppe, 60
gauchos, 1, 19, *20*, 26, 27, *30*, 54, 59–60, 66, 67, 71, 80, 81, 84, 88, 89, 95, *208*; lifeways, 28–30; nostalgia for, 101, 112; role in independence, 32–33, 35
gauchesca literature, 67–68
Gelman v. Uruguay, 201
General Assembly, 52
Generation of 1873, 101
gente decente, 101
GINI index, 198, 200
Global South, 144, 200, 203
Gómez, Leandro, 68–69
good *golpe* of 1942, 145–46
graduated income tax, 165
Graf Spee, 145, *146*
Great Britain: excessive profits, 116–19, 133n21; informal empire, 61, 74n7, 85–87, 91–92, 125; intervention by, 26–27, 57, 60, 61, 64; investments, 86–87, 138, 147; merchants, 17, 27; transnational influence, 26–27, 57–64, 68–70, 73, 138, 147. *See also* Anglo-Uruguayan Agreement of 1947
"The Great Dictator," 151
Great Depression, 129
green energy, 148, 198, 204
Grito de Asencio, 32
Gualeguaychú, Argentina, 60
Guaraní, 5, 8, 10, 13, 16, 31, 33, 40, 45
Guaraní War, 13, 26
Guerra Grande, 57–64
guerrilla warfare, 163, 168, 180
Guevara, Ernesto "Che," 169–70
Guillen, Abraham, 171

Hague Peace Conference of 1907, 115
health care, 196–97
Hernandarias (Hernando Arias de Saavedra), 8–9, 20, 22n16. *See also* yerba mate
Herrera, Luis Alberto de, 101, 112, 123, 127, 141, 164, 168, 191; leader of Nationalist Party, 144–45, 151, 156, 167
Herrera y Obes, Julio, 84, 87, 100, 101, 107n53
Hidalgo, Bartolomé, 68
highways, 130
human rights, 175, 176, 180, 190–91, 201
hunter-gatherers, 4–5
hydroelectric power, 148, 166, 198

Ibarbourou, Juana de, 143–44
Ibirapitá Plan, 205
Idiarte Borda, Juan, 101–2
illegitimate children, 123
IMF (International Monetary Fund), 165, 166, 179, 190, 193, 195
immigration restrictions, 139
immigrants, 66–67, 73, 79, 87–88, 94, 95, 96, 97, 102, 104n19, 113; Brazil, 64–65; East Europeans, 114; French Basques, 59, 66, 67; Italian, 52, 71, 97; Portuguese, 13; restrictions, 139; Spanish, 59, 66, 67, 87–88, 97, 123–24; statistics for Montevideo, 104n19
Immortal Thirty-Three, 42–45, 84

imperial preference system, 138
imports, 69, 80, 95
imprisonment, 175
income inequality, 198, 205
Independence Day, 53, 85
India Muerte, 40, 48n35
Indigenous people, 8, 20, 33, 54; near extermination, 55; pre-Hispanic, 4–6; post-contact, 8–10
industry, 96–97, 116, 119, 137, 147, 148, 149, 151–54, 163–64, 166, 194
inflation, 158, 167, 168–69, 178, 190
infrastructure, 91–92, 163, 204
Institutional Acts, 176
Instructions of 1813, 35–40, *37*
insurance companies and banks, 87, 116
International Court of Justice, 197
International Human Rights Court, 201
international markets and trade. *See* exports
interoceanic cable, 92
ISI (import substitution industrialization), 139, 163–64

Jackson, Ambassador Geoffrey, 172
jefe políticos, 52, 101, 127
Jesuits, 10–11
João, Prince and King of Portugal, 32, 40, 41

Kirchner, Néstor, 195, 197
kidnapping, *30*, 171–72
Kissinger, Henry, 173
Knight, Alan, 140
Kodak Camera Company, 124
Korean War, 137, 153, 157, 164

labor movement, 184, 191, 192, 206; batllismo and labor, 121, 147; early union movement, 97; labor protests, 168, 169, 174, 181, 184; recent reforms, 191, 19, 206
Lacalle, Luis, 184, 191–92, 202, 205
Lacalle Pou, Luis, 192, 205–8
Laguna del Sauce, 145
Laguna Merín, 1, 3, 5
Lamas, Andrés, 64
lances, 60, 91–102, 112

land reform, 38–39, 114
land taxes, 114
Langsdorff, Captain Hans, 145
laptops, 205
Las Piedras, battle of, 32, *33*, 47n14
Latorre, Lorenzo, 80–82, 86, 91, 98, 99
Lavalle, Juan Galo, 57, 58
Lavalleja, Juan Antonio: Blanco leader, 57–58, 65, 84–85; Independence and Immortal Thirty-Three, 34, 41, 42, 45; rebellions, 54–55; Triumvirate and death, 65
Law of General Expiation (Expiry Law) 191; statute of limitations and, 201
Law of Industrial Promotion of 1974, 178
Law of Urgent Consideration of 2020, 206
Law of Rent, 179
League of Nations, 125
Lecor, General Carlos Federico, 40–41
Legislative Palace, 130
lemas, 127, 129, 142, 151; abolished, 192, 208
leva, 81
Ley Fuga, 81
libraries in public schools, 86
liceo, 121
Liebig's Extract of Meat Company, 92
Liga Federal de Acción Ruralista (Federal League for Rural Action), 165
light industry consumables, 96–97, 119, 148
Lincoln, Merino, 67
Liniers, Santiago de, 26–27, 31
literacy, 102, 109, 199
Little Tigers, 204
López, Francisco Solano, 68, 69
lost decade, 164, 179, 190
Luisi, Paulina, 123, 124, 127, 129–30, 142–43
Lula de Silva, Luiz Inácio (Lula), 195

machine gun, 81, 110–12
Maduro, Nicolás, 195
manufacturing, 96, 147–49, 153–54, 158; stagnation, 164
marijuana legalization, 203
martial law, 168
Martínez Trueba, Andrés, 156–57

Martín García Island, 8, 60
Masoller (battle), 112
maternity leave, 155
Mauá, Baron de, 61, 65
Mauá Bank, 65, 71
Medina, Hugo, 183
megafauna, 3–4, *4*
Melo, 17, 91, 144
Mendoza, Pedro de, 8
Méndez Galain, Ramón, 198
Mercosur (Mercado Común del Sur), 194–95, 197, 208
MEVIR program, 204
Mexico, 79, 82
Michelini, Zelmar, 172, 176, 201
middle class, 69, 80, 81, 88, 97–98, 102, 109, 121, 131, 153, 154, 158, 178, 207
middle income trap, 203–4
military academy, 82
militia: colonial, 14, 16, 17; nineteenth century, 27
Minas, 17, 24n36
minimum wage, 128
Minuane, 3, 5, 13
Misiones district, 10, 54
missions, 10–11
Mitrione, Dan, 171–72
model country, 116
modernist movement, 143–44
Monetary and Foreign Exchange Reform Law of 1959, 166
Montevideo: during independence, 26, 34–35; founding of, 12, 13, 14, 16–17; Guerra Grande, 52, 54, 58, 59–61; New Town (Centro) 80, 87–91, 95, 97; port expansion, 102; urbanization, 91; urban renewal, 178–79
Montevideo Water Works Company, 86–87
Morales, Evo, 195, 196
Mortgage Bank, 117
mound cultures, 5
Movimiento de Liberación Nacional-Tupamaros. *See* Tupamaros
Mujica, José (Pepe): guerrilla, 169, 172; President, 190–91, 197–98, 201, 203, 205

Museo de la revolución industrial, Fray Bentos, 97, 105n29
mutual benefit society, 97

ñandu, 4
Nardone, Benito, 165, 167
national corporations (*entes autónimos*), 116–19
National Council of Administration, 127–28, 129, 139, 141
National Council of Government, 157, 164
National Housing Fund, 204
national identity, 55, 73–74, 84–85, 99
Nationalist Party, 101–2, 121, 126, 142, 144–46, 152, 165–68, 169, 172–73, 183, 190, 191, 205–8. *See also* Blanco party
National Public Assistance Law of 1910, 115
National Security State, 185; economic reforms and failure, 177–80; repression and torture, 174–76
National Women's Council, 123
natural gas, 92
Naval Club Pact, 183
Nazis, 144–45
neo-batllismo, 147, 153, 165, 167, 175, 190
neo-liberalism, 165, 166, 178, 179, 192, 193, 194
New Left, 163
normal schools, 98–99, *100*

"Oath of the Immortal Thirty-Three," 39–40, *43*, 84
Obes y Herrera, Julio, 71
obreros (laborers), 97
oil shocks of 1973 and 1979, 179
Old City, 12, 14, 59, 64, 95, 178–79
ombú tree, 18, 89
open range, 9, 89, 91, 95, 114
Operation Condor, 175
order, 102. *See also* centralism
Ordoñana, Domingo, 80, 81, 94, 98
Organization for Latin American Solidarity, 175
Oribe, Manuel: during independence, 41, 42, 45, 84–85; fusionist movement

and death, 65; Guerra Grande, 57–62; president, 55–57
Orsi, Yamandú, 209
OSE (National Water and Sanitation Company), 152
Otorgués, Fernando, 30, 34, 35, 41; character, 40; and Lavalleja, 49n45

Pacheco Arico, Jorge, 168–69, 171
Pact of Chinchulín (Pork Barrel Pact) 139
Pact of the Cross, 102
Páez Vilero, Carlos, 177
Palacio Salvo, 130, *131*
pampas, 2
pampero wind, 6
Pan-American Women's Conference, 123–24
Paraguay, 195
Paraná River, 8, 60
pardos, 14, 16
participatory democracy, 196–97
Paso de los Toros: dam, 148, 166, 200, 205; soft drinks, 119, 149
Patria Vieja, 37–39
patriciado (elite), 54–56, 60–61, 70
patronage, 127, 142, 165, 166, 167, 178, 179–81
Patti, Adelina, 96
Paysandú, 19, 34, 35, 60, 68–69
Peace Commission, 193
Pedro I of Brazil, 41–42
Pedro II, 64, 68–69
pensions, 128–29, 141, 155, 158, 192–93
peoples' university, 129
per capita income, 131, 154, 157, 163, 200
Perón, Eva Duarte de, 151
Perón, Juan Domingo, 151, 154–55, 156
personal liberties expansions, 198, 201–2
Pfizer vaccine, 206
philanthropy and MEVIR, 204
Pink Tide, 195, 202, 205
Pinochet, Augusto, 174, 180
Piria, Francisco, 97, 117, *118*, 133n18
Piriápolis, 117
Plan Nacional de Desarrollo, 1973–1977 (National Development Plan), 178
plebiscite of 1980, 180

Plenario Intersindical de Trabajadores (PIT) (Inter-Union Plenary of Workers), 181
plural executive, 126–27, 157
Pocitos, 95
police, 169, 175
political instability, 140
political party names, 56
political prisoners, 175
politics of ideas, 71
Ponsonby, Viscount John, 45, 85
Popham, Sir Home Riggs, 26
popular republicanism, 38, 53
Portugal, 1, 6, 11–14, 17, 20; occupation of Banda Oriental, 31, 40–42
positivism, 79–80, 81, 99
poverty reduction, 205
Prebisch, Raúl, 147
pre-school education, 193
presidential system, 52, 142, 168
primary products, 92–95. *See also* beef products; cattle; sheep; wool
principistas (1871 reformers) 71, 72
privatization. *See* neo-liberalism
progress, 99–100
progressive presidents, 195–98, 201–5
progressive reforms, 109, 129, 131, 154–55
Prompt Security Measures, 168, 169, 175
protectionism, 96, 114, 118, 157, 163. *See also* tariffs
public education, 79, 98–99, 150; Education reform law of 2008, 196; Law of Public Education (1877), 98–99
public employees (*empleados*), 152, 154, 165, 167, 178, 184
Public Enterprises Law of 1990, 192
public works, 102, 130. *See also* railroads
pueblos de ratas (rat towns or squatters), 95
pulperia (country store) 26, 28, 67
pulpwood mills, 197, 200, 204
Punta Carretas prison, 171
Punta del Este, 7, *149*, 171, 178
purificación, 34–35, 41

Quebracho, 82, 109
quillapis, 9
quilombo, 14

Radio Ariel, 152
Radio Femenina, 145
Radio Rural, 165
railroads, 81, 83, 87, 91, 112, 120; competitive lines, 119–20; nationalization of, 152
Railway General Routes Law of 1884, 91
reapportionment, 112
recession of 1981–1982, 180
recession of 1999, 193
redistribution of wealth, 152, 197, 199, 203
reducciones (missions), 10–11
referenda, 191, 192
refrigeration technology, 92, 94
regulations, 192
Remington rifles, 89
República Oriental del Uruguay, 51
Reus, Emilio, 87, 97
Rincón (battle), 44
Rincón de Bonete (dam and lake), 147, 148
Río de la Plata, 1, 3, 7
Río Negro, 3, 91, 148
Río Uruguay, 1, 7
Río Yi, 3, 54, 55
Rivadavia, Bernadino, 44–45
Rivera, Fructuoso: and Artigas, 34; character, 48n38, 49n44, 49n50; during Guerra Grande, 59–61, 64, 65, 70; during independence, 33, 42–45, 84–85; restanciero, 64; president, 53, 54–57, *58*
roads, 147, 148, 204
Roaring Twenties, 129–30
Robin Hood guerrillas, 171
Rocha, 4–5, 17, 91
Rodó, José Enrique, 99–100. *See also* positivism
rompecabezas, 6
Rondeau, José, 34, 45, 51, 53
Roosevelt, Franklin D., 144–45
Root, Elihu, 124
Rosas, Juan Manuel de, 55, 56–57, 61
Rural Association, 80–81, 88, 89, 94, 130
Rural Code of 1879, 89
rustling, 89

saladero, 14, 64, 66, 94
Salsipuedes, 55
Salto, 33, 35, 39, 60

same sex marriage, 207
Sanguinetti, Julio María, 183–84, 189–93
San Martín, José de, 11, 34
San Miguel (fort), 17
San Pedro de Timote (estancia), 11, 204
San Rafael casino robbery, 171
Santa Teresa (fort), 16, 17, 40
Santo Domingo de Soriano, 9, 11
Santos, Máximo, 81–82, *83*, 126; corruption, 82; reelection and assassination attempt, 8; railroads, 91
Sarandí, 44
Saravia, Aparicio, 101, 110, *111*, 142
Sarmiento, Domingo Faustino, 84, 98
sarnifugas (sheep dip), 118–19
School of the Americas, 174
School of the South, 144
second *colegiado*, 156–57, 168
secret ballot, 121
secularism, 100, 98, 115
Sendic, Raúl, 169, *170*, 171, 172, 173, 183, 190, 191
separation of Church and state, 127
Seregni, General Líber, 172–73, 190, 191
service economy, 194
Seven Mission territory, 13
sex education, 129–30
sex workers, 122
sheep, 66–67, 73, 89, 90, 92, 95
sheep dip (*sarnifugas*), 118–19
sheep ranchers, 97
sheepshearer, 67
"shield of the weak," 122–23
single party government, 70–71, 110
Sino-vac, 206
six-day workweek, 127
slavery, abolition of, 54, 64–65
Smoot-Hawley Tariff, 138
social democrat reforms, 112, 127, 128
socialism, 97
Social Security, 128–29, 155, 168, 192, 196
social welfare, 109, 206
Solano López, Francisco, 68–69
solar energy, 198
Un Solo Uruguay, 205
Sosa, Adelia Silva de, 150
Southern Cone, 174, 195

Spain, 1, 12–14, 31, 34; explorers and settlers, 6–10; immigrants, Chapter 4; rivalry with Portugal, 11–14
stability, 102, 163
stagflation, 167
standard of living, 180, 181, 198
State Insurance Bank, 122
state-led development, 163, 179, 190
State Railway Administration of Uruguay, 152
strikes, 115, 121, 127–28, 133–34n26, 168, 174, 182, 190
students, 168, 169–70, 181
Suárez, Joaquín, 32, 47n12, 55, 59, 64, 70, 74n10
sub-lemas, 157
subsidies, 178
suffrage, 52, 97, 101, 116, 121, 127; Suffrage Law of 1915, 121; Universal suffrage, 121; Women's suffrage, 121
sumptuary taxes, 138
sustainable energy program, 148, 198
Swiss colony, 95
Switzerland of the Americas, 109, 126, 137

Tajes, Máximo, 82, 84, 101, 147
tariffs, 80, 96, 114, 138, 148, 154, 157–58, 178
tasajo. *See also* beef products
Teatro Solís, 96
technology, 79, 81, 89–92, 204
telegraph, 81, 89, 91
telephone operators strike, 128, 135n45
tenements, 179
Terra, Gabriel, 129, 139, 141–43, 148
terrible year of 1875, 73, 80
Tidemann, August, 89
toldería, 6, 9–10, 17
toldo, 5, 6, 9
Torres-Garcia, Joaquín, *143*, 143–44
torture, 175
Toscanini, Arturo, 96
tourism, 151, 178, 193, 194, 197. *See also* Punta del Este
trade deficit, 138
trade unions, 97
trams, 87
tram workers strike of 1911, 115

transgender rights, 203
transnational, 1, 12–14, 19, 25, 28, 57–64, 73, 85–87, 91–92, 94, 98, 150–51, 171, 174, 175, 194, 207; allies in war, 68–70, 116, 144–47; colonial conflicts, 12–14, 19, 20, 31, 41–45, 51, 53, 55; feminism, 123–24; independence era invasions, 25–27; student movement, 129; territorial disputes, 61–62; twentieth century trading partners, 194–95, 197, 198–200. *See also*, Argentina; Brazil; China; France; Great Britain; Hague Peace Conference; League of Nations; Mercosur (Mercado Común del Sur); Operation Condor; United Nations; United States
transportation by, oxcart, stagecoach, and steamship, 66
Treaty of Asunción, 194
Treaty of 1851, 64–65, 68
Treaty of Madrid of 1750, 13
Treaty of Montevideo (1828), 45
Treaty of San Ildefonso (1777), 14, 31, 44
Trinquier, Roger, 175
two-party system, 56, 82, 127
Tupamaros, 172; and Blacks, 187n22; defeat of, 173, 184; formation of, 171–72; leaders, 171, 173, 175, 177
Tuyutí, 69

unemployment, 139, 141, 164
United Nations, 150
United Provinces of the Río de la Plata, 35, 44
United States, 124–25, 138, 145, 176, 193, 203; frigoríficos, 114; investments, 125; loans, 138, 156; progressive ideas, 124; trade, 124–25
University of the Republic, 99
university reform, 115
UPM (Finnish owned pulp corporation), 197
urbanization, 79, 95–96, 178–79
Uriarte de Herrera, Margarita, 123
Urquiza, Justo José de, 60, 61, 64, 68
Uruguayan investors and investments, 97–98, 148–49, 153
Uruguayan Women's Suffrage Alliance, 123

Usina Eléctrica de Montevideo (Montevideo Electric Power Plant), 115
Usinas Eléctricas y Teléfonos del Estado (UTE), 117, 139, 148, 200
usufruct rights, 9
utilities, 92, 116, 120

Varela, José Pedro, 71, 98
Vargas, Getulio, 156
Vázquez, Tabaré, 192, 193, 195–97, 203–5
vecino, 16, 17, 38
Végh Villegas, Alejandro, 178
Viana, Javier de, 68
Villa Serrana, 153
Villa Soriano, 9, 11
von Liebig, Justos, 92

wage councils, 150, 154, 164, 168, 190, 196
wage-price spiral, 168, 180
Wall Street crash of 1929, 137. *See* Depression of 1930
War of the Spears, 71
War of the Triple Alliance, 68–70, 80, 82, 85
Washington Consensus, 190
"Week of Tourism," 127
welfare state, 127–29, 150, 152, 155, 156, 164, 165, 167, 178
Whitelocke, General John, 27

Williman, Claudio, 112, 115
wind power, 198
wine industry, 149
women, 62–63, 98, 121, 122–24, 134n32, 143, 164, 202; legal equality, 123–24, 138, 147; property rights, 199; voting, 139, 150
women guerrillas, 172
Women's University, 123
wool, 66, 67, 86, 94, 138, 179, 199
wool tops, 154, 179, 199
wool uniforms, 116
workers, 141, 143, 148, 149, 152, 154, 155, 169, *170*, 171, 178, 190, 199
workers' compensation, 122, 124
workplace equality, 124
World Bank, 190
World Committee of Women against War and Fascism, 143
World Cup of 1950, *155*, 156
World War I, 124–25
World War II, 137, 144–47; British trade surplus, 147, 152

yerba mate, 9, 11, 26, 206–7, *208*
youth movement, 169

Zabala, Bruno Mauricio de, 12
Zorrilla de San Martín, Juan, 82, 84, 85, 144

About the Author

Peter V. N. Henderson, now a resident of Cape Coral, Florida, is professor emeritus at Winona State University. His books include *The Course of Andean History, Gabriel García Moreno and Conservative State Formation, In the Absence of Don Porfirio, Félix Díaz and the Mexican Revolution,* and with Virginia Garrard and Bryan McCann, *Latin America in the Modern World.*

www.ingramcontent.com/pod-product-compliance
Lightning Source LLC
Chambersburg PA
CBHW021839220426
43663CB00005B/312